[handwritten inscription:] Best to ... Jackson (Mac Low Binghamton 10/30/86

Representative Works: 1938–1985

Representative Works: 1938–1985

Jackson Mac Low

ROOF

SECOND PRINTING
ISBN: 0-937804-19-3 (cloth)
ISBN: 0-937804-18-5 (paper)
Library of Congress Catalog Card Number: 85-61017

Back cover: Photo copyright © by Anne Tardos, NY 1985

Front cover: Kurt Schwitters. *Merz 83: Drawing.* 1920.
Collage of cut paper wrappers, announcements, tickets, 5-3/4 x 4-1/2".
Collection, The Museum of Modern Art, New York.
Katherine S. Dreier Bequest.

This publication is funded in part by grants from the National Endowment for the Arts and the New York State Council on the Arts.

ROOF BOOKS
are published by
The Segue Foundation
300 Bowery
New York, NY 10012

Preface

Mac Low stands with John Cage as one of the two major artists bringing systematic chance operations into our poetic & musical practice since the Second World War. The resulting work raises fundamental questions about the nature of poetry & the function of the poet as creator. For raising such & other questions, Mac Low like Cage has sometimes met with strong rejection &, being primarily a poet, has found less public recognition for a work that's often sensed as "abstract" & that seems, by setting "chance" over "choice" in the making of poems, to act against the projection of personality usually associated with "the poet." Still he's widely influential & recognized by many (Cage among them) as the principal experimental poet of his time.

My own first response to Mac Low was one of resistance, which (since I was still inexperienced) I didn't recognize as a sign that something important & new was going on. The occasion I now remember was in 1961, a performance of his play, *Verdurous Sanguinaria,* at Yoko Ono's loft in what would later be New York's Tribeca district. Diane Wakoski, Simone Forti, LaMonte Young, & Mac Low were "acting" in it, & Wakoski was the one who had coaxed some of us to come along. We just couldn't get with it that night — although it touched off the obvious comparisons to things we said we admired: Dada or the works of Gertrude Stein: the great traditions of 20th century experimental poetry & art. But it's one thing to carry the torch for events already historical — another to tune in to the work of a contemporary moving in what (at the time) seemed like a bewildering, even a "self-indulgent" direction.

There followed a period in which one heard Mac Low perform his work more often than one read it. And a period in which one (I mean myself & others like me) began to push our own work past the initial breakthroughs of the 1950s—in our case expressionistic & imaginal—toward the even more open & unexplored terrain of the 1960s. For this, Mac Low—his work, I mean—began to appear more & more as a challenge & incentive. Then, very suddenly it seems in retrospect, it came to be something still more: an achievement of the first order.

I want to be clear about all this because I know that from then to now my own experience has been repeated by others—that it will be repeated, I'm sure, by still others for whom this book is a first encounter with Mac Low. The great block to Mac Low's work, as I observed earlier, lies with his use of random & chance methods of composition & performance—the very heart of his achievement & his challenge to our inherited ideas of authorship & authority in the work of art.

For myself I can recall three points of entry to his work. The first was through a series of poems from the early to the mid 1960s, in which "chance" & "choice" were both operative—notably *The Pronouns,* the early *Light Poems,* & *The Presidents of the United States of America.* The most chance-determined of these, *The Pronouns,* definitively answered my own lingering questions about Mac Low's "accessibility"; they were nothing but stunning—as I later wrote: "a masterpiece of language & a total joy." And once being stunned—& thereby vulnerable & open—the range of his contributions became clear, still clearer as more of his work appeared, to show him without limit.

In addition to numerous ways of making chance do the poem's work, what we were seeing were continuing experiments—both beautiful & outrageous—with a range of composition & performance modes: simultaneities & other group forms, music & language intersections, phonemic sound poems, collage & assemblage, intermedia, high-tech computer work, concrete & visual poetry, acrostics & syllabics. If that sounds overly formal, the corpus viewed differently runs the gamut from the "abstract"/impersonal *Stanzas for Iris Lezak* to the "expressionistic" but still highly structured *Odes:* a work of personal history that (in some of its sections not shown here) out-confesses the "confessionals." And there are still other magnificent choice-determined segments & whole poems: Mac Low, say, writing to a friend:

The traitorous light turns
as the
whirling earth
turns.
The traitorous light turns from pale
blue to grey.

My traitorous heart turns from one to the other loyally.
Faithfully my traitorous heart
turns
trying to make no promises or none it cannot keep
or none that cannot keep it
or none that cannot keep it keeping them . . .

or addressing a lover (he is in fact an incredible love poet), while simultaneously tracking the operations of chance that bring key words into the poem & his actual life:

I know when I've fallen in love   I start to write love songs
Love's actinism turns nineteens to words & thoughts in love songs
as your "A" & the date made "actinism" enter this love song...

or celebrating chance itself:

And chance—what else can I call it?—has opened my life now again
And again again beautiful life opening up and blossoming when it seems to have died
to the roots
Nothing but rotting at the roots...

that "blessed chance" to which he would again & again turn, to summon
poems whole:

Asymmetry 205

silence,
        island.

                Lordship eyes no
        cable eyes

island.

        silence,
                Lordship anchor no
        descended

Lordship oars rapidly descended silence,
        hand island.

                praying

—which is, well, simply beautiful. (The reader will get a sampling of all such
turns—& the rationales for their composition—in these "Representative
Works.")

    But nothing, come to think of it, is *simply* beautiful, & everything gets
back (crucially in Mac Low) to what Charles Olson spoke of as the poet's
"stance toward reality." This was, for me, the second point of entry to Mac
Low's work—the recognition, through what he himself revealed, of how that
work was placed in relation to the world, even to "reality" itself. And the fact
was that it really was so placed, that he was (even in his most chance-
determined work—or especially there) reporting the world to us with a
cranky accuracy. Poems like those already quoted, literally spelled out the
poetics of which they were a part, & where that wasn't enough, he wrote in
prose to clarify his methods & to show their link to ideology.

The basis of that ideology is anarchist & pacifist on its political side, Taoist & Buddhist in its reflection of what he calls "the world 'in general.' " The offering throughout is of a "synchronous" view of the world, in which coincidences of occurrence ("acausal connections" in Jung's writing about the *I Ching* — or, more simply, things happening together) are never meaningless, but allow the mind to experience the most diverse relations, *"across* any present, between any two things co-existing." And it's the turning to "chance"—"to produce a kind of art that is not egoic"— that lets things happen in this way. Speaking of all that, in 1975, he said:

That's the main motive for "letting in" other things than oneself, randomizing means or other people or the environment, as when performances include long silences: during silences when you, as a performer, don't do anything for a while, other things that are happening become part of the piece. All of these are ways to let in other forces than oneself. At first one thinks one can avoid the ego, make works that are egoless, by chance. This illusion passes after you work this way a while. You realize that making a chance system is as egoic, in some ways, or even as emotional, as writing a poem spontaneously. But at the same time you realize there *is* something more than just yourself doing it. & by interacting in that way with chance or the world or the environment or other people, one sees and *produces* possibilities that one's habitual associations—what we usually draw on in the course of spontaneous or intuitive composition—would have precluded, for our so-called intuition or taste is always involved with our biographies & habits, & you know that in Buddhism, the ego includes the Unconscious, in the Freudian sense; all the layers of the mind as dealt with in modern psychology are still within the bounds of the ego, & this includes the deep Unconscious.*

Beyond that, he tells us, he travels with those like Duchamp & Cage into something that "has to do with what in Zen is called the 'No Mind' ":

... that layer of mind below the Unconscious, the impulses, the instincts, the Id, the deepest layer, which is common to all people: the No Mind (Sunyata viewed as an aspect of mentality). From the No Mind, or from emptiness, everything arises. & if one can step aside a little bit, one can allow it to manifest itself.

The politics ("I've been a serious pacifist most of my life, & since about '45, I've also identified myself as an anarchist") are in some sense an extension of those other concerns—what he calls "the political side of Dharma." They move him, in other words, towards a "society without a coercive force pushing everybody around"—in which the world can be accepted with least interference; in which "the poet does not wish to be a dictator but a loyal co-initiator of action"; & in which performance together establishes a new

* The longer Mac Low quotes in this section are from his talk, "The Poetics of Chance & the Politics of Simultaneous Spontaneity, or the Sacred Heart of Jesus," in Anne Waldman & Marilyn Webb, *Talking Poetics from Naropa Institute,* volume one (Boulder & London: Shambala, 1978).

social bond or serves as model for "the free society of equals which it is hoped the work will help to bring about." Put this way, Mac Low's art returns to something like the stance of an earlier avant garde (Russian Futurism, Dada, etc.) for which artistic, spiritual & political renewals were all part of a single impulse. In no contemporary does it show through as clearly, movingly, this vision of experimental/language-centered art as social action.

An ideal of egolessness, then, which he pursues & never reaches, the failure itself, like the failure of all great art, a goad to more reflection; thus:

Despite the fact that the ego is going to make up these systems & pride itself on becoming "Jackson Mac Low, the great poet who makes up chance systems," nevertheless, there is something or other happening, though now I'm not sure what it is . . . .

Or again:

I think it is rather hard to think concretely about anarchist politics. In the 60s, many many people went through semi-anarchic situations in communes & so on, & all of the theories of government were probably born again in people's minds as they went through those experiences, when the communes fell completely to pieces because no one would take responsibility, or some guy took over, or a small clique took over: nearly every possibility worked itself out.

The disappointment shows through; it underlies the great fervor & yearning with which he continues to give himself to projects like those David Antin describes: "Jackson the modernist at an avant garde festival in the early '60s, treating us to a formalized prophecy of the death of our cities; . . . Jackson the concrete poet at Bryant Park, where we had been expressly forbidden to read 'sexual or political poetry,' reading his 'non-political poem,' which he explained 'expressed no attitudes or opinions or ideas of a political nature,' and nearly causing a riot with a single litany of names."

And it's all the more moving, to me, because the stance is so devoid of fanaticism—is, rather, generous & open to "the world 'in general' " & to other poets, rejecting few in his own thought, whatever crankiness he may show as a matter of style or instinct. ("How can I reject *anyone* who's risked this much?" he said to me with respect to my own work with anthologies & the need to exclude therefrom, etc.) An inclusive rather than an exclusive avant garde, then—& that's a pretty rare bird in itself.

The third entry I found into Mac Low's work was through performing it. He's undoubtedly one of those who has contributed most to reviving a poetics of performance—from the side of music in his case, since he's a composer & sometime pianist himself, who tends to conceive performance works in musical terms. For myself—as for other poets & artists in the vicinity—the invitation to perform with Mac Low became the occasion for hearing the work from within it. If this made us part of "a free society of equals," then it was as well a society in which one figure exercised a curious & quirky

ix

leadership, to bring us towards our own experience & understanding; for, along with the anarchist commitment, was a desire that the others act as real "co-initiators," in an atmosphere of mutual attention.

I got the "idea" early along, but I really *got* the idea sometime mid-60s in a performance of one of the "gathas," scores & instructions for which appear within. The text, as I remember, was the Japanese Buddhist prayer or mantra, *namu amida butsu* ("praise Amida Buddha"), a repetitious, quite familiar formula of Pure Land Buddhism. Mac Low's directive, as it would be thereafter, was to *listen! listen! listen!* & to observe & interact while "listening intensely to everything in the performance & in the environment"—though our inclination back then was more likely to take his "anarchism" in the colloquial sense as each man/or woman for him/or herself. It didn't matter that night. The old Japanese words, resonant from earlier readings, & the recognizable *aum* as mantric axis line that held the piece together, appeared & disappeared as phonemes & syllables began to move around the space in which we had dispersed ourselves. I had never so clearly heard or felt my own voice or Voice Herself as carried by the others—the separation & recombination of sounds that related back to a fixed string of sounds & to a meaning that I didn't reach but that I knew was there. It was something very old & very new: Jackson's arrangement & invention but vibrant with the source itself.

Part of the intention of the series in which *Representative Works* was originally intended to figure as the second book — its principal intention — was to place the poetry of our time in relation to other times & places. Mac Low, who is one of our true inventors, creates new modes & brings us back to the oldest possibilities of sound & language as they enter poetry & music & performance. If it's possible to see that here "objectively" & through a silent reading of the work presented, it's also possible through what he offers, to follow his directions for composition & performance into one's own creation or into one's own realization of the work. The more one does that — treats the book not only as a text but as a score & manual — the more one realizes the service of this work, its lasting power. It is in this sense that the book becomes, in Ezra Pound's words, "a ball of light in one's hands."

Jerome Rothenberg
October 1980

Table of Contents

Introduction

The title *Representative Works* originated during a telephone conversation between Buzz Erikson and myself. I remember liking it, when one of us thought of it, not only for the reasons given below, but also for its echo of Emerson's title *Representative Men,* which I'd long admired.

My main reason for adopting this title is to distinguish the present collection from a possible *Selected Works.* The latter title would imply that the book includes all, and only, "my best works"—or as some writers put it, "all the works I care to keep." This is not the case. Space limits have precluded inclusion of many other works I'd like to see in such a collection.

What I mean by "representative works" is that each is an example of one of the *kinds* of work I've made between 1938 and now. Some of these, e.g., "H U N G E R ST r i kE wh A t doe S lifemean," are *sui generis.* Of other kinds there may be one or few other examples: "Night Walk" has a near twin called "Subway Ride," untyped from 1960 to 1985, and a poem called "Dufay" is similar to "Machault," though written much later. Of other kinds—the Stanzas, Asymmetries, Matched Asymmetries, Gathas, Odes, Light Poems, Pronouns, Vocabularies, etc.—there are many examples other than those in this book, some of which may be "better" than those included. But the latter are good examples of their kinds—each adequately represents its "genre."

The kinds of work are not equally represented—there's only one scene from one play—and some are not represented at all. But the works in this book are good representatives of what I've produced during the last 40-odd years.

However, as readers will quickly discover, the years since 1954 are much better represented than those before. This isn't because I think badly of my earlier work. I can imagine a fairly substantial *Selected Earlier Works.* But with the "5 biblical poems," begun in December 1954, I started producing poems and performance pieces markedly different from both my own previous works and those of other verbal artists—much to the bafflement of most of my friends.

Why did this happen? I can point to influences that came to bear on me in the early 1950s: the *I Ching or Book of Changes* in Cary Baynes' English translation of Richard Wilhelm's German version; Gershom G. Scholem's *Major Trends in Jewish*

Mysticism, especially the chapter on Abraham Abulafia; Dr. D. T. Suzuki's books on Zen Buddhism, and later his classes at Columbia University; and especially, some of the early chance-generated compositions of John Cage—(but also the early works of Morton Feldman, Earle Brown, and Christian Wolff and the dances of Merce Cunningham), and later, discussions with Cage about chance operations and his reasons for using them.

But why did these, and such earlier influences as the writings of Gertrude Stein and the collages, and much later the poems, of Kurt Schwitters—as well as my involvement for more than a decade with the pacifist and pacific-anarchist movements—lead me at that time to begin following compositional practices so different from my earlier ones?

Why did I begin at that time composing poems, musical works, group performance works ("simultaneities"), and plays by means of chance operations? Why did I begin to view *performance* as central and texts as primarily notations for performance (if only by a silent reader)? Why did my work begin to include silences longer than those occasioned by punctuation marks (sometimes *much* longer) as well as indeterminate features (ones realized differently at each performance)?

Certainly, no one—least of all, Cage—tried to *persuade* me to change my ways. And when I first encountered aleatoric methods, I felt strong reservations about them which I openly expressed. Nevertheless, not much later, I found myself employing systematic-chance methods of my own—and composing both determinate and indeterminate works with them—with great pleasure and gusto. The explanation, if any, must be sought not only in the realm of my artistic activities, but in the wider sphere of my life in general.

What seems to have happened is that a kind of crystallization took place in my life then. Not only my work changed. In fall 1955 I returned to school, since I'd not obtained a bachelor's degree when I'd left the University of Chicago in the early 1940s (though I was doing graduate-level work in philosophy and structural criticism when I left). Thereafter I attended Brooklyn College at night for 2½ years, earning an A.B., cum laude, in Classical Greek in February 1958, which led to several reference-book editorial jobs and later to seven years of teaching at New York University. (Before, I'd worked intermittently as a factory or office worker, tutor, parents' helper, music teacher, or messenger—all for miniscule pay.) I cannot explain why these changes happened then, though I can see why my economic situation had become intolerable at 33. Suffice it to say that they did, and that most of the work in this book was made after these changes.

I feel sympathy for my self of the middle 1950s since in the 1980s other changes have been happening in and to me. I find myself questioning all my beliefs and ways of working—questioning though not rejecting. Some beliefs, such as my opposition to warfare, interpersonal and interspecific violence, exploitation, and authority depending on violence, are stronger than ever. About others I have reservations of varying intensity.

Without rejecting compositional methods followed over a quarter century, I am exploring new ways as well as reexamining older ones. I am, for instance, much more interested in texts per se—works primarily for readers, though they can also be read aloud or performed—and in works written or composed directly (sometimes spontaneously), rather than by means of chance operations.

The day after completing this introduction's first draft on 6 December 1981, I began a book of poems completed at the end of the following month and published soon after as *From Pearl Harbor Day to FDR's Birthday* (College Park, Md.: Sun & Moon Press, 1982). Those poems and the ones in the 1982–83 section of my next book, *Bloomsday* (Barrytown, N.Y.: Station Hill Press, 1984), were written without use of aleatoric systems. (The few permutational poems in these books are systematic, but their composition involved no chance operations.)

However, in the period December 1981–May 1983 I also completed two large aleatoric projects begun previously: *French Sonnets* (Tucson: Black Mesa Press, 1984) and "Words nd Ends from Ez" (Part I published in *Unmuzzled Ox;* Part IV in *Abacus;* II and IX in this book). The latter is a "reading through" of all of Ezra Pound's *Cantos,* composed by a "diastic-aleatoric" method that selected words and "ends" (fragments) of words successively from the *Cantos.*

Moreover, during the 1980s I have also composed several musical works, notably the *Milarepa Quartet for Four Like Instruments,* by "translating" the successive letters of verbal texts into musical notation, a method that is aleatoric insofar as pitch classes and note values were not chosen by me, following strictly from the orthography of the "translated" texts, but in which choice determined other parameters.

In addition, my love of performance has continued during the 1980s, but it has given rise to works combining in new ways previously adopted principles and procedures. These performance works have included both determinate texts and musical notations and instructions for performances minimally dependent on texts or notations and including much free improvisation.

For instance, I composed four radioworks, or *Hörspiele,* in 1981–84. Of the first three, produced by Klaus Schöning at Westdeutscher Rundfunk Köln, *Dialog unter Dichtern/Dialog among Poets* (1981) comprises ten superimposed chance-regulated solo performances by myself: nine of poems of mine made of words or phrases drawn by chance operations from poems of other poets (seven in English, two in German) and one of a chance-generated performance score based on a Tibetan mantra. The parameters of the stereo mix-down were also chance-determined. The other WDR *Hörspiele*—*Thanks/Danke* (1983) and *Reisen* ("Traveling"; 1984)—and the fourth radiowork, *Locks* (produced by Brian Flahive and Ray Gallon at Sound Foundation, Inc., New York) comprise written-out conversational speeches and free vocalized, spoken, and instrumental improvisation. (*Thanks/Danke* and *Locks* were performed by Anne Tardos and me; in *Reisen* the German *Hörspiel* composer Peter Behrendson joined us.)

Other 1980s performance works include "arrangements" of spontaneously written poems: in some, silence notations were chance-determined; in others, pitches of phonemes and changes therein are regulated by freely composed graphic notations on musical staves. Other recent works are minimal instructions for improvised performances, some including materials from which performers may choose.

A last category of recent work comprises prose texts, most of which are parts of my book-in-progress *Pieces o' Six* (to be published by Sun & Moon Press in 1987), or which one is in the present collection: these include many prose poems and some stories and essaylike pieces on writing, speech, language, poetics, and related topics.

The foregoing indicates some directions in which my new and reawakened older interests are leading me. Others of course are unpredictable, but I'm looking forward to their revealing themselves. Right now I am happy to be sharing these "representatives" of my work and life from 1938 to the present.

Jackson Mac Low
6 December 1981
and 22–31 March 1985
New York

Acknowledgments
&
Previous Publications

Representative Works has taken a long time in coming to press, and many people have contributed to its final form. Here I acknowledge those whose efforts were most crucial to the initiation and completion of the project. In 1979 Jerry Rothenberg brought my writing to the attention of the Santa Barbara publisher Ross-Erikson and recommended that a large book of my work be published as part of a series he was editing for them. He thus began the project, and his editing, suggestions, and support largely determined the book's form. That year Buzz Erikson agreed to publish the book, and in a transcontinental phone conversation we arrived together at its present title. Regrettably, circumstances prevented his completing its publication. From late 1979 to about 1982 George and Susan Quasha of the Open Studio Print Shop, Rhinebeck, N.Y., provided the original design and tirelessly watched over the typesetting and layout of the book. During much of this period Charles Stein acted as its copy editor and spent countless hours working with me on its details. Then late in 1984 Michael Coffey, former production manager at Open Studio, who had worked on the book there, brought it to the attention of the Segue Foundation, publisher of ROOF Books; since then he has given great devotion and effort to its final editing. He, along with Diane Ward, the ROOF Books production manager, and James Sherry, director of the Segue Foundation, have brought the book to its present form and to publication. Their suggestions as to additions of recent work have been invaluable. I thank all of these friends and also, especially, Anne Tardos for her continuing support of my work and of myself throughout these years.

Some of the poems and performance works in this book have appeared previously in the following periodicals: *Abyss, Alcheringa, antipiugiù* (Turin), *The Atlantic Review* (London), *Bread &, Caterpillar, ccV TRE* (Fluxus newspaper), *Center, Chelsea, Chicago Review, Choice, Conjunctions, El Corno Emplumado/The Plumed Horn* (Mexico City), *East Side Review, E Pod, The Insect Trust Gazette, joglars, The Lampeter Muse, L.A. Weekly, Le Lumen* (Amiens), *Mandorla, Mèla* (Florence), *Nadada, The New York Quarterly, Paper Air, Poems from the Floating World, Poetry Review* (London), *Pogomoggan, Precisely, Randstad* (Amsterdam/Antwerp), *Shantih, sixpack, Some/Thing, Spectacular Diseases* (Peterborough, Cambs., U.K.), *Stony Brook, Sumac, Sun & Moon, trobar, Volume 63* (Waterloo, Ont.), *vort, V TRE* ("proto-

Fluxus" broadsheet), *WIN, Woodstock Poetry Review, words worth* (London), *The World*, and *0 to 9.*

In the following anthologies: *A Controversy of Poets,* ed. R. Kelly & P. Leary, Garden City, N.Y.: Anchor/Doubleday, 1965; *Happenings,* ed. J. Becker & W. Vostell, Reinbek bei Hamburg: Rowohlt, 1965; *The American Experience, A Radical Reader,* ed. H. Jaffe & J. Tytell, New York: Harper & Row, 1970; *A Caterpillar Anthology,* ed. C. Eshleman, Garden City, N.Y.: Anchor/Doubleday, 1965; *Open Poetry,* ed. R. Gross, G. Quasha, E. Williams, et al, New York: Simon & Schuster, 1973; *America a Prophecy,* ed. G. Quasha & J. Rothenberg, New York: Random House, 1973; *Revolution of the Word,* ed. J. Rothenberg, New York: Continuum/Seabury, 1974; *An Active Anthology,* ed. G. Quasha, Fremont, Mich.: Sumac Press, 1974; *Deciphering America,* ed. M. Gibbs, Amsterdam: Kontexts, 1978; *Text-Sound Texts,* ed. R. Kostelanetz, New York: William Morrow, 1980; *Aural Literature Criticism,* ed. R. Kostelanetz, New York: Precisely-RK Editions, 1981; *The Poetry Reading,* ed. S. Vincent & E. Zweig, San Francisco, Momo's Press, 1981; *The Postmoderns: The New American Poetry Revised,* ed. D. Allen & G.F. Butterick, New York: Grove Press, 1982; and *A Century in Two Decades: A Burning Deck Anthology 1961-1981,* ed. K. & R. Waldrop, Providence, R.I.: Burning Deck, 1982.

In *A Report on the Art and Technology Program of the Los Angeles County Museum of Art 1967-1971,* ed. M. Tuchman, Los Angeles: Los Angeles County Museum of Art, 1971; and in the catalog *1984 New Langton Arts,* San Francisco: New Langton Arts, 1985.

And in the following books: *The Pronouns—A Collection of 40 Dances—For the Dancers,* 1st ed., New York: Mac Low, 1964; 2nd ed., London: Tetrad, 1971; 3rd ed., Barrytown, N.Y.: Station Hill, 1979. *August Light Poems,* New York: Caterpillar Books, 1967. *22 Light Poems,* Los Angeles: Black Sparrow, 1968. *Stanzas for Iris Lezak,* Barton, Vt.: Something Else, 1972. *4 trains,* Providence, R.I.: Burning Deck, 1974. *36th Light Poem: In Memoriam Buster Keaton,* London: Permanent Press, 1975. *21 Matched Asymmetries,* London: Aloes Books, 1978. *phone,* New York & Amsterdam: Printed Editions & Kontexts, 1979. *Antic Quatrains,* [Minneapolis:] Bookslinger, 1980. *Asymmetries 1-260,* New York: Printed Editions, 1980. *"Is That Wool Hat My Hat?",* Milwaukee, Wis.: Membrane Press, 1982. *From Pearl Harbor Day to FDR's Birthday,* College Park, Md.: Sun & Moon, 1982. And *Bloomsday,* Barrytown, N.Y.: Station Hill, 1984. The final work in the book will appear in *Pieces O' Six,* Los Angeles: Sun & Moon, 1987.

Representative Works: 1938–1985

HUNGER STrikE whAt doeS lifemean

&

Water and water and water and water
Whater you thinking about
Or are you doing
what areyou doing
Fire in grates are greates
Ingrates in grate
great ingrates in great grate
great grate greasy great grate
grating
g r a v e r l o w
        GRATE
God and god and god and god
G r o d an d grod in grate
in great ingrate in grate in great grate
Growl great grate
Grin g r o w l i n ggreat grate
Great grown ing grateS
Grod and grod and grod and grod

A N D   G R O D

G L O W
_____

G L O R Y   G L O W

g l o r y and g lor y and g lory andglory

G R U U C H
_____

3

```
Grow grouc h
G r o w and grow and grow andgrow

A n d   Grow          (grunt)
Great gracious grunt
G O and go a n D
go  go g o gogo go
go  go go go


         Ğ  Ŏ  Ď
         _____


Go god go god go
  g o d   g o g o D


        O   G O D
        _____

        _____


 g ain   g a m e s  gain
           g a m es
    g a i n  g  a y  gam e S
 g̶ a̶m̶e̶  gain games

G o L l Y  god agog agog
gog gog goggog  g o g  gog gog gog


         G  R  O  G

GRUCH  g r u c h  gruch
  g r a g  gr ag  grag


        g l u g
        _____
```

And the bathtub went down the drain
Ukraine
Cranium U k r a i n i u m
        (Uranium)
    You   c r a n i u m   crane
Crane yum you crane
You crane Ukraine
Krake and krake and krake and krake and cake (krake)
G a k e^{gage}cake gag gag gaggag gaggaggaggag gag
              g o n g
gog gog gawg gawg gawg
        goug goug

            G O D (cod)
            _____

Gay cake gotta gay cake go gotta gay cake
gaga gotta gay cake
gong gong gonk

                    God in his mercy is good
                    God in his mercy is good
                    God in his mercy is good
                    God in his mercy is good
                    God in his mercy is good
                    God in his mercy is good
                    God in his mercy is good
                    God in his mercy is good
                    God in his mercy is good
                    God in his mercy is good
                    God in his mercy is good
                    God in his mercy is good
                    God in his mercy is good
                    God in his mercy is good
                    God in his mercy is good
                    God in his mercy is good
                    God in his mercy is good
                    God in his mercy is good
                    God in his mercy is good

```
God in his mercy is good
God in his mercy is good
God in his mercy is good
God in his mercy is good
God in his mercy is good
God in his mercy is good
God in his mercy is good
God in his mercy is goog
Gog in his mersy iz goog
Gog im fis merky ib goog
Gog ig gis mergy ig goog
Gog ig gig gergy ig goog
Gog ig gig giggy ig goog
Gog gg ggg ggggy gg goog
Gog gg ggg ggggg gg gggg
ggg gg ggg ggggg gg gggg
```

ggggggggggggggggggggggggggggggggggggggggggggggggggggggggggggggggggg

```
ston ston tont tont ston stant stont stint stit
         Hi stonet stont stit
stit stlit stold stlott stlit stoldstlott
  stloff stlow slow slow slowly
slow        slow        slowbly
       s l a b l y        s l o w l y
 s l o w b l y
    slob  blob
blob  blob  blob
blob  blob blob blos blop
blob blob blobg blog
b r a g   b r i m   b r a g
b r a g   brimming   brraag
```

                b l o o g l y   blagly
        blagly bloogly
bland   blagly bloogly
        bloogly blong

                        Blong
                        Blong
                        Blong

        g

        G   L   O   S   T   E   rrrrrrrrrrrrrrrr

G l a b b e r   glabber glabber
glad to be of service
so glad to be of service
sinfully glad to be of service

                for his hit surface
                            (surflakes)

good guy can't carry cash
            crash
good guy can't carry cash
cood cguy cgan't gary gpash

g la ss   g la ss   g la ss   g la ss   g la ss
                                            (gloss)

                g r o u c h

```
Can't go
Can't go carry nothing
scant   ko   scary   sluthing


                 s     l     o     p

slinguliar slop

     slaresly    slasely

     slap              slap              slap
                 slooker


          s


     S      L      A      P
            SLANK
```

plap plaster plap psplap

                    prask

                         pony

November 1938
Kenilworth, Ill.

The Scene

Thrown forward by the deafening concussion,
blinded by the fragments, we sink down;
dream images & memories blot our thoughts:
the dragons from our storybooks, the elephant
with writhing proboscis who scared us in the park,
the big bird with red hackles who gobbled at us like an irate uncle:
they swim thru our brains like minnows.

We recover lost toys: Teddy-Bear who burst,
covering the dining-room rug with sawdust, the puppy
who died of distemper, the tootsie-toys that broke
(red cars & fire engines that never ran us down)—
here they are again: look! we can play with them forever!

Mother comes in and bandages our red knees;
the clock on the kitchen wall hurries us thru breakfast,
but we get to school late again anyway; Teacher looks up,
then slashes at our papers, savagely, with red pencils;
the bully humps our nose—but what's all this mud?!
Mother will scold us for dirtying our clothes! Let me alone!
Stop pinching! Why are we crawling on hands & knees?

This isn't the war: this is every day.
The dragons are invisible & real.
For God's sake, somebody bandage our knees! Teddy-Bear has burst!
The puppy has died again! Get away, Uncle, get away!

22 October 1945
New York

9

Selections from "The 11th of July"
(19 Cubist Poems   New York, 11 July 1946)

Hear I Here

Hear I here I hear!
In between the between in between.
I listen. no. no. no.

Here I hear I here!
Between the between!
I here!

No. no. no.

Between the hear the here!
No. no. no. Hear!
The between.

Memory

Cleats, cleavages, the freedom, the freedom;
Horns on the haunted, the hinted;
Clatters of Christians flintly.
The Cleavages.

Memory (the cleavages) memory.
I hint I hunt.

Memory eagerness memory,
I hint I hunt I hear.

Memory memory memory
The cleavages!

Memory

Clear Reapers Pleasing

Clear reapers pleasing.
Help the heed the, heedful.
Clear reapers pleasing.
Help the herd the, heard.
Clear reapers pleasing.

Molly Go

Molly go many go memory
Molly go many go
Molly go many go memory.
Flan.

Many go when to go.
Many go when to go where to go
Molly go many go when to go
Where to go. Flan. where to go

Molly go many go memory
Molly go marry go
Merry go Mary go merry go.
Where to go.

Molly go many go memory.
Where to go.
Flan.

& The

At tear the & when the & when the.
And.

At tear the & when the at tear the:
And the at, where,

At the.

And the at, tear the, and the,
At the at tear the at the
And the when the (where), and the,

& the.

Clear Being

Clear being freer seeing freer.
Being.

Clear being.

Freer seeing freer.   Being.
Freer seeing be-er:—Freeing.
Clearer freeing: Being.

Freeing

Clear being freer.
Seeing.
Clear freeing.
Hearing!
Clear seeing being hope hearing!
Freeing!
Hearing!   Hope!
Clearing!

Clear.   Seeing.   Being.

Whenas My Love

Whenas my flattering love it flew the crate the weight
Whenas my flattering love,
When the flew the.   Crate the weight.
When the flew the—
Crate.

Weight.

Whenas my flattering crate the weight
The flattering, crate the
When, my,

Whenas.   My flattering.   Crate.

Whenas my crate the flattering crate the when
Whenas my.
When.

When my flattering when my love my flew
It flew.

Whenas my love, weight
Whenas my.   Crate.
Whenas my love my weight my crate

It flew!

Whenas my love it flattering flew
When it flew
Whenas my; flew,
Whenas my love.

Whenas my love it flew!

Crate!   Flew!   Weight!

Whenas my love!   Flew!
Whenas!   Flew!
When!

Whenas my love.

11 July 1946
New York

Headline Material

In crawlers trail thin lives among fat towers
Hankering leaps to lave the self in space
Free from maze encumberments: contrivances,
Eagling sweetly over a swarming labyrinth.

Their gazes soar to fierce unlikely tors:
Temptation vibrates through gnarled vertebrae:
—So death's fine ally gains the vagrant wheel
To steer a lubber's launch from a stone shore.

Hardly a woe leads the consummation:
Bent echoes of foregone eventuation
Join tones of inwit's brash deliverance:
Resolve in eyeblink fugue,—glean a fluttering benison....

February 1954
New York

14

Glass Buildings

WHEN FIERY WATER THIRDS FLAUNT SOLAR FUSION

PURGATION WILL SUBLIME MILIEUS OF TINKLING

SO CONTINGENT GLEAMS HIGH FOLIAGE GLINTING

BEQUEATHES A VITROUS SKIN NO FOUNDRIED BONE

WHEN FUNGOID GEYSERS OVERFLAME THE SUN

NASCENT ARCTIC ISLE GLACIAL ABORNING

METALLOPHONIC JOINERS TOLL THE MORNING

SERACS OF LUCENCE FLEE CHILL COME PERFECTION

August 1954
New York

5 biblical poems

Methods for Reading the "5 biblical poems"

"7.1.11.1.11.9.3!11.6.7!4.,a biblical poem" and "4.5.10.11.2.8.4.2.,the 2nd biblical poem" are the first works I composed by means of chance operations (30 Dec. 1954–1 Jan. 1955). With three similar poems (1–27 Jan. 1955) they comprise the "5 biblical poems," of which the 5th is a three-voice simultaneity, my first such work. The number series in each title gives the stanzaic structure of the poem. Each stanza has the same number of lines as the number of integers in the title, and each poem has as many stanzas as lines in each stanza. The integers show how many *events* (single words or silences) occur in each line of a stanza. Continuations of verse lines are indented. Silences are represented by boxes and are each equal in duration to any word the reader chooses. One of the following methods must be followed throughout the reading of each biblical poem.

1) *Indeterminate Method:* Lines may be read at any tempo within the limits of normal conversational speech, and within these limits the tempo may change freely, and individual words, including those determining silence durations, may have *any duration,* but the spoken words must always be coherent and intelligible.

2) *Pulse-Beat Method:* The reader's pulse rate is determined at the beginning, and a uniform rate of one or more events per pulse beat is followed throughout. Durations of words are equal without regard to numbers of syllables, and each silence lasts one beat, but all spoken words must be intelligible. While it is best not to deviate from the beat, a reader may sometimes find it necessary, in order to speak a polysyllable intelligibly, to slow it slightly by use of *rubato,* i.e., by "robbing" a little time from the following word, but getting back on the beat immediately afterwards.

To make structures audible: Since no pauses may occur except for silences symbolized by boxes, instruments or noisemakers may be used to indicate ends of lines and stanzas: single short sounds at ends of lines within stanzas; longer single sounds or groups of two or more short sounds at ends of stanzas. Use of two contrasting timbres is desirable, e.g., percussive for line ends, nonpercussive for stanza ends. These nonverbal sounds must be fitted in so that they do not interrupt continuity, especially in the pulse-beat method, where they should occur between the last beat of each line and the first of the next.

Simultaneous performance: All biblical poems but the 5th (which *must* be read by three voices) may be performed either as solos or as simultaneities, by either method.

1) *Indeterminate simultaneities:* Any number of people, beginning together, may either:

A) all read a biblical poem from beginning to end, so that their different choices of tempi and durations produce a canon with irregularly varying relations between the voices; or

B) separate the stanzas of all but one reader's copy and rearrange them so that they are differently ordered within each reader's copy; all begin together, and each order of the stanzas, original or new, is read from beginning to end; or

C) separate the stanzas of one or more copies, shuffle all of them together thoroughly, and distribute them evenly among the readers (a poem with an odd number of stanzas requires an even number of copies); after beginning together, each reads all stanzas in the individual group in the order in which they were dealt.

Readers produce line and stanza sounds in all three methods.

2) *Pulse-beat simultaneities:* Any of the above three ways of reading a biblical poem as a simultaneity may be used with either of two pulse-beat methods:

A) One pulse beat is agreed upon and followed by all readers (method 1A becomes an exact unison); a conductor or mechanical time-beater is required for most performers to do this well; a nonreader should produce the sounds at ends of lines and stanzas, and that performer's entrances must also be conducted, in most cases.

B) Readers take their own pulses at the beginning, and each follows that beat throughout; as in indeterminate simultaneities, readers produce their own line and stanza end sounds, carefully fitting them in between pulse beats.

Delivery (all methods, solo and simultaneous): All words must be audible and intelligible to everyone present. Readers must listen intently to their own voices and (in simultaneities) to those of other readers and to all ambient sounds audible during a reading, including those of the audience, if any. Amplitudes are free, within the range of full audibility, but readers in simultaneities must never drown each other out or try to outshout each other. Words must be read soberly and seriously, but without fake solemnity or any other artificial type of delivery. Even in the pulse-beat methods, the regular beat ought not to seem mechanical. *Silences must never be hurried.* In simultaneities, *all must begin together.* In all methods except 2A, they'll get apart soon enough.

(First worked out in Jan. 1955; earlier forms written in the late 1950s and in Nov. 1961; revised June-July 1963; completely revised and rewritten for publication in Bernadette Mayer and Vito Acconci's magazine *0 to 9*, 15 June 1968, and this version was revised for publication in this book, 8-10 June 1980.)

"...how God had wholly entered his heart, so that like a child, he would cast dice whenever he did not know what to do."   Georg Büchner: "Lenz"

"Can't you hear it then? Can't you hear the terrible voice that is crying out the whole length of the horizon and which is usually known as silence?..." *Ibid.*

[These quotations were added some time after the composition of the poems.]

7.1.11.1.11.9.3!11.6.7!4.,a biblical poem

In/_____//_____/wherein the/_____//_____/
made
/_____//_____/eat lest they/_____/and taken/_____//_____/the
eight
/_____/twenty/_____//_____/shalt waters the ark/_____//_____//_____/
heart any/_____//_____/servant same sons/_____//_____/
And and of
/_____//_____//_____/in/_____/thou against unto took/_____//_____/
/_____/of/_____//_____/Kadesh/_____/
be that and/_____/and/_____//_____/
/_____//_____//_____/left

them live/_____/lay/_____//_____//_____/
he
closed/_____/Hagar this to thy thy Abraham this ran his
/_____/
/_____//_____/master's mother/_____//_____/Sheba/_____/gathered
      /_____/he
looked with the/_____/a and these/_____//_____/
/_____/thou went
that/_____//_____/and beguiled that/_____//_____//_____/because
      /_____/
/_____/thence/_____/in of/_____/
/_____//_____/carried/_____/my/_____//_____/
/_____/felt Mizpah saying

18

thou/_____//_____//_____//_____//_____//_____//_____/
sun
/_____//_____/with me/_____/daughter in/_____/came/_____/and
Eliphaz
Timna/_____/of words him doubt went and with mock unto
/_____/dungeon ears they Pharoah years I be/_____/
/_____/is/_____/
/_____/said he/_____/the/_____/the/_____/indeed bore/_____/
me households I Beriah and How
/_____/said lived/_____//_____/way is
For the utmost saying

/_____//_____//_____/that fear of/_____/
hard
she Who/_____//_____/of with will/_____/believe in their
of
/_____/the unto the spoke water thine/_____/hearkened land between
/_____/that/_____/of/_____//_____/among out land
/_____/in blemish
in promised/_____/they in/_____//_____//_____/may/_____/by
/_____//_____//_____//_____/of/_____/
And Lord the pass right/_____/the
/_____/that called/_____/

thy/_____//_____//_____//_____//_____/Moses'
/_____/
and it together thereof/_____//_____//_____/keep before/_____//_____/
/_____/
And/_____/Notwithstanding and the/_____//_____/the/_____/
    righteous land
I Then and cherubim shaft/_____//_____/thou tabernacle
and/_____//_____/
of/_____/about/_____/the/_____/of/_____//_____//_____/And/_____/
thou/_____/upon/_____/and/_____/
/_____/the/_____/over/_____/Lord This
I the them which

up∠___//___//___/onward. and∠___/
hand
God; not words∠___/of bring∠___/came∠___//___//___/
each
∠___/the∠___//___/of∠___//___/like∠___//___/ with
sockets∠___/is,∠___/twined∠___//___/the the
∠___//___//___/
∠___/of∠___/to∠___//___//___//___/when of out
∠___/a∠___//___/bring meal-offering
∠___//___/present∠___//___/through it
the∠___//___/take

wherein for∠___//___//___//___/him
∠___/
It∠___//___/and and Moses, Aaron∠___//___//___/upon
∠___/
∠___//___/legs∠___//___/sprinkled which upon∠___/carry
      ∠___/
∠___/are∠___//___/not∠___//___/all raiment,
with∠___/meeting
But hair priest he and to∠___//___/of for priest
∠___/he∠___//___//___/wash
a and linen∠___//___//___//___/
∠___//___/bullock,∠___/

∠___/put of there do, woman∠___/
∠___/
∠___//___/which with∠___//___/eaten.∠___/or∠___//___/
∠___/
man∠___//___//___//___//___//___/walk profane∠___/
      ∠___/
or shall∠___//___//___//___//___/of leave
the the∠___/
∠___/dwellings. in∠___/children Moses neither∠___/kinsman
        means∠___/
And∠___//___//___//___/statutes,
you: unto∠___//___/with∠___//___/
∠___/twenty sanctified ox

20

whether/_____/Lord congregation Judah, number numbered
were
as/_____/fifty/_____/shalt were the Take/_____/blue, Eleazor
sons
/_____//_____/Kohathites, fourscore. /_____//_____//_____/ be man
    before that
before/_____//_____/give/_____//_____/the/_____/Shedeur.
/_____//_____/shekels,
/_____/Dan: sacrifice/_____/as wave-offering. shall/_____/it/_____//_____/
Lord/_____//_____/you host the
/_____//_____//_____//_____//_____/when/_____/
/_____/we the 'Come

/_____/the/_____/therein,/_____/that of
/_____/
/_____/of/_____//_____//_____//_____/which But done/_____//_____/
gave
man/_____/said us from/_____/altar−/_____//_____//_____//_____//_____/
/_____//_____//_____/died made/_____//_____/I, shalt
/_____/ye the
days. for with/_____/because/_____/much from of face/_____/
/_____/unto/_____/the/_____/thee;
/_____/from/_____/said, that against of
the/_____//_____//_____/

And/_____//_____/them to/_____/families:
of
/_____//_____//_____//_____//_____//_____/the daughter,/_____/
    /_____//_____/
the
with/_____//_____/thou the/_____//_____//_____/And/_____/for
This /_____//_____/make kings/_____//_____//_____//_____/
/_____/the/_____/
Moses. /_____//_____//_____//_____/of And of/_____//_____//_____/
/_____/that/_____/stages Rephidim/_____/
/_____//_____/And land/_____//_____//_____/
/_____//_____/of Jogli.

Genesis 1:1−Numbers 34:22
****
Thu.Fri.Sat.30-31.dec.54.1.jan.55. 152 Ave C,NY9NY

21

4.5.10.11.2.8.4.2.,the 2nd biblical poem

thither;/_____/to/_____/
not/_____//_____/tribe/_____/
every/_____/the not/_____//_____/the before lest/_____/
Arabah, a thy/_____/All/_____//_____//_____//_____/the/_____/
Get/_____/
/_____//_____/thy/_____/them,/_____/thy/_____/
/_____//_____/shalt/_____/
/_____/this

/_____//_____//_____//_____/
/_____//_____/of this/_____/
which round many slack/_____//_____/the might/_____/fathers
of is/_____/from/_____/the/_____/great Israel;/_____/you.
I/_____/
and ye shalt/_____/God there, and of
/_____/lent/_____//_____/
/_____//_____/

If the the/_____/
/_____/God to/_____//_____/
thou/_____//_____/chosen/_____//_____//_____/spoken. shall
    established.
/_____/not/_____//_____//_____//_____//_____//_____/Jebusite;
    neck/_____/
son/_____/
thou took/_____//_____//_____//_____//_____/die:
to/_____/be/_____/
house,/_____/

/_____//_____//_____/shall
/_____//_____/the her and
/_____/out/_____/set/_____//_____/a set thou/_____/
upon/_____/thee with/_____//_____//_____//_____//_____//_____//_____/
thy thou
your nations;/_____/it/_____//_____/the /_____/
/_____//_____/witness He
them,/_____/

/____//____/be thy
And/____//____//____/with
Even will Me/____//____//____/the/____//____/And
/____//____/Naphtali/____//____//____/and children/____/
       Moses/____/
/____//____/
Have we/____/you. /____/doors 'Sanctify/____/
the cut And/____/
the of

/____/And/____//____/
/____/the/____/the/____/
/____/us he/____/And/____/and out/____//____/
on the/____/and/____//____/and against down be remaining.
/____/Israel
beforetime/____/that/____//____//____//____//____/
/____//____/the/____/
the cities

/____//____/the of
/____/this along Anak−/____/
In the/____//____/the/____/unto the/____//____/
/____/Moses the their their were city/____/in out families
/____/about
/____//____/there/____//____//____/much that
/____//____//____/children,
/____//____/

not/____//____/of
the/____//____/them through
/____/and/____//____/up after/____//____/Hebron the
/____/drove pass, as/____/war,/____/was/____//____/of
/____//____/
/____//____//____/And Lord/____//____//____/
and heart/____/doth
/____/her

****
Numbers 35:6–Judges 5:27
****
Sat.1.jan.55. 152AveC.NY9NY

5.2.3.6.5.,the 3rd biblical poem

sustenance/_____/and/_____//_____/
/_____//_____/
/_____//_____/bullock,
of twenty/_____//_____//_____/children
hands,/_____/came and/_____/

/_____/weight threescore/_____/the
upon/_____/
Shechem/_____//_____/
/_____//_____/he/_____/his against
/_____//_____/Jephthah, cities/_____/

/_____//_____//_____/not children
/_____/thee? .
ten the/_____/
/_____/said for eater But/_____/
/_____//_____/done to and

in pray/_____/sons,/_____/
they this
/_____/the Ephraim,
man/_____//_____/young/_____/unto
/_____/now up/_____/Israel

/_____/in men of/_____/
we/_____/
/_____//_____//_____/
/_____//_____/unto/_____//_____/man
prayed/_____//_____//_____//_____/

****
Judges 6:4—First Samuel 1:10
****

Sat.1.jan.55. 152AveC.NY9NY

24

11.15.22.4.15.15.11.15.2.1.7.15.,the 4th biblical poem

her. not/____/judge Lord/____//____//____/and/____//____/
said: it/____//____/they/____//____//____//____//____/
        /____//____//____/hath/____/
ground the/____/Beth-shemesh, Abel and /____/ he /____/
        shall goodlier/____/draw/____/answered/____/at
        him, was the/____//____/
men, When shall/____/
land,/____/myself hand and/____//____/unto of/____//____/
        people the/____//____/
/____//____/spared fly for/____/'Peacefully; thy/____/valley
        /____/Philistine taunted/____//____/
the/____/know/____//____//____//____/him, /____/
        /____/
/____/it/____//____/'Speak/____/slay let his/____//____/
        for/____//____//____/
/____/side-ward
/____/
/____//____//____//____/to/____//____/
/____//____//____//____//____//____//____//____/
        /____/the/____/I the my Edomite

Lord, thy/____/Saul/____//____/cut unto/____/away/____/
David thine after, to cried/____/young David/____//____/
        /____//____//____//____//____/
divined/____//____//____/of?' I/____/of behold, am
        /____//____//____//____//____//____//____/
        will/____/the when
/____/it/____/that
Lest/____/of/____//____//____//____/and came and thing
        /____/that thy/____/
And king/____//____/more/____/Geba/____/house. vain
        off O and that son
said:/____//____//____//____//____//____/hand/____/the I
So/____/was unto/____//____/Lord/____//____/ love stronger
        son, king's/____//____/
/____//____/

25

/___/
that/___/to/___//___/as was
strong;/___/him. his prostrate and will on it and mule/___/
      bear up/___/

the/___//___/Joab.'/___//___/came/___//___//___/the
/___/have/___//___//___/which/___/'Art/___/house,
      /___/for/___/there/___/
/___//___//___/did/___//___/a/___//___/refuge/___/
      Thou by he was Ithrite,/___/people. Gad/___//___/
            /___/
/___/the David and
and/___/so him/___//___/sword.' there sat/___//___/hold
      /___/upon/___/
/___/daughter/___/life son, victuals flour/___//___/And
      desire, cubits. /___/not/___/
cherub/___//___//___//___//___//___//___/to/___/
      had
/___/And foursquare,/___/of/___//___//___//___//___/
      month congregation and/___//___/
When/___/
mighty
Thee;/___/of Me: gold,/___//___/
These/___//___/of/___//___//___//___//___/of
      sycomore-trees/___/away/___//___/

And the himself and/___/will/___/of/___/to the
/___//___//___/words shall places/___/from to them in And
      /___/according the
and/___//___//___//___/acts/___/the/___//___//___/
      /___/oil/___/Jezebel/___/will they/___/the Jezreel./___/
/___//___/jealous/___/
have/___//___/in/___/after did Then go sent Thus his/___/
      him and
/___/they the of Israel/___/a/___//___//___//___//___/
      hast/___//___/
here,/___//___//___//___/spirit Samaria. son the vessels;
      answered:

/____/to/____//____/up the hand master man man of any/____/
    also, word
/____//____/
/____/
/____/that, 'The reigned said:/____/which
/____/hands,/____//____/blood take he/____//____/they valley
    about, of man brought

/____/he the days to/____/death/____//____/the/____/
in/____/book/____/of/____/king the/____/up/____//____/ and
    /____/so
former/____//____//____/pieces Judah/____//____/ a and /____/
    the/____//____/and/____/his a/____//____//____//____/
/____//____//____/it
/____//____//____/all he it, slew king,/____/shall the /____/were
    places/____/
house reigned servants in/____//____//____//____/about. captain
    son/____/Judah devour/____/
I/____/not/____//____/house And gold, not/____/
/____/the/____/of that psaltery, bitter/____//____/ their
    /____/in was/____/
will a
/____/
And their name/____/teacheth from done
And the/____/counsel/____//____//____/ resting-place for
    mountains,/____//____/more there.

The this/____/break For And wail of/____//____//____/
/____//____/eyes portion/____//____/earth and/____/head Lord
    upon will From What
offspring merchants upon do/____//____/of The/____//____/
        /____/And soul./____/a day. /____/Therefore/____/as
            of by
/____/the and/____/
But/____//____//____//____/offender profit, out/____// ____/the
    /____/Lord/____/to
Turn his/____//____/a leap everlasting/____//____/is /____/of the
    /____/that

/____/shall/_____//_____//____//____/come/_____/ /____//____/
    /____/
/_____//___//____//____//____/the/____/him/_____//____/Now/____/
    that Lord. degrees, had
said the
And
Have to that/_____//___//____//____/
/____//____/make/_____/may upon/_____//___/His/____//____/
    For/____/For/____/

years/_____//____/shall/_____//____//____/spoil/____/upon/____/
/____//____//____//____//____/be/_____//___//____/ head
    Lord upon/____/inquire, the
/____//____/thee issue, Whose/_____//___//____//____//____/
    gain/_____//____//____/that/_____//____/trap; hast/____/
        Even the
/____/they it shall
And/_____//___//____/the through,/____/with a /____//____/
    /____/Me/____/that
That a/____/hear, of/____/a have ungodliness, fruitful/____/
    /____/for speaketh/____/
/____/shall/____/people up And And/____/without/____//___/
/____/they/____//____/will they/____/Yea, this/____/sun /____/
    peace/____//____/
said/____/
And
And/____//____/understood hath the/____/
Behold,/____/that/____//____/upon song, unto thee, Ye/____/
    old./____/have declare.

And/_____//___//____/A/___//____/shall the/____/level
I/____/not shall be thy/_____//___//____/neck am Me./____/
 back pasture;
All they/_____//___/I Behold, heavens,/_____//___/art two Lord
    /____/Go esteem/_____//___//____//___/did/____/Lord
And/____//____/make
Except within/_____//___//____/with/____//___//____//____/
    /____/hast and 'Wherefore/____/

And I is stumbled/_____/thy/_____/Mine/_____/call/_____/also /_____/
    And forth;
'Ye in will/_____/Father;/_____//_____/worked for Jacob,/_____/
Shall While/_____//_____/which/_____/like/_____/declare/_____/
    /_____//_____/another, in build,
thereof, I
The
Of according thy/_____//_____//_____//_____/
And/_____//_____//_____/family their/_____/away this of/_____/
    fleeth;/_____//_____//_____/

They/_____//_____//_____/against/_____/them: sleek And/_____/
    /_____/
Their/_____/for/_____//_____/come/_____/after/_____/not evil men
    /_____//_____/My
For, they/_____/not haste, earth; King without/_____/his every fruit;
    evil/_____/Believe/_____//_____/the/_____/was the/_____/
By our a us,
    /_____/I Lord,/_____/Lord/_____/when/_____//_____/sin/_____/
    /_____/thou,/_____/which
/_____/said the do for place,/_____/of and/_____/But,/_____//_____/
    /_____//_____/
'Inquire, not of by to destroy/_____/is/_____/them/_____/
/_____/if am/_____/Babylon/_____/concerning among and/_____/
    doth Josiah, worthy/_____//_____/
And/_____/
/_____/
/_____//_____//_____//_____//_____/given you.
that/_____/Nebuchadnezzar/_____//_____//_____//_____/saying: and
    /_____/have/_____/the/_____//_____/

/_____/be/_____//_____//_____//_____/an shall bring/_____/I as
/_____/like/_____/hosts shall Take/_____/against is/_____//_____/and
    /_____//_____//_____/
/_____//_____/for/_____//_____//_____/whereby Abraham, to/_____/and
    Lord, drink
        /_____/all the/_____//_____/sent/_____/the/_____/shall
Babylon.' not it not

out the of/_____//_____/then/_____/day Nethaniah eyes Lord/_____/
    ye of/_____/
/_____//_____/that/_____/an of into/_____//_____//_____/prophet
    handle/_____//_____//_____/
/_____//_____/fell/_____/is land/_____//_____//_____/and hath
/_____/is/_____/wail where; of Thy/_____//_____/it And/_____/the
    man is
/_____/be
Cut
/_____/is her a counsel cup men,
/_____/with/_____/land upon/_____//_____/midst though that/_____/
    no of the/_____/

captive it side; lifted my/_____//_____//_____/that/_____/spirit
and, side,/_____//_____//_____/be/_____//_____//_____//_____/
    /_____/not/_____/have
Lord; The wish to of with Lord And I and shall/_____/I/_____/
    /_____//_____//_____//_____/anxiety; that in lies
against if so oil.
/_____/hast/_____/strangers satisfy/_____//_____/thou/_____/the
    /_____/fruit,/_____/army As
/_____//_____/if/_____//_____/return for/_____//_____//_____//_____/
    mountains God: fury/_____/
Mine/_____//_____//_____/with/_____/ye/_____//_____/any/_____/
/_____//_____//_____/heart/_____/mitre the thee./_____//_____/
    My/_____/rulers,/_____/soul
/_____/so
/_____/
/_____/their/_____/with/_____//_____//_____/
saith profane a the/_____//_____/the And/_____//_____//_____//_____/
    /_____//_____/time,

/_____/thy/_____/Javan/_____//_____/They/_____/I/_____//_____/
/_____//_____//_____/unto and In/_____/be In/_____//_____/go
    /_____//_____/and
My not/_____/and thee the lie with/_____//_____/watchman/_____/
    he/_____//_____//_____/the have/_____//_____/I I
thy/_____//_____//_____/

unto shall/_____/the/_____/of there/_____/caused/_____/transgressions;
     /_____//_____/in/_____/
Lord/_____/brimstone. of till year were was/_____//_____/to and
     /_____//_____//_____/
/_____/post wall/_____/wood; the/_____//_____/round/_____//_____/
/_____//_____//_____/in/_____//_____//_____/horns. the/_____/
     holy at/_____/And/_____/
chambers./_____/
of
/_____//_____/for/_____/Lord/_____//_____/
/_____//_____//_____//_____//_____/of of/_____/after side. and/_____/
     the/_____//_____/

****
First Samuel 1:19—Ezekiel 48:18
****

Sat.thruThu.1.thru.6.jan.55
152AveC.NY9NY

21.21.29.,the 5th biblical poem(for 3 simultaneous voices)the 1st biblical play

VOICE I:

L____//L____//L____/one Lord children/____//____/My the/____/
L____//____//____/Lord,/____/lying,/____//____//____/
     unto
L____//____/O Judah that/____/the Ephraim/____//____/their
L____//____//____/And/____//____/of them/____/for
Therefore/____//____/turned/____//____//____/prevailed;And
L____//L____//____//____/tear/____//____//____/
L____/thou/____//____/Make laid cry before
L____//L____/His/____/

L____//L____//L____/Thy/____/full/____//____//____/
those nation in Edom/____//____/And/____/the To naked
And/____/unto/____/were I uprightly/____/thee, To innermost
L____/Lord Thy/____//____/shall may/____//____//____/
L____//____//____//____/upon/____/And/____/heart/____/
L____/thee,/____/had/____//____//____/of the
L____//L____//____/before/____//____/
from of

The/____/her Achzib preach; gone/____/lips;/____//____//____/
L____//L____//L____//____//____//____/And/____/pain,/____/
L____/goings/____/go/____/up weights?'/____//____/Their
her;/____/ retaineth the so They filled upon canker-worm,
     slumber,/____/
Their/____//____/empty violently/____/of/____//____/mount
for of the/____//____//____/voice And be/____//____/bone
L____//L____/Him more.Haggai corn,/____/

****
Ezekiel 48:25—Haggai 1:11
****

Thu.27.jan.55.
152AveC.NY9NY

32

VOICE II:

/____/side:/____/the/____/children/_____//_____/My the/____/
 /____//____/the Swearing/____/And the them/____//____/
/____//____//____//____//_____/watereth the Ephraim not; his
 /____//____/is/____/house;/____/his spoiled/____/anger,
 /____/
/____//____/strove blood/____/them/____/ripped/____//____/
 fragrance lion, the them,/_____//_____//____/camp say will
 the this And/____/children/_____//____/turn into

/____//____//____/the/____//____//____/deliver/____/And
 /____/Lord/____/Me, house/____/from the unto/____/
 thee?'
The/____//____/against/____//____//____//____/every/____/
 said:/____//____//____/name. will in off/____/ Zion And
I/____/flood on me; that/____//____//____//____/all/____/of
 they before God./____/And in/____/she lifted sent/____/their
 /____//____/is/____/

Then/____/by/____//____//____//____//____/cast/____/and
 /____/in/____/lionesses, that as Thy/____/at And
/____//____/that with And anger./____/unto/____/to near drive
 /____//____/hosts./____/desert,/____/name Thou/____/
In no it so/____/the and the/____//____/that hosts: upon of the
 /____/even/____//____//____//____/The/____/so/____/eye
 /____/ass,/____/

****
Ezekiel 48:25—Zechariah 9:9
****

Thu.27.jan.55.
152AveC.NY9NY.

VOICE III:

/‾‾‾//‾‾‾//‾‾‾/one/‾‾‾//‾‾‾//‾‾‾//‾‾‾//‾‾‾/the
/‾‾‾/the/‾‾‾/oil/‾‾‾/them,/‾‾‾/respond/‾‾‾/
/‾‾‾//‾‾‾/
Because/‾‾‾//‾‾‾/new priests, like/‾‾‾/earth.' /‾‾‾/robbers
like silver builded/‾‾‾/fool, I/‾‾‾//‾‾‾/counsel.
/‾‾‾//‾‾‾/
/‾‾‾//‾‾‾/a/‾‾‾//‾‾‾//‾‾‾//‾‾‾/compassions He his wild
/‾‾‾/unto They/‾‾‾/the house/‾‾‾//‾‾‾//‾‾‾/
A he is years/‾‾‾/shall Stir/‾‾‾/

So shall/‾‾‾//‾‾‾/the palaces the/‾‾‾//‾‾‾/ he the
/‾‾‾/hath Saith/‾‾‾//‾‾‾/The exactions /‾‾‾//‾‾‾/
/‾‾‾//‾‾‾//‾‾‾/pass the/‾‾‾/that shall Therefore/‾‾‾/
mourn Smite/‾‾‾//‾‾‾/name. /‾‾‾//‾‾‾//‾‾‾/as
/‾‾‾//‾‾‾/
/‾‾‾//‾‾‾//‾‾‾/despised./‾‾‾/thy down,/‾‾‾//‾‾‾/
/‾‾‾//‾‾‾/the heaven, Passed of live.' /‾‾‾/and of
/‾‾‾/O/‾‾‾//‾‾‾/of/‾‾‾/I of/‾‾‾//‾‾‾/

For thy forth go up/‾‾‾//‾‾‾/For/‾‾‾/Their her; He into
/‾‾‾/so/‾‾‾/jostle his thee Make O
Their/‾‾‾//‾‾‾//‾‾‾//‾‾‾/net, thee, glory, from forth
/‾‾‾//‾‾‾//‾‾‾/son the/‾‾‾//‾‾‾/the shall
/‾‾‾/
/‾‾‾/they/‾‾‾/the turn enemy;/‾‾‾//‾‾‾//‾‾‾//‾‾‾/sixth
And/‾‾‾/eyes?/‾‾‾//‾‾‾/is Zechariah to/‾‾‾/do?'
/‾‾‾//‾‾‾//‾‾‾//‾‾‾/thee'; day, answered behold,

****
Ezekiel 48:25—Zechariah 5:9
****

Thu.27.jan.55.
152Ave.C.NY9NY

34

Machault

it wits it it by the lasso)
tired animal." tired lasso) it
wits it that it

it by lasso) that by that
the so lasso) lasso) tired lasso)
the by wits it

lasso) the lasso)
it it it lasso) lasso) by lasso) by lasso)
it by that it lasso)

off off proverb, off
ran may may
proverb, confessed as

the by that it that
it
it by it the by by it it it

it by the lasso) tired
lasso)
wits it wits it it by the lasso)

and circle, larger wits it
lasso)
circle, and circle, the wits it lasso)

as confessed proverb, off ran
off as confessed as
his as confessed proverb, off

it wits
wits it it by the by it it
wits the
by by the by lasso)

lasso) it by
by by the lasso) tired lasso) tired obedience
the the
it by

circle, wits wits
larger it larger it and and it
wits
circle, larger wits it

his confessed
in as his in
as
Of in

tired animal." tired lasso)
it that it by it it
lasso) it it it by
the lasso) tired lasso) tired animal." tired

by it by the by
by the lasso) tired
animal." tired so lasso) tired lasso)
the by wits it

it the by the
lasso) the it by
the lasso) lasso)
larger wits larger circle, it

as his confessed proverb,
off confessed as
almost as in
his in as Of

lasso) lasso)
wits it that it by it
by
wits it that it by that
it

it by it the by lasso)
lasso) the animal." tired lasso) the
by
lasso) the animal." tired lasso) the
lasso)

it by
wits the circle, larger circle, wits
larger
wits the lasso) by that
it

off proverb, confessed
as confessed as his
in
as confessed as as
Of

it it that it by it by the by
lasso) lasso)
by lasso) the by that it that

by by it the
by the by
it it by the lasso) tired

circle, it wits it circle, larger wits
wits it lasso) lasso)
circle, larger wits it that

Of Of his
in as as
Of his in as

it it
it it by the by the obedience obedience

lasso) by that the by it
the by it it it it wits it it that

it lasso)
it the by that

Of proverb, off
ran confessed ran off proverb, confessed

the it that by
the by the by the by that it wits

it it that by the so
so animal." tired lasso)

it lasso) lasso)
larger circle, larger wits it wits it that

as
as his in as

it it it by
wits it that it by
that

lasso) by the by the by
it by the by the obedience
the

it lasso) larger
circle, larger wits larger wits Wild
wits

Of as
his as almost in
as

it wits
that it
obedience the by tired lasso) the lasso)
the by lasso) by it

tired lasso)
the by the by lasso) it
that it wits it it that
it by

it it
the lasso)
wits it that
it lasso) lasso) lasso)

ran confessed
proverb, off
ran off proverb, confessed
as confessed

wits wits wits it that
it that it by that it
lasso) it it it by

by it by the by
lasso) by the lasso) tired
animal." tired so lasso) tired lasso)

it by the by the
lasso) the it by
the lasso) lasso)

his confessed proverb,
off confessed as
almost as in

the lasso) tired lasso) animal." tired
lasso) lasso)
wits it that it by that
it

the by wits it
it by it the by lasso)
lasso) the animal." tired lasso) the
lasso)

larger wits larger circle, it
it by
wits the lasso) by that
it

his in as Of
off proverb, confessed
as confessed as as
Of

Written in January 1955 at 152 Avenue C, New York 9, NY, by translating the pitches of Guillaume Machault's motet QUANT THESEUS (p. 6 in Lehman Engel's *Renaissance to Baroque,* Vol. 1 French-Netherland Music, Harold Flammer Inc., New York, 1939) into a gamut of words from T.H. Bilby's *Young Folk's Natural History with Numerous Illustrative Anecdotes,* published by John W. Lovell Company, New York, copyright 1887, by Hurst & Co.

A Sonnet for Gérard de Nerval

Constantinople. from writers The it surely, This interesting it violent
of ringleaders contemporary this was the the and at age.
influence into married to age. Seventeenth dream This *Contes* him
descriptions and Gautier's work This back a married Gérard
    ringleaders

but Constantinople. Nerval inspiration the lover way to or references.
suffered day. work This interesting it violent of ringleaders but
of the as patina dreams), descriptions married Constantinople. or then
contracted and or This France, is *Aurélia,* who writers or

age. influence into married Nerval ringleaders as called his the
and at age. longing the of this age. ringleaders This
occasional or longing memory, it violent of comme age. Duke's

of to magnetic healthier But medieval thought genre. important to
to grandeur grandeur influence into married Nerval a to fall
a married Gérard the was, of patina Nerval's Méry or

Spring 1958
The Bronx

Sonnet of My Death

I feel my death approaching through my time
and leaning forward we two greet each other
as friendly dog and cat put forth their muzzles
to nuzzle briefly though so unalike.
But we two recognize our mirror-likeness:
I know my death as what I will become;
my death must know me also but is dumb
to tell of death as I to tell of life.

My death arises through the limbs like wine
and nuzzles silently the heart and tongue;
it rubs against the brain and through the eyes
it gazes like a wistful dog whose one
communication is to lick and touch
and claim the body I do not call mine.

28 December 1958
The Bronx

Syllabic Sonnet

God only knows how people can stand it!
Lurching to work every morning, mashed
into a steaming mass of half-squashed
resentful sleepiness, ready to quit
by the time they get to work, made to fit
in by petty harassments, the clock-lashed,
fringe-benefitted mules of ready cash
deny their sorrows. Through mere lack of wit?
"People who stand for a politics of
imminent disintegration would stand
for anything!" "They need a good hard shove
to wake them from their television trance!"
"The trouble is they've had too little love!"
The trouble is God only understands.

February 1959
The Bronx

42

September Pack

Overflame arctic.

       Foundried once
glass will fusion chill
yet.

   Flaunt orange of sun bone
thirds.

     More and bequeathes glacial need the fungoid joiners
and several yet fiery gray nascent friends skin Cimabue ashes
dear come high isle lucence morning tinkling consumed purgation
more solar the thanks
metallophonic scarlet from so
O leafmeal of
no
foliage milieus more
me anxiety tan vitrous
a a to red when shades conduct
deeper.

    Of in through glinting aborning seracs
when
gleams.

   Khaki yet.

     Pipe perfection the and toll sublime
to.

  Geysers once.

25 September 1959
The Bronx

A Short Introduction to *The Marrying Maiden,*
a play of changes

The Marrying Maiden, a play of changes, is a play for nine characters in six scenes based on the *I Ching*.[1] The actors' nonverbal movements and the total duration of any performance are not predetermined by the text, but the order of the scenes and of speeches within scenes, as well as the latter's words, are fixed, and the delivery of the speeches—tempo, dynamics, "manner," and many pauses—are relatively determined by explicit notations. The text was composed in summer 1958 and the delivery regulations completed in summer 1959.

All determined aspects of the play, from its title and the number and names of characters to the words of speeches and delivery regulations, are results of chance operations rather than the author's choices—conscious, preconscious, or unconscious (see below for details). They result from the systematic use of objective hazard.

As source material for the play I used ten classes of material from the *I Ching* and its "Ten Wings" (verses and commentaries suggested by the hexagrams): only ancient material translated directly, not Wilhelm's summaries of other commentary traditions. The words of Scene 3, entitled "Enthusiasm," were all drawn from Chapter III of the so-called "Eighth Wing"—"Shuo Kua," a discussion of the trigrams. From this chapter, which presents the symbols with which each trigram is associated, I have drawn words and phrases of various lengths. The symbols include the trigrams' "attributes" (e.g., "The Creative is strong") and symbolic animals (e.g., "The Creative acts in the horse"), parts of the body (e.g., "The Creative manifests itself in the head"), family members (e.g., "The Creative is heaven, therefore it is called the father"), and additional symbols (e.g., "The Creative. . .is round,. . .the prince,. . .jade, metal, cold, ice;. . .deep red, a good horse, an old horse, a lean horse, a wild horse, tree fruit") associated with each trigram. Because both of the names of each trigram (e.g., "The Creative" and "Heaven") and their associated symbols appear in this chapter, both names and symbols appear in this scene's speeches.

In composing *The Marrying Maiden* I first obtained a long series of hexagrams by the "coin oracle" method. Then, having coded the ten classes of *I Ching* material relevant to each hexagram and its trigrams, as well as the individual words and word groups within each class, to digits or digit groups, I used a random digit table (*A Million Random Digits with 100,000 Normal Deviates,* by the Rand Corporation: Glencoe, Ill.: The Free Press, 1955) to specify all details of the play's

---

[1] *The I Ching or Book of Changes,* as rendered into English by Cary F. Baynes from Richard Wilhelm's German translation (Bollingen Series XIX: New York: Pantheon Books, 1950).

text. All verbal materials—including the titles of the play and of its scenes, characters' names (except for those of the "Three Ancient Kings"), as well as the actual words and word groups in each scene's speeches—were drawn from one or more of the ten classes of *I Ching* materials connected with the successive hexagrams in my series. Random digits also determined which class was to be the source for each verbal element. Each scene's speeches were drawn from a different class or group of classes, as those of Scene 3 came solely from Chapter III of the "Shuo Kua."

The delivery regulations were drawn by means of random digits from three gamuts: five levels of tempo and five of dynamics and 500 adverbs and adverbial phrases indicating "manner" of delivery, ranging from "comically" to "like a stage American." Tempo regulations are printed above the first words to which they apply, dynamics notations below, and manner adverbials between pairs of virgules placed between words of speeches. Pauses are determined by line endings and by punctuation.

The number of words to which each regulation applies were also determined by random digits, and in some scenes series of dynamics and/or tempo regulations were repeated, sometimes in reverse order. Often the scope of one regulation runs on from one line to another and even from one character's speech to another's. Such "run-ons" are indicated by placing continuing regulations in parentheses at the beginnings of typographical lines.

Each character has only two continually persisting attributes: his or her name and the number of verbal units (single words or word groups) he or she speaks in each verse line of a speech. While most speeches consist of single verse lines, some comprise two or more lines. Each verse line begins at the left margin, and when it extends over two or more typographical lines, continuation lines are indented. (I first used this type of verse, in which "events"—here words and/or word groups—rather than feet, syllables, or accented beats act as metrical units, when writing my first chance-generated poems, the "5 biblical poems," in December–January 1954–55.)

The order in which the characters' names were obtained during composition from the Judgements of the first hexagrams in my series determined their relative taciturnity or loquaciousness. The Marrying Maiden herself speaks only one word or word group in a line; The Superior Man, two; Ancient King I: Pharoah, three; Ancient King II: David, four; Ancient King III: Abdullah bin Fazil, A Moorish King, five; The Ruler, six; The Great Man, seven; A Maiden, eight; and The Merchant and Stranger, nine words or word groups. (A Maiden and The Ruler do not appear in Scene 3.)

The Marrying Maiden has only been produced once—by The Living Theatre in the loft playhouse it occupied at 14th St. and the Avenue of the Americas in Manhattan in the late 1950s and early 1960s—opening in June 1960 and continuing once a week thereafter for about a year. Judith Malina directed it; Julian Beck designed sets and costumes; Nicola Cernovich lighted it; and John Cage, assisted by the late Richard Maxfield, composed music for it in the form of audiotapes made by submitting a tape of a rehearsal to various chance operations.

These tapes were of two types: a long tape made by cutting the rehearsal tape at breath pauses and reassembling the segments, along with silent segments, through chance operations; and six short tapes produced by means of "hands-on" tape-recorder manipulations which modified the actors' voices. The latter were played between scenes and between the two parts of Scene 5, along with short rehearsal films by Julian Beck. The long tape was turned on and off at random intervals by a silent dice player (a "10th character" introduced by Ms. Malina) when he threw a certain number; it had the effect of superimposing word groups from other parts of the play upon those being spoken on stage.

The actors' nonverbal actions were determined by two factors: a fixed scenario composed by Ms. Malina, which was suggested to her by the titles of scenes and characters' speeches; and an "action pack" originally comprising about 1400 playing cards upon which Iris Lezak had lettered a series of action commands I had devised. These cards were given to actors by the dice player when he threw a certain number, and had the effect of interspersing new actions every night among those required by Ms. Malina's scenario. The action commands ranged from ones as specific as "Walk forward six steps" to ones as general as "Do something romantic." As used by the Living Theatre actors, they often led to interesting nonverbal improvisations.

derived from the longer introduction
written in November 1960
completed 2 September 1981
New York

from *The Marrying Maiden, a play of changes*

Scene 3: ENTHUSIASM

CHARACTERS IN SCENE:

> Ancient King III: Abdullah bin Fazil,
>   A Moorish King
> The Great Man
> Ancient King II: David
> A Merchant and Stranger
> The Marrying Maiden
> Ancient King I: Pharaoh
> The Superior Man

ANCIENT KING III: ABDULLAH BIN FAZIL, A MOORISH KING:

> *fast*   *very fast*
> /*loathingly*/ foot tongue /*exhaustedly*/ fire The Joyous thunder
>   *(p)*

THE GREAT MAN:

> *slow*   *fast*
> /*(exhaustedly)*/ a large wagon the strong horses /*gratingly*/ with wild
>   *(p)*
> *(fast)*   *slow*
> courage firm and gnarled /*withdrawingly*/ trees deep red mare
> *(p)*
> *(slow)*
> The Creative
> *(p)*

ANCIENT KING II: DAVID:

          (slow)   *fast*
/*(withdrawingly)*/ pleasure /*righteously*/ a large wagon a sorceress the
          (p)
        (fast)
various kinds /*comically*/ of black-billed birds
(p)

THE GREAT MAN:

        (fast)   *slow*
/*(comically)*/ dryness hard and salty soil The /*politely*/ Receptive a
        (p)
            (slow)
/*poetically*/ spreading out brightness wood watchmen
            (p)

A MERCHANT AND STRANGER:

        fast
/*(poetically)*/ tongue /*as if reading a letter aloud*/ eye form heaven a kettle
         (p)
        (fast)   *very fast*
hard and salty /*quarrelsomely*/ soil frugality hard and salty soil
(p)
           (very fast)
/*lispingly*/ the middle daughter
        (p)

ALL 7 CHARACTERS:

        (very fast) *fast*
/*(lispingly)*/ a sorceress head horses which /*insinuatingly*/ can neigh
        (p)
        (fast)
  well round
        (p)

ANCIENT KING II: DAVID:

(fast)   *slow*
/*(insinuatingly)*/ rush the concubine bursting open /*hurrayingly*/ The
            (p)
(slow)
Creative
(p)

A MERCHANT AND STRANGER:

        (slow)
/*(hurrayingly)*/ horses which /*righteously*/ can gallop the goat
            (p)
moderate
big-bellied men deep red /*puffingly*/ the fingers rush the sun
(p)
very slow
horses which can /*yieldingly*/ gallop the middle son
(p)

ANCIENT KING I: PHARAOH:

    (very slow) very fast
/*(yieldingly)*/ rush horses which can gallop dragon
            m

A MERCHANT AND STRANGER:

        (very fast)   *very slow*
/*offensively*/ horses which can gallop The Gentle /*virtuously*/ yielding
            (m)
    (very slow)   *fast*
    wind ice foot lake /*jokingly*/ bamboo that is green /*like a stage*
    (m)
        (fast)
African/ and young pig
        (m)

ANCIENT KING II: DAVID:

(fast)   *very fast*
/*confidently*/ vehement the undecided pod-bearing useful plants firm
(m)
                (very fast)
/*briskly*/ and /*lovingly*/ gnarled /*quaveringly*/ trees
                (m)

THE SUPERIOR MAN:

        slow
/*(quaveringly)*/ wheel The Joyous
        ff

A MERCHANT AND STRANGER:
        (slow)   *fast*
/*(quaveringly)*/ advance /*embarrassedly*/ men with sick hearts the
        (ff)
(fast)   *slow*
guideline seeds fruits frugality /*solemnly*/ cloth fruits
(ff)
(slow)   *fast*
men with earache
(ff)

THE SUPERIOR MAN:

        (fast)   *slow*
/*(solemnly)*/ The Receptive horses with /*inconsequantially*/ beautiful
        (ff)
(slow)
backs
(ff)

50

ALL 7 CHARACTERS:

(slow)   *fast*
/*(inconsequentially)*/ the /*dreamily*/ snail wheel an old /*sexually*/ horse
                    (ff)
(fast)   *very fast*
melancholy men dangerous
(ff)

THE GREAT MAN:

(very fast)   *fast*
/*(sexually)*/ the middle daughter /*like a stage American*/ The Creative
              (ff)
(fast) slow   *moderate*   *very slow*
horse big-bellied men metal pod-bearing useful/*haughtily*/
(ff)
(v.slow) v.fast   *very slow*   *fast*
plants men with much white in their eyes
(ff)

1958-1959
Stony Point, N.Y.
and The Bronx

Night Walk

Reading Directions, Structure, and Vocabulary

I. Reading Directions

Each line of "Night Walk" is preceded by indications regulating the degrees of rapidity & loudness with which it is to be read, & is followed by a number indicating the length of the silence following the line. The readers are free, within certain limits, to set the meaning of the levels of rapidity & loudness & the length of the standard count or "second" of silence, but these meanings must be followed consistently throughout a reading of the poem.

1. Rapidity

There are 9 levels of rapidity in the poem: Very Very Slow (vvs), Very Slow (vs), Slow (s), Moderately Slow (ms), Moderate (m), Moderately Rapid (mr), Rapid (r), Very Rapid (vr), & Very Very Rapid (vvr).

The readers shd always try to make the words as intelligible as possible. Therefore, altho they are free to set the rapidity levels, they shd not make "vvr" a rate of reading so rapid that the words are rendered unintelligible. The author finds it possible to read a typical 10-word line of this poem in 3 seconds. Probably some readers can do so in 2 seconds, but certainly not much less than that. The following is a suggested (*not mandatory*) gamut of rapidities:

```
        /vvs/vs /ss /ms /m /mr /r  /vr /vvr/
seconds/11 /10 /9 /8   /7  /6  /5  /4  /3  /
```

Some readers will, however, want to make the spaces between the rates greater & shd feel free to do so. Thus, a reader who can read 10 words intelligibly in 2 seconds might use the gamut:

```
        /vvs/vs /s  /ms /m /mr /r  /vr /vvr/
seconds/18 /16 /14 /12 /10 /8   /6  /4  /2  /
```

or, a reader with a "vvr" rate of 10 words in 3", wd possibly use:

```
        /vvs/vs /s  /ms  /m /mr /r   /vr  /vvr/
seconds/15 /13 /12 /10½ /9  /7½ /6.  /4½ /3  /
```

Any such gamut is permissible.

2. Loudness

There are 5 levels of loudness in each section of "Night Walk." In Sections I, II & IV, these levels are: Very Very Soft (ppp), Very Soft (pp), Soft (p), Moderately Soft (mp), & Moderately Loud (mf).

In Section III, Very Very Soft (ppp) is dropped from the bottom of the loudness scale & Loud (f) is added at the top.

As with the rapidity-levels, the exact values of these loudness levels are to be determined by the readers, but each reader shd be consistent in keeping loudness levels throughout a performance at the values decided for these levels.

3. Silences

At the end of each line there is a figure or group of figures indicating the number of seconds of silence which shd follow that line. All lines ending within stanzas are followed by silences of from 1 to 10 seconds. (1"-10"). All lines at the ends of stanzas, but not at the end of a section, are followed by silences of from 11 to 70 seconds (11"-1'10"). All lines at the ends of sections are followed by silences of from 71 to 180 seconds (1'11"-3'0"). In a group reading of several parts made from this poem (of which the present version wd be one of the parts) it is best that these seconds of silence really be seconds. In a solo reading, the "seconds" may be each reduced in length, but such a reduction must be consistent throughout any one reading. Thus, if each "second" is reduced actually to ½", silences of 5 "seconds" shd last 2½", silences of 53 "seconds" shd last 26½", &c.

4. Word Grouping—Punctuation—Pauses within Lines

The lines of "Night Walk" are unpunctuated in order that readers may freely group the words within them in any ways they see fit. The attempt shd be *made,* however, to *group* words, & not merely to read single words mechanically throughout the poem. *Some* such mechanical reading may be found desirable here & there, & many words will probably have to be read alone (i.e., as if they formed rhetorical sentences of their own, such as "Night."). Pauses may be made within lines in accordance with the groupings chosen, but each such pause must last less than a second. Where the standard "second" used for silences (as in some solo readings) is of shorter duration than a clock second, pauses within lines must be shorter than the standard "second" used.

II. Structure

Night Walk consists of 4 sections, each of which consists of 6 stanzas. In each section the stanzas are of 2 different forms which alternate *abbbab*. The 2 different stanza forms are different in each section.

A line is defined as a group of 1 to 10 successive words followed by a silence of 1 to 10 seconds (1″-10″). In three cases, "one o'clock," "two o'clock," & "three o'clock," a group of words functions & is counted prosodically as one word.

A stanza is defined as a group of 1 to 10 lines followed by a silence of from 11 to 70 seconds (11″-1′10″).

A section is defined as a group of 6 stanzas of 2 different forms, alternating *abbbab*, which is followed by a silence of from 71 to 180 seconds (1′11″-3′0″).

The actual structures of the sections of "Night Walk" are as follows. Roman numerals indicate section numbers. Arabic numerals indicate the number of words in each line (zeros indicate 10-word lines). Virgules indicate stanza breaks. Double virgules indicate section breaks.

I: 2/3223/3223/3223/2/3223//
II: 16326/940570/940570/940570/16326/940570//
III: 573023/011289/911289/911289/573023/911289//
IV: 949932922/84299048/84299048/84299048/949932922/84299048///

III. Vocabulary and Meaning Groups

The words in "Night Walk" are all taken from a list of 100, representing objects, actions, and states of mind remembered as having figured in an actual situation. All of the words may function as nouns, i.e., be subjects or objects of sentences. Most of them may function also as verbs, or adjectives, or either verbs or adjectives. Thus, the word "looking" may be taken as a gerund, and thus a noun, or a present participle with either its verbal function emphasized or its adjectival function. The word "coats" may be taken as either a plural noun in either the subjective or the objective case, or as a singular or plural noun in the possessive case, or a verb in the 3rd person singular of the present tense. The words "streamsound" and "ease" may function as singular nouns or as verbs in the 3rd person plural of the present tense.

Thus, in presenting the words in each line with no punctuation, the maximum of ambiguity is preserved & the reader has the opportunity of forming any number of different groupings of words, often with widely different meanings. Thus, "darkness quiet streamsound darkness remembering teeth" may be taken as a series of single words, each denoting a separate situation or aspect of a situation; or as "Darkness. Quiet streamsound. Darkness remembering teeth."; or as "Darkness quiet. Streamsound darkness. Remembering teeth."; or as "Darkness, quiet streamsound darkness: remembering teeth."; or in other ways. The line "three o'clock hands knowing hair clouds learning tongues twigs sweaters" may be read as one sentence ("Three o'clock hands knowing hair clouds, learning tongues, twigs, sweaters.") or as "Three o'clock. Hands knowing hair, clouds learning tongues, twigs learning sweaters." or in other ways.

Readers may want to punctuate their lines for a particular performance or leave them unpunctuated & make the decision as to groupings during the course of the reading. Either method is permissible, the 2nd more appealing.

Night Walk

for VBW

I

ms/ppp	standing halflight	41
vs/p	water woman silence	7
s/ppp	two o'clock friends	10
vr/ppp	cold hills	6
vs/mp	twigs darkness talking	49
mr/p	needing meaning memory	3
m/mf	meaning finding	2
r/mp	hair two o'clock	7
ms/mp	man teeth revealing	24
m/p	slipping learning finding	4
vvs/p	air fingers	2
r/p	touching freezing	2
vvr/ppp	trees sky hearing	19
s/p	standing quiet	51
ms/p	peace sweaters freezing	9
vs/p	feeling dimness	9
vvs/mp	fingers resting	4
vs/pp	lips memory cheeks	107

vs/pp   air   6

ms/p   happiness ease silence sweetness needing
                  halflight   9

mr/pp   delight walking needing   7

vr/p   standing ease   1

r/pp   darkness quiet streamsound darkness remembering
                  teeth   33

ms/mp   warming warming warming water clothing
                  clasping stars revealing bears   5

vvs/p   dimness sky needing dark   5

s/mp   sweetness wondering wondering hugging finding
                  resting bodies clothing woman pointing   9

s/mp   knowing woman grey being delight   5

vvs/ppp   water hearing hearing quiet pockets kissing
                  memory   7

vr/ppp   sky night seeing black looking memory wondering
                  revealing attention eyes   41

vvs/mf   morning wet grey looking lips dimness tongues
                  hugging grey   7

ms/mf   wet sweaters kisses man   1

vvs/p   eyelids stories loving streamsound knowing ease
                  bodies halflight meaning tongues   10

vvr/pp   hairsmell light hairsmell eyelids peace   2

vs/ppp   ease water liking warming attention bears
                  eyebrows   7

vvr/pp   ice listening white foreheads kissing thankfulness
                  evening touching walking sliding   54

vr/p   seeing night touching pointing white listening
                  talking cheeks desiring   6

vvs/p   touching liking morning eyebrows   7

mr/pp   clouds memory being sweetness pointing white
                  streamsound one o'clock light cheeks   3

r/mp   sweetness one o'clock dimness feeling kissing   1

r/p   sweetness coats dimness ease quiet hands
                  hugging   4

m/ppp	meaning constellations touching sliding pointing bodies memory liking peacefulness finding 91
mr/mf	clouds 1
s/p	hearing warmth starlight ice coats talking 8
vvs/ppp	constellations freezing peacefulness 8
r/pp	white sky 4
ms/pp	ice eyes bodies remembering clothing constellations 60
vvs/mf	thankfulness loving happiness grey talking needing telling happiness ice 8
ms/mf	white hairsmell starlight thankfulness 8
vvs/p	dimness knowing learning learning slipping foreheads resting black sweaters teeth 2
vs/pp	resting light touching needing hugging 1
vs/ppp	white sky foreheads walking stories noses two o'clock 1
s/mp	looking ease night walking loving friends eyebrows sky freezing foreheads 158

III

mr/mf	coats twigs being tongues revealing 3
vvr/mp	silence walking coats bodies delight learning man 1
s/p	clouds meaning noses 7
mr/f	attention delight feeling foreheads light halflight night hearing two o'clock eyebrows 6
r/mf	sweetness teeth 3
m/pp	foreheads happiness revealing 47
r/pp	stories eyebrows clouds dark hairsmell standing revealing black dark 2
vr/mp	kisses 8
vvr/mp	telling 4
vvs/pp	finding dimness 5

vvs/f	cold coats desiring clothing three o'clock evening clothing feeling 9
r/f	sky cold learning clouds trees desiring touching memory clasping 42
m/p	kisses black delight wondering desiring freezing bodies listening learning 9
ms/p	light 10
vvr/mp	clothing 4
vvr/mp	sliding dimness 10
vr/f	pointing dark looking cold hearing stars streamsound white 9
vr/f	clasping knowing sweaters fingers quiet meaning revealing being silence 21
r/f	hugging needing sweetness loving halflight ice dimness ice streamsound 9
vs/mf	warming 7
s/f	kissing 5
vvs/pp	friends kisses 6
mr/mp	sky resting tongues trees being eyes hugging air 1
vr/f	eyebrows talking man hearing coats hearing coats hearing peace 52
m/f	walking pockets delight eyelids dimness 10
r/p	slipping being eyes lips resting night being 10
vvs/p	liking talking kisses 6
m/mf	grey meaning tongues memory warmth trees attention warmth touching needing 8
ms/mp	feeling listening 8
r/f	bodies three o'clock man 48
vr/pp	noses starlight tongues noses cheeks darkness wonder three o'clock sliding 9
mr/pp	delight 2
vs/pp	clasping 4
mr/pp	trees pockets 5
vs/pp	revealing trees listening trees trees teeth stories black 1
vr/p	being friends clothing hairsmell light hairsmell telling eyes clasping 141

IV

vvs/mf	clouds man delight listening looking eyebrows telling memory warmth 5
ms/mf	revealing cheeks woman cold 1
vvs/mp	kissing streamsound touching white listening halflight learning eyebrows coats 5
vr/pp	smiling sweaters wet cheeks cold looking friends listening darkness 8
m/mf	warmth sky water 6
m/pp	stars lips 5
s/mp	telling trees slipping stars talking evening three o'clock black meaning 3
vs/mp	water dimness 9
r/pp	revealing talking 53
mr/pp	being fingers pointing twigs light eyebrows smiling seeing 9
mr/pp	cheeks kisses cheeks walking 6
mr/p	feeling lips 3
mr/p	hairsmell listening hairsmell tongues noses pockets sky hearing darkness 5
m/ppp	touching coats looking white sky teeth stories memory kissing 10
r/mf	stories halflight dimness white wonder resting friends darkness clothing noses 5
vr/pp	touching air slipping hands 4
s/pp	pointing twigs hair constellations lips dimness delight bodies 50
vs/pp	teeth lips sky hands light sky sky hair 9
s/pp	silence looking eyelids eyelids 8
vvs.ppp	peacefulness night 5
vvr/pp	night hearing halflight smiling constellations standing streamsound silence wet 5
mr/mp	walking bears one o'clock foreheads delight hands slipping meaning light 5
m/mp	sky peace grey thankfulness trees ice friends streamsound peacefulness delight 1
vr/mp	loving meaning sky pockets 9

vr/p   trees light hands pockets slipping thankfulness water
            needing   32

ms/p   liking teeth hands bodies wondering constellations
            listening peace   9

m/mf   water ice eyes evening   6

vr/mf   clothing attention   4

ms/p   three o'clock hands knowing hair clouds learning
            tongues twigs sweaters   9

vr/p   attention sliding thankfulness friends stars coats
            warmth peacefulness bears   3

m/mp   quiet lips talking cheeks touching starlight seeing
            morning resting fingers   8

vvs/mf   kissing talking stories smiling   5

mr/mp   sweaters looking delight ease morning trees ease
            kisses   42

vvr/mp   wonder cheeks touching peacefulness seeing
            revealing halflight memory revealing   3

vs/ppp   man wet sweetness stars   5

vvr/mp   dimness remembering dimness kissing noses hands
            clothing kisses silence   6

s/mf   resting black revealing hearing kissing darkness
            snow warming peacefulness   8

vvr/mp   grey man resting   4

m/mp   looking loving   1

s/p   teeth lips standing hugging dark starlight smiling
            tongues memory   4

vvs/ppp   ease wondering   2

vr/ppp   kisses constellations   49

vvs/p   delight evening evening warmth freezing revealing
            starlight ice   4

vr/p   sliding meaning standing coats   10

m/mp   twigs dark   1

s/pp   woman lips grey eyes memory remembering
            finding telling clothing   1

m/mp   sweetness eyebrows teeth hairsmell evening
            streamsound hands night dimness   2

vvr/pp   finding being constellations darkness hugging

<pre>
                   darkness wet listening sliding smiling   1
s/mp   smiling lips constellations listening   1
s/p   hugging walking grey telling friends bodies
                   thankfulness clasping   126
</pre>

End of Night Walk
27 February 1960
The Bronx

Friendship Poems

NOTE. Each line of all but one of these poems is regulated, for expressive purposes, as to speed of delivery, loudness and duration of silence following it. Speeds include *very very slowly* (vvs), *very slowly* (vs), *slowly* (s), *moderately slowly* (ms), *moderately* (m), *moderately rapidly* (mr), *rapidly* (r), *very rapidly* (vr), and *very very rapidly* (vvr). Degrees of loudness include *softly* (p), *moderately softly* (mp), *moderately loudly* (mf), *loudly* (f), and *very loudly* (ff). Durations of silence are given in seconds and/or fractions of seconds. In carrying out these regulations naturalness is more important than finicky exactitude.

1

29 February 1960

mr/mp	I have started again to write poems that say things to people 1
r/mf	I even wrote a chance poem that says & says & says ½
vr/mf	Tho I let chance order the words and structure them as I've usually done for the last five years 3
r/mp	And chance—what else can I call it?—has opened my life now again ½
vvr/f	Again again again beautiful life opening up and blossoming when it seems to have died to the roots 1 ½
ms/p	Nothing but rotting at the roots 3
s/mp	And the *I Ching* called me a dry poplar 2
ms/mf	"A dry poplar takes a young wife" is a line near the end of part 5 of the Ode to Iris ½
mr/mf	Written with the *I Ching,* a book of a million random digits, and a half-inch red die 3
m/mp	And now by chance— /r/f/ O blessèd chance continue to happen to me! ½
s/p	For I wd never plan so well—/r/mp/ I wd have died of my planning— ½

62

mr/mf	A new happiness has come which I never cd have imagined— 2½
m/mp	A new happiness which may not last at all ½
r/mf	For all happiness that happens to us passes as all happenings do— ½
vs/mp	But while it is here—now— 2
m/p	I thank you ½
m/mf	I thank you ½
m/f	I thank you 5

2

m/mf	Here I am on the subway again ½
m/mf	Writing poems as I used to do ½
ms/mp	The ink is green and spring is not so far 1½
r/f	What is it that enlivens the spirit ¼
mr/mf	The spark that opens the cage door ½
m/mf	And sets the bluebird flying? 3
ms/mp	A simple turning toward ½
mr/mf	Not even the most important ½
r/f	But here it is, teaching me a world full of possibility! 5

29 February 1960

r/mp   I went to a rehearsal today wearing only
                    sweaters   1
vr/mf   Yesterday I got up at 9 & worked on a poem tho I'd
                    gone to sleep at 5   ½
m/mf   And I'd done the same the night before & looked
                    like a king all day next day   4

s/mp   This is the happiness   1
r/mf   That will not—I have to keep telling
                    myself—cannot—   ½
vs/mp   Last—at least not like this   3

m/mp   But for the while it does, thank you, smiles   ½
mr/mf   Thank you, earnest loving looks & kisses   ½
vr/f   Thank you thank you thank you   5

4

29 February 1960

m/mp   The way things happen—Lordy!—   ½
m/mf   A friend turns toward a friend   ½
mr/mf   And the fact that he turns allows her to turn toward
                    him: 2

s/p   As simple as 2 seconds of a stageplay   1
ms/mp   But when it has happened   4

mr/f   Radiance!   7

5

29 February 1960

mr/mp	I like the way your hair smells ½
r/mf	I'm so sick of hair that smells of synthetic shampoo perfume ½
mr/mp	Never the smell of a person 2
r/mf	You said with a laugh "Probably because it's not washed" ½
s/mp	If that's the reason—good—½
vr/p	I sit on a couch in the Bronx bent forward—sniffing even—remembering—trying to remember more strongly—the way your hair smells 6

6

29 February 1960

m/mf	I'm like high on pot ½
r/f	Keep goofing and doing the wrong things ½
vr/ff	Starting to do one thing and then doing something else 1
ms/mp	And all the time not caring at all—it's a pleasure to take a breath 2
m/mf	Not caring at all and caring all the time ½
mr/f	I'm high all right, ¼
r/ff	Like, this is what they mean by high! ½
m/mp	And none of that medicinal smell, that sticky tar, that droopy haze 2
m/mp	I'm high like on pot ½
vr/f	And wide awake as I can be ½
m/mf	I'm liking what I never like— ¼
r/f	The cold air— /vr/ff/ the cold air?!— /r/mp/ I *must* be high if I'm liking the cold air! 4

29 February 1960

r/mp	After I left the theatre Saturday night	½

m/p   After working on your *Night Walk* from 8 or so till
                    2 ½

vr/mf   I stopped at a party a block away on 14th Street on
                 the way to the subway 3

r/mp   The party was nothing but I like Walter Mullen
                  who'd invited both casts from the theatre 1

m/mf   And when I saw Jamil, with whom I'd smoked a
                 couple of times ½

s/mp   He looked at me close, saying, */vr/f/* "Man, are you
                 stoned out of your *mind?*" 5

1 March 1960

Yesterday afternoon I framed your drawing
of people—grownups & children—and balloons
or whatever those round things are
that float with a stem to the ground
—flowers?—trees?—visiting Martians?—
all seeming to go to a little copse of tree trunks at the top
and a little to the right

that little drawing whose foreground is quite empty
so that the bottom third of the paper is white
and the watermark
—BODLEIAN—
is clearly visible amid the calendaring.

I mounted it asymmetrically
on old russet velvet

near the left bottom corner of the frame

but the velvet overwhelmed it
until I painted a black stripe of India ink
across the top of the velvet
and a thicker stripe down the right side.

It's in a 11-by-14 98c frame from the 5 & 10
black & unobtrusive
and I've hung it on the hall wall
opposite the kitchen doorway
that has no door

so that now that I sit writing on the kitchen table
with the dimmish/brightish light coming and going as the
        clouds move far above
I'm looking at it in the light of the hallway bulb
that counteracts the glare from the opposing window.

Yesterday I kept taking it with me
as I moved from room to room
putting it on the piano rack
when I was in that room
and on an upended wooden letter tray
in the middle of the top bookshelf
when I was in the front room

so that when I was lying in bed
it faced me there
and when I was sitting at the writing table,
or on the couch, in the front room,
it faced me there too.

That's why I framed it—
because the day before
I'd been carrying it from room to room
in a dark mahogany letter tray
that upended, framed it and boxed it
and I was afraid
that if that continued

the paper wd curl
or the drawing wd fall
and get soiled or creased.

Now the white is not so vivid behind the glass
but if it wasn't behind the glass
it probably wd darken
or the drawing might get spoiled, as I said,
dirty, creased, torn, waterspilledon, fingermarked,
all or any of the spoilages drawings may suffer—

but now, carrying it under glass from room to room,
there's always a chance the glass may break,
like, if I tripped on the dog or cat,
and the drawing got torn.

Well one or two of several things may happen:

I'll get used to it and stop carrying it from room to room
but be content to leave it on the hallway wall
facing my right side when I sit at the kitchen table:

you'll probably give me another drawing or two
so I will have those to look at in the other rooms:

my whole feeling may change—
—O God forbid this happiness shd pass
where I go about in a cloud of poetry
high as a kite
like a 15-year-old
like a man who suddenly likes the cold winter air he's always hated
like a man who's kicked marihuana and finds himself higher than
        when he got on it
like a foolish 37-year-old who knows it can't last like this but
        hopes—hopes—hopes—

so that the drawing—beautiful as it is—will again be only a drawing
and my need to see it, satisfied
when I pass wherever it hangs

and I no longer try to remember the smell of my friend's hair
on a snowy path deep in a forest in February
at one or two in the morning under the stars,
the only light the starlight
reflected up from the crusty top of the snow.

9

6 March 1960

m/mp   I wish we knew a language nobody else we know
                     knows   ½
m/mf   Ancient Greek or Sumerian or Yucatecan   2
ms/mp   Why? I don't know   3

mr/mf   Maybe it's because there are some things   1
m/mp   I only want to say to you   ½
mr/p   I only want to be able to say to you   4

s/mp   You'd think there was nothing like that   1
ms/mp   We seem so interinvolved & interenmeshed with so
                     many others   ½
mr/mf   But that's just the reason   2

m/p   No, not *just* the reason   ½
mr/mf   Not the *only* reason   1 ½
ms/mp   But the others, the other reasons, are much harder
                     to speak about   4

vs/p   They're like   1
ms/mp   The way we seem so familiar & related   ½
s/mf   The way   2

mr/mp   We turned to each other   6

69

6 March 1960

ms/mp	The kids sliding on	½
mr/mf	The dirty grey snow mountain	1 ½
ms/p	Remind me of yours	3

February–March 1960
New York (Manhattan & The Bronx)

Selected Poems from *Stanzas for Iris Lezak* in Roughly Chronological Order (May–October 1960)

A Note on the Methods Used in Composing & Performing *Stanzas for Iris Lezak*

Stanzas for Iris Lezak comprises all of the poems I wrote between some time in April or May & Halloween Week, 1960. They were written in 3 school composition notebooks with black & white marbleized covers, designated as "1960 #2," "1960 #3," & "1960 #4" (here called the "first, second & third notebooks"), of which "1960 #2" is the thickest & bound upside down—which may have led to my writing the first group of poems (see below) at the back of it. Poems were written in these notebooks (especially in the first) in random places, so that the chronological order is completely mixed up within each notebook.

Iris had come to live with me on April 10th; we were deeply in love, & our sexual life was very happy. It may have been these circumstances that led me, in late April or early May, to select a book of love poems in prose, *Gitanjali* ("Offerings"), by the Bengali poet (Sir) Rabindranath Tagore (1861-1941), as a word-source for a group of systematic-chance poems, & to use an acrostic (tho aleatoric) word-selection method in composing them, thru which the initial letter of the words of each of the poems spell out the exultant sentences, "My girl's the greatest fuck in town. I love to fuck my girl." These poems were the "6 Gitanjali for Iris".

In composing the "6 Gitanjali" I combined acrostic chance selection with a numerical method which seems to have been (as nearly as I can reconstruct it from my notebooks) as follows:

I used the number corresponding to each letter's place in the alphabet (that is, the place of each letter in the "index sentences" quoted above) to determine the page of Tagore's *Gitanjali* from which a word beginning with the letter was taken (along with any accompanying punctuation). Thus in the first of the "6 Gitanjali for Iris," the first word, "My," is the first word beginning with "m" on p. 13 of the book; "you" is the first word beginning with "y" on p. 25; & so on. When a word beginning with the required letter did not appear on the page corresponding to the letter's place in the alphabet, I read thru the subsequent pages until I found one. The end of a word in the index sentences determined the end of a line, with the "'s" of "girl's" determining a whole line since it stands for a separate word, "is." Each time a letter reappeared in the index sentences, the word corresponding to it was repeated in the poem. When the first index sentence was spelled out, I made a strophe break & then spelled out the second index sentence. Later I obtained random-digit couplets from the Rand Corporation's *A Million Random Digits with 100,000 Normal Deviates* (The Free Press, Glencoe, Ill., 1955) to determine durations of silence, measured in seconds, between the two strophes of each of these poems.

In composing the 2nd of them, I took the 2nd word beginning with "m" on p. 13, the 2nd word beginning with "y" on p. 25, & so on. As before, I read thru subsequent pages to find words beginning with the letters of the index sentences when none appeared on the pages corresponding to the letters' places in the alphabet. Carrying out this method six times produced the "6 Gitanjali for Iris."

The method used in composing these poems was a bridge between the systematic-chance methods I had used previously in composing poems, plays, verbal & mixed simultaneities, & instrumental works, beginning with the "5 biblical poems" (Dec. 1954–Jan. 1955), & the methods used in composing the other poems in *Stanzas for Iris Lezak*. The former methods had been largely numerical & had involved various auxiliary means: dice, playing cards, random digits, the *I Ching* ("Book of Changes"), tossed coins, & the "translations" of the notation of musical works (via numbers) into words. However, I had not previously used any chance-acrostic method. I soon realized that the most obvious advantage of such a method was its doing away with the need for auxiliary means. (The use of random digits to determine durations of silence between the strophes of each of the "6 Gitanjali" was an afterthought.) This proved to be very practical in that it allowed me to compose during my long subway rides between the Bronx & Manhattan, going to & from jobs, visits, performances, &c.

At the distance of 11 years, I find it difficult to remember which poem was the first purely acrostic-stanzaic chance poem. I think it was either "The Blue and Brown Books," drawn from the volume containing those two short works of Ludwig Wittgenstein (precursors of his *Philosophical Investigations*), or "Mark Twain Life on the Mississippi Illustrated Harpers," drawn from the book with those words on its spine. The former seems more probably the earlier, since it is written on the first pages of the notebook which I had begun by writing the "6 Gitanjali for Iris" on the last pages, & because it was written with the same pen & ink as that with which the "6 Gitanjali" were written. However, I have no memory of the process of writing it, whereas I remember that while writing "Mark Twain . . ." I spelled out all the words on the book's spine by trying to take every consecutive "m," "a," &c., from the beginning of the book, going back, when necessary, to find the required words. That is, having found the first "m" word in the book, I may have gone back to find the first "a" word, forward to the first "r" word, & possibly back once more to the first "k" word. Then, having spelled out the whole "index string" (the poem's title), repeating words when letters recurred in the poem's title, taking each word's type-face species (Roman, italics, boldface), capitalization (if any), & punctuation (if any) as an integral part of it, & ending verse lines at ends of word strings spelling out title words, I went back to find the second "m," "a," "r," "k," &c., words in the book to make the 2nd stanza, & so on.

However, I found this going forwards & backwards in a source text too cumbersome, so that after generating a few poems that way, I generated the rest of the poems by going straight thru each source; that is, each time after I had taken a word into a poem, I went forward to the next word in the source text that began with the required letter.

After a while, I got tired of the frequent recurrence of the same structure words (especially articles & prepositions) in the stanzas, so that I began taking into poems only lexical words (nouns, verbs, adjectives, & adverbs) & occasional pronouns & other structure words that seemed to have "lexical weight." I also began the practice of using different words in each stanza; that is, just as I now skipped most structure words in taking "each next" word with the required initial letter into a poem from a source text, I also skipped any words that had appeared in a previous stanza.

Soon I introduced two other procedures: the use of units larger than single words (i.e., word *strings* beginning with the required letters) & of nonrepeating units (i.e., taking a different unit into the poem each time a letter recurred in the index string—almost always the title of the poem—rather than repeating the unit within the stanza). Word-string units were repeated in stanzas of some poems, not repeated in others.

The type of word string I used most frequently as a unit was one beginning with the next word in the source text having the required initial letter & ending with a punctuation mark. The next most frequently used string ran from a "letter word" to the end of a sentence. Possibly the third most frequently used word string was a whole sentence beginning with a "letter word."

By later summer, 1960, I was sometimes using several types of units in the same poem. A chart at the back of the 3rd notebook lists 40 types of units & combinations of units. The code index following each unit or combination name allowed me to use random-digit triplets to determine the type(s) of units to be used in a whole poem or in a particular stanza ("o" means "odd digit"; "e" means "even digit").

List of Types of Units & Combinations of Units From Inside of Back Cover of 3rd Notebook ("1960 #4") Containing *Stanzas for Iris Lezak*

1	Non-Repeated Line-Fragments	oo1
2	Non-Repeated Phrases	oo2
3	Mix 7 Types	oo3
4	Repeated Altered Sentences	oo4
5	Mix 6 Types	oo5

As it turned out, this list was not often used to determine the types of units to be used in a poem (altho it *was* so used from time to time, both in making later *Stanzas* poems & in making the numbered Asymmetries which followed them) because using it requires a source of random digits as well as a source text, & this was not often feasible when I was writing poems in subways, restaurants, or elsewhere outside my home. The same holds true of a number of the listed units & combinations: those requiring auxiliary means were rarely used. All combinations required a random-digit table to designate which units on the list were to be combined. "Altered" units required a systematic-chance means of designating certain words or other subunits for replacement & of selecting the replacements—usually from elsewhere in the source text. & while many of the listed units & combinations were used in poems, some were never used. The poems containing combinations & infrequently used units were mostly written in the 2nd & 3rd notebooks & on yellow legal-size lined paper.

Throughout the *Stanzas* I continued to take into the poems the punctuation & typeface species of the source texts. However, enclosing punctuation (parentheses, brackets, quotation marks) often presented a problem, which I usually solved by inserting extra initial or final parentheses, &c., at what seemed appropriate places in the poems, so that quotations or parenthetical passages wd not begin without ending or end without ever having begun.

Poems were ended in various ways. Often I simply stopped working on a poem after one or two sittings or after I had finished reading the source text. In other cases I read all the way thru the source text, taking words or strings with the required initial letters as they appeared & stopping the poems when I'd gotten to the end of the text—often in the middle of a stanza. Thus the short poem "Poe and Psychoanalysis" ends where it does because I found no second "y" word before arriving at the end of the essay.

Still other poems had the number of stanzas predetermined by random digits or other chance means. This was especially true of some of the more complex poems toward the end of the book, of which random digits also determined the types of units or combinations of units that appear in each stanza.

Probably the most "personal" aspect of the *Stanzas,* aside from the title-dedication & the initial impulses which led to the invention of the generative method which produced the "6 Gitanjali for Iris," is the variety of source texts, which included practically everything I happened to be reading from May thru October of 1960. The titles of many of the sources appear as titles of poems—book titles, chapter titles, titles of articles, &c. Among them were books on Zen & Tibetan Buddhism, politics, poetry, & botany; *The New York Times,* especially the *Sunday Times Magazine;* the current issues of the *Scientific American* & the *Catholic Worker;* bulletins of other pacifist groups such as the Committee for Nonviolent Action & the War Resisters League; Spencer Holst's mimeographed edition of his *Twenty-Five Stories; Drugs and the Mind,* by De Ropp; Dorothy Day's autobiography, *The Long Loneliness;* an Olympia Press translation of de Sade's dialogue *Les Philosophes dans le boudoir;* the Wilhelm-Baynes translation of the *I Ching* ("Book of Changes"); "La Jeune Parque," by Paul Valery; a copy of *The National Enquirer;* & various leaflets & pamphlets, such as ones on using soy beans & on the Catholic

Church of the North-American Rite. The most frequently used book on Tibetan Buddhism was W.Y. Evans-Wentz's *Tibetan Yoga and Secret Doctrine,* while most of the Vedanta poems come from René Guenon's *Man and his Becoming according to the Vedanta,* altho at least one long one comes from Sri Ramana Maharshi's *Who Am I?* I don't remember the Zen sources, except for *Zen Buddhism and Psychoanalysis,* by Erich Fromm, Richard De Martino, & others; & of the many botany texts I borrowed from our local branch library (Hunts Point Regional Library, on Southern Blvd. in the Bronx) that summer, I remember only one title, *The Story of Mosses, Ferns, and Mushrooms.* One long poem incorporates, in one place or another, almost all of Robert Louis Stevenson's *A Child's Garden of Verses.*

A number of other books & periodicals also served as sources for the *Stanzas.* Many of their titles serve as titles for the poems drawn from them, but trying to trace & list any more of them here does not seem useful.

By August 1960 a large number of these poems had been written. In order to present them as a simultaneity in a concert at The Living Theatre which was being organized by Dick Higgins, Al Hansen, & others, & which eventually took place on 8 August 1960, I typed the poems on 5″-x-8″ filing cards. Each stanza that was short enough was typed on a single card, using both sides of a card when necessary. Longer stanzas were divided among several cards. The resultant 700 to 800 cards were shuffled, distributed, & read from by 5 performers (John Coe, Dick Higgins, Spencer Holst, Florence Tarlow, and myself) whose delivery was regulated as to speed, loudness, silence durations at line endings, & production or nonproduction of instrumental sounds or noises within some of these durations, by means of playing cards & number cards. The details of this method of performing the *Stanzas* as a simultaneity constitute the second part of this Note.

Subsequently, this simultaneous version of the *Stanzas* was presented at the Phase 2 coffeehouse (along with Lionel Shepard's mimes, who worked from the "action pack" for The Living Theatre's production of *The Marrying Maiden*—about 1200 different actions that had been lettered on playing cards by Iris Lezak), at the AG Gallery, at Le Metro & Les Deux Mégots coffeehouses, at my concerts at Yoko Ono's studio on Chamber St. (8 & 9 April 1961), at St. Mark's Church in-the-Bowery, & at the University of British Columbia in Vancouver. It was also broadcast by WRVR-FM, New York, & by the Canadian Broadcasting Company.

Soon after the first simultaneous performance, I used the stanza cards as sources of prose works consisting of complete sentences with normal English syntax, namely, "A Story for Iris Lezak" (pub. in *CENTER* #1, Fall, 1970, Woodstock, N.Y., ed. Carol Bergé), "A Sermon," & "A Greater Sorrow" (pub. in *AN ANTHOLOGY,* ed. La Monte Young, pub. by Mac Low & Young, New York, 1963; 2nd ed., Heiner Friedrich, New York, 1970).

To do this, I produced a selection template by spattering 10 green ink blots onto a 5″-x-8″ filing card, rapidly cutting out irregular quadrilaterals around each blot with a razor blade, producing 10 slots, & using chance operations to assign the name of a lexical part of speech (noun, verb, adjective, or adverb) & a different number, from 1 to 10, to each slot.

This template card was placed successively over each stanza card, the whole set having been thoroughly shuffled. In composing "Story," "Sermon," & part I of "Sorrow," when words showed thru more than one slot, the one in the slot labeled with the highest (or lowest) number was used as the part of speech assigned to that slot, suffixes being added as necessary (e.g., the noun "wind" was converted to the adjective "windy"). In composing part II of "Sorrow," all words showing thru were used in the order of their slot numbers as the assigned parts of speech. Function words were supplied freely, when necessary, to connect the chance-given lexical words. Tense, number, & person of verbs & number & case of nouns were usually chosen.

In "Story," only narrative statements were written, but in "Sermon," six types of sentences—positive & negative statements, questions, & commands—were used, the sentence type being determined by a die throw before any lexical words were drawn from the stanza cards.

In writing "A Greater Sorrow," I used as a "matrix" the complete text of "A Great Sorrow," a 19th-century children's story printed on a crumbling book page sent me by the collagist & mail artist Ray Johnson. I began by eliminating one type of sentence (negative questions) from the gamut of possible synthetic-sentence types by a preliminary die throw. Then whenever the number assigned to that sentence type (six) came up, I brought in a sentence from the old story instead of synthesizing one. When the last sentence of part I of the old story came in, I began to use *all* the slot words instead of only one from each card. When I reached the old story's last sentence, my story ended. Thus my story "expands" the old story by the insertion of five types of synthetic sentences with lexical words drawn (with the exception of "said" & its near-equivalents, which were drawn from a separate list) from the previously composed *Stanzas*. As a result, the title adjective changes from "Great" to "Greater."

Before & after writing the prose pieces drawing words from the *Stanzas* cards I wrote seven poems, using the shuffled set of cards as a source text, but without employing the template card used in composing the prose pieces. Three of these, "Stanzas for Iris Lezak," "ONE HUNDRED AND NINETY DOLLAR POEM FOR VERA", & "A LITTLE DISSERTATION CONCERNING MISSISSIPPI AND TENNESSEE FOR IRIS" consist of one or more stanzas, each of which "spells out" the poem's title by initial acrostic as do the stanzas of the other stanzaic poems in the book. The others—the First, Second, 3rd, & 4th "Asymmetries for Iris"—were composed by a slightly different method, which I will describe below. In some stanzas of the first three poems the metrical unit is the single word; in the other stanzas & in the four Asymmetries for Iris, the unit is a word string beginning with a "letter word" & continuing to the first punctuation mark. This is the most frequently used multiword unit in this book & is inaccurately designated "phrase" in the list given above. In the poems drawn from the cards, these units are often very long because some stanzas on the cards have little or no punctuation. Since the cards were drawn from in their shuffled succession, a word string beginning with a word on an unpunctuated card includes all the rest of the words on that card & all those on the subsequent card(s) up to the first punctuation mark. Thus a unit running to a punctuation mark may be as short as a single word or as long as 100 words or more.

The "Asymmetry" method produces poems that are, in a sense, "self-generating." Beginning with the first or a chance-designated subsequent word in a source text, the first line of such a poem spells out this word; the second line spells out the second word of the first line; the third line, the third word, & so on. A strophe break occurs after the last word of any line has been spelled out. These poems are otherwise similar to stanzaic poems in that the words are drawn from many source texts by reading thru such texts until words or strings beginning with the required letters are found.

These poems are "asymmetrical" in that each strophe spells out a different series of words, whereas each stanza of a stanzaic- acrostic poem spells out the same word series—either the title or some other word string. The Asymmetries included in *Stanzas* are transitional between the stanzaic poems & the 500 numbered Asymmetries written between Halloween Week 1960 & some date early in 1961. The essential difference between these transitional Asymmetries & the numbered & later ones lies in their format, which is very similar to that of the stanzaic-acrostic poems that form the bulk of this volume. The format of the numbered & later Asymmetries is like that of such stanzaic poems as "Federacy", in which lines break at punctuation marks. Such poems are much more fragmented in appearance & have certain rules for their reading which cause the reader to fall silent for longer or shorter durations, according to the sizes of spaces, or to substitute sustained instrumental tones, &c., for those durations. Examples & rules for reading such Asymmetries are included in *AN ANTHOLOGY* [as well as in *Asymmetries 1-260* (Printed Editions, New York, 1980) and the present volume].

In a number of the transitional Asymmetries, other methods were used, some of them only slightly different from the one described above, others quite different. For instance, in *"The Courage to Be*—Paul Tillich **(Headlines from Tillich)**," which may have been the first Asymmetry-type poem composed, the first word & line determine the first strophe, but in the second strophe, tho the first line spells out the first word of the 2nd line of the first strophe, the subsequent lines spell out *that* first line, & the third strophe begins with a word that only begins like the second word of the first line &

78

the first word of the second line of the second strophe, & partially spells *that* word out. In the "Asymmetry from *Birth* 3 (&c.)", the first words of the 2nd & other strophes only have initial letters in common with the words of the first line of strophe 1. A number of other variations of the strict Asymmetries method are also to be found, & the compositional methods followed in *some* of the poems with "Asymmetry" in their titles, notably the one to Lucia Dlugoszewski—which was drawn from several different source texts, including a poem of Hart Crane, a book on Hindu astrology, an article on plant growth in the *Scientific American*, a book on Paracelsus, & a Scots poem—cannot be reconstructed at this time, but seem not even to have involved acrostic.

Asymmetries were ended in various ways. Some do not end until they have spelled out their own first strophes, but various contingencies, ranging from getting to the end of the source text to my not having taken them up after the first sitting, ended many of them. (Later, in writing the numbered Asymmetries, I let the edges of notebook pages end lines & the bottoms of the pages end the poems themselves, when other contingencies didn't intervene before that.)

Further compositional notes on the poems in *Stanzas* are not needed. Some readers will, doubtless, find even the amount of information here excessive, but they, of course, need not read all of it. In the last part of this Note I will describe how the poems in *Stanzas* may be used in group performances—theatre or concert events of the kind which I have come to call "simultaneities."

How to perform *Stanzas for Iris Lezak* as a simultaneity

Any number of persons may perform *Stanzas for Iris Lezak* as a simultaneity. I use the term "simultaneity" to designate each of my works (or as in this case, versions of works) in which each of a group of people performs a relatively independent series of actions (reading, producing nonverbal sounds, &/or doing predominantly visible physical actions) & all of these series of actions take place *simultaneously,* that is, during the same period of time, the duration of the performance.

Each performer of the simultaneous version of *Stanzas* is provided with a large random collection of text cards & of number cards (each described in detail below), a full pack of playing cards (including jokers, if possible), & several musical instruments or other sound producers.

The description below is divided between *Preparation* up to the beginning of the performance & the *Performance Method* itself, which is followed by a *Summary* of the performance method that ought to be copied & distributed to the performers for use during performances.

Preparation:

1. Procure a plentiful supply of large (5″-x-8″) plain index cards. Transfer the separated stanzas of the poems to the index cards, placing one whole stanza, if possible (see below) on each card, using both sides of cards for long stanzas. The same procedure shd be followed with the separated strophes of the nonstanzaic poems (Asymmetries) & the separated paragraphs of the three prose pieces, "A Story for Iris Lezak," "A Sermon," & "A Greater Sorrow." The latter are the only prose pieces in the book, aside from this Note; all the other works, even those having a proselike format (see below), are verse, by reason of their structure. For convenience, I only refer to *stanzas* below, but whatever is said of stanzas applies equally to nonstanzaic strophes & prose paragraphs, except, of course, that the latter do not divide into verse lines.

Any convenient method may be used to transfer the stanzas to cards. One may type them, as I did, duplicate the pages of this book by xerography or other means, or use the actual pages of two copies of this book. When duplicated or actual pages are used, cut them at stanza breaks & glue each stanza on a separate card; it is important to join segments of stanzas that begin on one page & end on another. Thus, for instance, the last four lines of page 4 & the first line of page 5, which constitute the ninth stanza of "THE BLUE AND BROWN BOOKS," must be cut out & glued on the same card.

Whenever stanzas that are too long to fit on one side are continued on reverse sides of cards, "(OVER)" shd be typed or hand-lettered in red ink in the right corner of the first side of each such card and "(2ND SIDE—READ OTHER SIDE FIRST)" shd be typed or lettered in red at the top of the second side. Red ink shd be used or the words shd at least be encircled with red ink to remind readers during performances not to read these words aloud.

It shd be noted that stanzas of these poems have two formats. Some stanzas have a format like that of conventional verse; that is, each verse line begins at the left margin, & if any verse line extends over more than one typographical line, each additional typographical line is indented to indicate that it is not a separate verse line but a continuation of a verse line begun on a line above.

Other stanzas, altho they are also verse, appear in a prose-like format originally adopted because most of their lines are very much longer than most verse lines. In stanzas having this format, each verse line has the appearance of a prose paragraph, since its first typographical line is indented, while each additional typographical line begins at the left margin. (See "**Pattern Recognition by Machine**.") However, many such prose-format verse lines end, not with periods, question marks, or exclamation points, as do prose paragraphs, but with commas or other non-sentence-ending marks, or even with no punctuation mark at all.

When transferring stanzas to index cards, care shd be taken to follow the format of each stanza exactly. When it is necessary to continue a stanza on the reverse side of a card, it shd be indicated at the top of that side—again in red or red-encircled letters—whether the first line on it is the beginning of a new verse line or the continuation of a verse line begun on the first side of the card.

2. Prepare a pack of "number cards" as follows: Procure 200-300 blank cards the size of calling cards. If such cards are not obtainable, cut 3″-x-5″ plain index cards into exact thirds.

In addition to the cards, a table of random digits shd be obtained. However, if no such table is available, a telephone book may be used as a source of pseudo-random digits.

On one side of each of these cards, an integer from "1" thru "20" shd be written in blue or black ink. They may be obtained by going down the columns of random digits, two adjacent columns at a time. (If a telephone book is used, the two columns farthest to the right in each successive column of telephone numbers shd be used.)

Digits in right-hand columns must be copied as they appear. If a digit in a left-hand column is a "1", it is copied. Any other *odd* digit appearing in a left-hand column must be changed to a "1". If the left-hand digit is *even* or a "0", & the right-hand digit is other than a "0", the left-hand digit is omitted & only the right-hand digit is copied. If the left-hand digit is "2" & the right-hand digit is "0", both digits are copied (as "20"). However, if the right-hand digit is "0" & the left-hand digit is either "0" or an *even* digit other than "2", the left-hand digit must be changed to "2" to produce a "20".

Thus digit-couplets from "10" thru "20" are copied as given; left-hand "0"s & *even* digits are omitted when beside digits from "1" thru "9" & changed to "2"s beside "0"s; & left-hand *odd* digits other than "1"s are changed to "1"s.

When every small card has some integer from "1" thru "20" written on one side in black or blue, write a similarly random collection of integers from "21" thru "120" on the other sides of the cards *in red*. Obtain such integers by going down adjacent columns of random digits (or telephone numbers) as before, copying all couplets from "21" thru "99" but adding "1"s before all couplets from "00" thru "20", so that they become integers from "100" thru "120".

One will now have 200-300 number cards, each with some integer from "1" thru "20" written on one side in black or blue & some integer from "21" thru "120" written in red on the other side.

3. Procure as many complete packs of cards, if possible including jokers, as there are performers.

4. Procure many musical instruments, noisemakers, &/or other sound producers—enough so that each performer will have at least three or four of them to use during the performance.

5. Make as many copies of the "SUMMARY OF REGULATIONS" [omitted from this book] as there are performers.

6. Just before the performance, divide the text cards, number cards, &

sound producers as evenly as possible among the performers, & give each one of them a full pack of playing cards & a copy of the "SUMMARY OF REGULATIONS." Each performer arranges the groups of cards in front of him or her, places the "SUMMARY" for ready reference, & arranges the sound producers so that they are readily at hand.

Performance Method

Loudness & Speed

The playing cards are used to regulate the loudness & speed of the reading of the text cards, one playing card regulating each text card. The *denomination* of the playing card gives the *speed*. An *ace* indicates the *slowest* speed, a *king*, the *fastest*. However, after a performance has begun, each speed is relative to the previous one. Higher denominations indicate a change to a faster speed; lower denominations, to a slower speed; & the *gap* between denominations indicates *how much* faster or slower one card shd be read than the previous card.

Clarity is of the utmost importance, so that no performer shd read at a rate faster than one at which he or she can produce clearly enunciated, intelligible words, or slower than one at which it is possible to keep the words from completely falling apart into an unintelligible series of syllables.

The *suit* of the playing card indicates the *loudness* of the reading of the text card. There are four degrees of loudness: *red* indicates *loud, black soft; pointed-top* suits, *fully* loud or soft; *rounded-top, moderately* loud or soft. Thus *Spades = p* (quite soft), *Clubs = mp* (moderately soft), *Hearts = mf* (moderately loud), *Diamonds = f* (quite loud).

Each reader's *p* shd be no softer than the minimum amount of sound needed to make that individual's voice heard intelligibly throughout the space in which the work is performed. An *f* shd be no louder than the maximum loudness at which the reader can speak intelligibly, with a relatively "good" tone, & without shouting or other unnecessarily ugly sounds.

Silences & Instrumental Sounds

The number cards are used to indicate durations of silence measured in seconds. One may measure these silences either with a stopwatch or other clock with a second hand or by counting "one thousand and one," "one thousand and two," &c.

The *red* side of a number card is used to obtain the duration of the silence that is to be observed *before* the reading of each text card. Thus the first action of a performer is to observe an initial silence.

When the red number is *even*, the *black* or *blue* numbers on subsequent cards indicate durations of silence *after each verse line* of the stanza on the text card.

When the red number is *odd, no measured silences* are to occur *after verse lines,* but a *single* instrumental sound or *simultaneous group* of sounds (e.g., a chord) *must* be produced at the end of each verse line of the stanza. Produce a different sound after each line, i.e., never produce the same sound after two lines in a row, & in general, make the sound as varied & non-repetitious as possible. These sounds may be produced on any musical instrument or other sound producer, but relatively "musical" sounds ought to predominate.

The production of these sounds shd not interrupt the reading of the stanzas. That is, there shd be *only* short hesitations at the ends of unpunctuated lines & slightly longer pauses after punctuation, but the time taken to produce the musical sounds must be minimal. If the sound is such as to persist after the first attack, the voice shd go on over that sound. In general, after the lines of these stanzas without verse-line silences, only relatively *short* sounds ought to be produced. Longer sounds, & wind instruments generally, shd be reserved for the *optional* sound-production situation described below.

During each of the measured silences before stanzas & each of those after verse lines, the performer has the *option* of producing a single sound or simultaneous group of sounds at any time within a silence. This option shd be exercised with great discretion, that is, not too often, & only when producing such a sound will *add* something to the total performance (see the "little sermon" below).

It is to be emphasized that silences &/or instrumental sounds are to occur only at the ends of *complete verse lines* (not at the ends of *typographical* lines that are merely the beginnings or middles of long verse lines). As described under "*Preparation 1.*" above, verse lines in "verse format" begin at left margins, & continuation lines are indented. In the "proselike format," the verse lines look like prose paragraphs & *begin* with indentations; continuation lines begin in this format at left margins. (Paragraphs of the three actual prose pieces shd be treated like the verse lines in the proselike format.)

The performers shd pay close attention to all the sounds they produce & make only sounds which they wd *like* to hear.

Technical & Stylistic Considerations in Reading of Text Cards

It shd be noted that some stanzas are continued on reverse sides of cards. Technical indications of continuations & (in the "6 Gitanjali for Iris") of pauses of definite durations within stanzas are typed or circled in red & are, of course, not to be read aloud.

All punctuation shd be followed scrupulously & interpreted by definite voice changes, as in normal reading. That is, the voice shd be *dropped* at periods & semicolons, raised slightly at commas, raised (or raised-&-lowered) questioningly at interrogation marks, &c.

Lines & stanzas ending without punctuation shd be "left in the air"—not brought to a close. This applies also to stanzas ending with commas, dashes, &c.

Capitalized words, non-foreign words in italics, & all words in boldface shd be *emphasized*, but such emphasis shd be in keeping with the loudness & speed of the whole stanza as determined by a playing card.

The *long dashes* (usually six-em dashes) that occur in some stanzas are to be interpreted as silences, each as long as any word the reader wishes to say silently. The measured silences in the "Gitanjali" must have the durations indicated.

Five *stylistic* considerations are paramount:

Clarity: All words must be *clearly* enunciated & connected. Never speak too fast or too loud to do this.

Seriousness: All the stanzas, even the funny ones, are to be read *seriously* & *soberly*. This quality is to be attained by paying close attention to meaning & by thinking seriously & concentratedly about all the words one reads & their possible meanings, separately & in conjunction with each other.

Straightness: No special colorations shd be given to words, *no special interpretations* except those brought about by serious concentration on meaning.

Audibility: All words shd be audible within the audience space, that is, soft & whispered speech ought not be so soft that a careful listener cd not perceive it. Also, no words shd be so overpoweringly loud that words & sounds happening simultaneously with them are utterly drowned out. This requires careful listening to both oneself, the other performers, & the environing sounds.

Sensitivity: Performers must try to be as sensitive as possible to the qualities of both the sounds of the words & of the instrumental sounds. They must pay close attention to the *timbres* of their voices & never let themselves feel forced by the chance-given parameters to produce sounds they find distasteful. That is, they shd adjust all the chance-determined speeds & loudnesses to their individual capabilities, so that they only produce sounds with their voices & instruments that they really like to hear. They shd also listen to the others, &c., & make sure they like the combination of sounds as modified by their contributions.

In general, performers of *Stanzas for Iris Lezak* shd follow the spirit of the following:

A Little Sermon on the Performance of Simultaneities
by Jackson Mac Low, Written on his 44th Birthday
(12 September 1966)

Firstly: Listen!   Listen!   Listen!
Secondly: Leave plenty of silence.
Thirdly: Don't do something just to be doing something.
Fourthly: Only do something when you have something you really

84

	want to do after observing & listening intensely to every-thing in the performance & its environment.
Fifthly:	Don't be afraid to shut up awhile. Something really good will seem all the better if you do it after being still.
Sixthly:	Be open. Try to interact freely with the other performers & the audience.
Lastly:	Listen! Listen! Listen!

While some of these admonitions apply more strictly to performances of simultaneities in which the performers make more kinds of choices & are less regulated by chance means than they are in performing the simultaneous version of the *Stanzas*, the general *spirit* of the "sermon" shd be followed, even to the extent of slightly *extending* the silences before reading text cards, especially when the total performance seems *too* thick.

Ending

A performance may end at any agreed-upon time or at a time found appropriate by the performers during the course of the performance. In either case, an ending signal shd be agreed upon beforehand & used, if necessary, to stop the performance. At this signal, all reading &/or playing of instruments shd stop immediately, no matter at what point in a stanza the signal is given.

New York (The Bronx & Manhattan)
1971 & 1982

Selected Poems from *Stanzas for Iris Lezak*

6 Gitanjali for Iris

I

My you
Gain is rainy life
See
The Here end
Gain rainy end again the end see the
Feet. Utter. Cry know
Is Now,
The outside when Now,

(18 seconds of silence)

Is
Life outside void end
The outside
Feet. Utter. Cry know
My you
Gain is rainy life

II

Midnight, your
Gifts is river, light,
Sing
Thy humble every
Gifts river, every and thy every sing thy
Flute unbreakable captive keep
Is not
Thy of whom not

(10 seconds of silence)

Is
Light, of voice every
Thy of
Flute unbreakable captive keep
Midnight, your
Gifts is river, light,

III

Me You
God is renew life
Sleep
The heart even
God renew even again, the even sleep the
Fear undisturbed. Come keep
Is noontide
The on with noontide

(13 seconds of silence)

Is
Life on venture even
The on
Fear undisturbed. Come keep
Me You
God is renew life

IV

My your
Ground is resting languidly
Sack
To He earth,
Ground resting earth, and to earth, sack to
Frayed unbreakable, court knew
Is not
To only weeping not

(5 seconds of silence)

Is
Languidly only voyage earth,
To only
Frayed unbreakable, court knew
My your
Ground is resting languidly

V

Master, your
Garment is renew linger
Strength
Trust hard entrance
Garment renew entrance a trust entrance strength trust
Finery, unholy colour knew
Is not
Trust on wall not

(3 seconds of silence)

Is
Linger on vaguest entrance
Trust on
Finery, unholy colour knew
Master, your
Garment is renew linger

VI

Morning You
Gleam in resonant life
Shame
Thee. He eyes
Gleam resonant eyes and thee. Eyes shame thee.
From up come Kindle
In not
Thee. Of wall not

(15 seconds of silence)

In
Life of vain eyes
Thee. Of
From up come Kindle
Morning You
Gleam in resonant life

Call Me Ishmael

Circulation. And long long
Mind every
Interest Some how mind and every long

Coffin about little little
Money especially
I shore, having money about especially little

Cato a little little
Me extreme
I sail have me an extreme little

Cherish and left, left,
Myself extremest
It see hypos myself and extremest left,

City a land. Land.
Mouth; east,
Is spleen, hand mouth; an east, land.

Graded City Speller Chancellor Eighth Year Grade

Guard raises against daily eliminate daily
Chrysalis identity Tuesday yearn
Subterfuge plight eliminate lessons lessons eliminate raises
Chrysalis he against neither chrysalis eliminate lessons lessons
            obvious raises
Eliminate identity guard he Tuesday he
Yearn eliminate against raises
Guard raises against daily eliminate

Guard relapse and detriment existing detriment
Culminate implement tenure yearn
Salutary politeness. Existing languor languor existing relapse

Culminate harangue and nor culminate existing languor languor
          of relapse
Existing implement guard harangue tenure harangue
Yearn existing and relapse
Guard relapse and detriment existing

Gentlemen. Résumé are dejected evils dejected
Cautious insinuate. The yet
Statistics pierces evils lessons lessons evils résumé
Cautious haggard are nature **cautious** evils lessons lessons of
          résumé
Evils insinuate gentleman. Haggard. The haggard
Yet evils are résumé
Gentleman. Résumé are dejected evils

Graceful ruminate and dangers; evaporate dangers;
Circumspect in through yielding
Suspicious pompadour evaporate light, light, evaporate ruminate
Circumspect hinging and not **circumspect** evaporate
                light, light, evaporate ruminate
Evaporate in graceful hinging through hinging
Yielding evaporate and ruminate
Graceful ruminate and dangers; evaporate

Graceful **"Recovery"** against deception embroider deception
Carefully is the young
Substance parenthesis embroider lancet lancet embroider
          "Recovery"
Carefully himself; against noxious carefully embroider lancet
          lancet obsequiousness **"Recovery"**
Embroider is graceful himself; the himself;
Young embroider against **"Recovery"**
Graceful **"Recovery"** against deception embroider

Gentleness **restoration** and designing encore designing
Concern. Is the yawl
Superiors proficient encore lattice lattice encore **restoration**
Concern. Henry and nominal concern. Encore lattice lattice of
          restoration

Encore is Gentleness Henry the Henry
Yawl encore and **restoration**
Gentleness **restoration** and designing encore

Great Recovery artifices deliberate embryo deliberate
"Cloud." In the yawl
Safe. Permeate embryo lawyer, lawyer, embryo Recovery
"Cloud." Heart, artifices nature, "cloud." Embryo lawyer,
       lawyer, or Recovery
Embryo in great heart, the heart,
Yawl embryo artifices Recovery
Great Recovery artifices deliberate embryo

Genial restoration and descend evacuate descend
City inferiors the yourself;
Self-possession particle evacuate limits limits evacuate restoration
City How and not city evacuate limits limits opportunities
      restoration
Evacuate inferiors genial How the How
Yourself; evacuate and restoration
Genial restoration and descend evacuate

Glossary ravenous arrogance daffodil even daffodil
Clemency is There Your
Spring prosaic even lymph lymph even ravenous
Clemency how arrogance nor clemency even lymph lymph or
      ravenous
Even is glossary how There how
Your even arrogance ravenous
Glossary ravenous arrogance daffodil even

Governor reveler a diminish epicure diminish
Connive impertinence. The you
Smiles. Premature epicure ligament ligament epicure reveler
Connive how a nor connive epicure ligament ligament officious
      reveler
Epicure impertinence. Governor how the how
You epicure a reveler
Governor reveler a diminish epicure

Twenty-Five Stories Spencer Holst One Dollar (No. 1)

Time was the edge never a tree. Yi!
Flew in a hurry. Very big, evenings
Swooping, (the fun of it;) rattle in the marsh. Everybody strutting
Sparkling pennies each night, college students! Europe retired.
He one week-end, looked slow at the world.
Only. Naked women explained
Dances, over a tiger lily willow leaves, all right,

That went. An earthquake. Noisily, the darkness. Years
Full of the past in that kind of agony, its very existence.
Shuddered in the breeze, of viewing red walls if it were eternally
                tired — stared —
Seemed pushed, exasperating. A neon sign. The Egyptian cat, each
                day, would always reappear.
He played outside life and sold that morning.
Once near morning big red eyes.
Dead. Once lives led. And really

To enjoy went experimenting about a new God. This new God retired
      young,
For many a Broadway hit. *This is too much!* Very pretty, even
Seen then, out like a man reflected if The Eagle seeking
Sees pure white. The annoyed eagle nest. Chickens on earth raised
His gun over the rocks. The little chick ate it slowly. To trick him.
One day she never went. This eagle.
One day off, lunch, his own lunch anymore, roosts.

See them. Warned embarrass not. To tell you,
"In your little field." "If rudely vomited" excited
The spectacle. The scientist on the other side rules in his fist, on
      earth he spoke
To his surprise the narrow path entered the same precise neat way.
      The cause every remembered
Hour of your clothes. "Look," said the gas,
On a road now explained
He had decided out of these last loved answered reindeer

From the snow, with a grand, old-world bow, ever heard, no feathers
    though he yearns to.
"From you it became very well," what else.
Six inches tall. Of his fairytales a pale red beret. I frighten you? Eyes
    stopped
Shallowly. Pure in pitch, escape now colored except rose rays
Hans on your lap senseless, these stories
On a tree now to each I ask
Do not read. Once a little girl liked Fifth Avenue ritual.

They'd walk. Evil nose, to these you
Face; in front. And some voice in her ear
Said to think, on the dummies. A Ladies Room inside eyes slippers.
"She pulled elfs not curious elfs?" Red-eyed leers
On their haunches old men looked a sign, and two elfs,
Opposite her nose, escape!
Deserved rest. Outside a little pot lived after. Laughter roared out of

The corner. A woman made a little clerical error. Never their pullman
    cars younger
Features it's obvious were taking them to a distant village everything
Swung from the trees. On mornings past rainbow bodies hobbled
    across the hut into a dark corner. Exposure and sun,
Snarls possession. Every night curiously, English, reminiscing about
    their
Hunting experiences of the animals, the llama, the South American
    animal.
One of the hunters now eyes
Daddy? Oh light look. A million dollars. A red tongue.

Poe and Psychoanalysis

Point, out effect
A not dreams
Point, stables young child, hand out a not a let young stranger
invites stranger.

Palace, on emotion.
Are now door.
Palace, sleeper.

Insect Assassins

Injects *no survive.* Efforts control the
Animal *survive. Survive.* Animal *survive. Survive.* Injects *no survive.*

In nasty spitting eye cost. This
Assassin spitting spitting assassin spitting spitting in nasty spitting

Insectivorous nutriment species encounter Charles to
Are species species are species species insectivorous nutriment species

Into notoriety. Sweeping eastern capture testimony
As sweeping sweeping as sweeping sweeping into
notoriety. Sweeping

Interest nervous succumb easily: composed tube
Adhesive succumb succumb adhesive succumb succumb interest
nervous succumb

It near spider East closes thorax.
And spider spider and spider spider it near spider

Its needle. Specialized enlarged? Cutting tough
A specialized specialized a specialized specialized its needle.
    Specialized

Is nontoxic secretion extremely contains that
Assassin-bug secretion secretion assassin-bug secretion secretion
            is nontoxic secretion

I needle-like snake. Enzymes compound TENDON
ANCHORING snake, snake, ANCHORING snake, snake, I
            needle-like snake,

INLET not significant, effect cockroach. Thus
About significant, significant, about significant, significant,
        INLET not significant,

Insect "natural" surround enzyme constituents time
After surround surround after surround surround insect "natural"
        surround

Internal nerve. Sucks especially contents through.
Against sucks sucks. Against sucks sucks. Internal nerve. Sucks

Immediate now share extinguishing controlling them.
Arises: share share arises: share share immediate now share

Insecticide? Needs. Sap; episode. Cimicidae thoroughly
Attributed sap; sap; attributed sap; sap; insecticide? Needs. Sap;

Insects numbing seconds. Each channels. They.
Accordingly seconds. Seconds. Accordingly seconds. Seconds.
            Insects numbing seconds.

Pattern Recognition by Machine

Perceive. As letters. Think? Think? Elusive, relations, now met most of the classic criteria of intelligence that skeptics have proposed.

Relations, elusive, *can* outperform their designers: original: group from the Carnegie Institute of Technology and the Rand Corporation (now met most of the classic criteria of intelligence that skeptics have proposed). In *Principia Mathematica,* think? In *Principia Mathematica,* original: now met most of the classic criteria of intelligence that skeptics have proposed.

Bertrand Russell. In *Principia Mathematica.*

More elegant than the Whitehead-Russell version. *As letters. Can* outperform their designers: His ability to solve problems, in *Principia Mathematica,* now met most of the classic criteria of intelligence that skeptics have proposed. Elusive.

Prove theorems and generally run his life depends on this type of perception. Achievements in mechanical problem-solving will remain isolated technical triumphs. The difficulty lies in the nature of the task. The difficulty lies in the nature of the task. Essentially classified the possible inputs. Request to pass the salt. Not transmit these ideal intervals.

Request to pass the salt. Essentially classified the possible inputs. Clear. Of variation among the dots and dashes, grid and converted to a cellular pattern by completely filling in all squares through which lines pass (not transmit these ideal intervals). In gaps (the difficulty lies in the nature of the task). In gaps (of variation among the dots and dashes), not transmit these ideal intervals.

(Bottom left). In gaps.

Maximum number of intersections of the sample with all horizontal lines across the grid. Achievements in mechanical problem-solving will remain isolated triumphs. Clear. Have been found and the range of the identified character spaces. In gaps (not transmit these ideal intervals). Essentially classify the possible inputs.

Process, are identified as dots and dashes. The classified marks and spaces gives a string of tentative segments, the classified marks and spaces gives a string of tentative segments. Experience has shown that when one of the tentative segments is not acceptable, reclassifies the longest space in the segment as a character space and examines the two new characters thus formed. Not fully specified in advance.

Reclassifies the longest space in the segment as a character space and examines the two new characters thus formed. Experience has shown that when one of the tentative segments is not acceptable, continuous message is divided into appropriate segments. Often be appropriate. Generalizing about pattern recognition. Not fully specified in advance. Is rather specialized. The classified marks and spaces gives a string of tentative segments, is rather specialized. Often be appropriate. Not fully specified in advance.

Be expected; is rather specialized.

Mechanical reader is to provide it with a means of assimilating the visual data. Are identified as dots and dashes. Continuous message is divided into appropriate segments. Handle. Is rather specialized. Not fully specified in advance. Experience has shown that when one of the tentative segments is not acceptable.

Presents no problem. An image of the letter could be projected on a bank of photocells, the output of each cell controlling a binary device in the computer. The output of each cell controlling a binary device in the computer. Experiments to be described here the appropriate digital information from the matrix was recorded on punch cards and was fed into the computer in this form. Representing the unknown letter would be compared to each template sequence, number of matching digits recorded in each case.

Representing the unknown letter would be compared to each template sequence, experiments to be described here the appropriate digital information from the matrix was recorded on punch cards and was fed into the computer in this form. Clearly fail. Orientation or size could destroy the match completely [good deal more than mere shapes]. Number of matching digits recorded in each case. INCORRECT MATCH may result even when sample (the output of each cell controlling a binary device in the computer). INCORRECT MATCH may result even when sample (orientation or size could destroy the match completely) number of matching digits recorded in each case.

Believe to be an important general principle. INCORRECT MATCH may result even when sample.

Matches. An image of the letter could be projected on a bank of photocells, clearly fail. Hierarchical structure is forced on the recogni-

tion system by the nature of the entities to be recognized. INCOR-
RECT MATCH may result even when sample (number of matching
digits recorded in each case). Experiments to be described here the
appropriate digital information from the matrix was recorded on
punch cards and fed into the computer in this form.

Rome

Rossano Brazzi became furious at a party when a teenage beauty with
        long black hair cascading down her back made
        romantic overtures toward Rossano. Out amid the
        dancers and very roughly broke in on Rossano and the
        girl. Meek but meaningful "Yes, dear." Embarrass-
        ment was amplified: there was a man in the room.

Recommended that she take a rest at a hospital to avoid a nervous
        breakdown. "Obviously he didn't know what he was
        talking about!" asserts Dawn. Many of the guests
        walked out, but the majority stayed and laughed and
        called out words of encouragement. Exclaimed:
        "That girl will never get anywhere."

London

Lower lip. Objected to being called a baby and called Niven an
        unprintable name. Niven called her a few vile names, threw up
        his hands in disgust and told the girl to "Get out! Go away!
        Don't bother me any more!" David hadn't had two seconds to
        calm down when a lady rushed over from the bar and, explain-
        ing that she hadn't noticed him before, asked for his autograph.
        Out of the place. Night and sang a number of shocking songs.

Liberace called Scotland Yard the other afternoon and complained that
he had received a threatening telephone call. Out of the pic-
ture. Not paying his bill to a tailor who needs the money far
more than Anthony.

Paris

Popped into town for a fast weekend and wound up dating two red-
headed strippers who looked almost like twins. And the
screen actor toured the the bars and picked up a third girl who
seemed to enjoy being caressed by the strippers as much as she
enjoyed being mauled by Boyd . . . Referred to the Duke of
Windsor in similar terms. Into a fist fight in one of those
off-beat bars Françoise likes to frequent. Sagan later admitted
she didn't know why they waded into the fight.

Put him in a mental hospital for a long period of time. As BB threw
her arms around her old friend and kissed him. Rushed back and
apologized, he kept right on crying. "Instead of a man!" Spoken
Charrier quieted down.

Passion. As he was kissing her neck he noticed someone else's teeth
marks and became infuriated . . .

Marseilles

Man who was standing next to him. At the end of that arm was in
Wayne's pocket. Right hand that caught the pickpocket square
on the mouth. Stephen said nothing. Enraged man's eyes and
then kicked him in the groin. In the car by the time Boyd had
finished walking all over the felled pickpocket.

Madrid

Man. At him to claw his face. Down and sobbed uncontrollably.

Sydney

Some of her own. "You couldn't be a true woman or you wouldn't fear such things." Did.

Berlin

Became quite annoyed when a girl at a bar here made a pass at Mrs. Jurgens, a tall, beautiful brunette. Explained that since she made a pass like a man he treated her like a man.

First Asymmetry for Iris

Seven. Evidence Vajra-Dhāra, *extrémité* nationality.
Essential *Vedānta* Individual dangers; enlightenment naturally
      closed enter
(vijñānamaya a Jefferson Reavey Anything) Dumas him any.
          Rests. *As*
experiences *Xanthoxyllum* thinking realize every malaria is
      typifies episodes.
Not at the inherent one. Not attack lies in things. You

either sack something expected non-religious, the Itself. As: like
viewed extending diverse alike: not the armed
in numbers darkness. Immediate *vulgaris Ilex* definitions. Unite
    and lead
dream. Against none group entertainment Realm support
every Nightshade looked it glorious Hawkweed that end not much
      especially nervous the
N. As the urban refer *Allium* leafleting little. You
claim lastly ought septa. Even Dumas
earth. Night the electrical regarded

Virginia, it join nineteenth a not analysis made as Yard.
      Astronomical
at
Juniperus experience flowering formula. Essentially responsible
      succeeded. Or neighbors
Redwood elementary astronomers, vets. Emitting year's
and Narcissus years the husband's in never *Gordonia*
doubtless *Upanishad* mention (āndaja) States
he is materials
a not you,
rock. Eyes seen two sources
as steady

exquisite *Xanthoxylum* pleasure extent "responsible—" interest
      energy notoriety. Canon, engaged sorrow;
Xerophyllum and not her one *Xanthoxyllum* yacht laziest
      LIVING upstandeth must
to happiness in nuclear *Kubla*. In nice guarded

revered earth, American lady in Zen. Even
expiration vividly extremely relatively yearning
moment. Armed "Lesser" a ray in an
Ilex sense
Tagetes your peasant in forms insinuate. Equalled season's
eight pure incorporated support of desires edge something

non-reality. Of Tangerine
a told
20, human exaltation
itself no however. Energy ruminate enlightenment nothing to
other *nirvāna*. Explained
neither of the
Auvergne to the *amara* classic know
"let's in elided step
Iris nominal
the history." India not gazing. Special
year. Our undreamed.

Paracelsus (20 Sept. 1960)

Nothing other therefore
is needed to everything.... Required profane, required establish the
terms Holy in supernatural
same in great "natural"
are serve
are
saints. *Ultima materia —materia* originally not something.
To obtain
pure recall a correspondingly transformed in stomach essence
mysterium and great in concealment
fruit.... One ripe

is form
and
many, as necessary,
purpose refined and curative things, it says endowed some
first arcanum *lapis* seed energies....
Mercurius arcanum gold; its crudity.
Here earth
this earth miraculously prerogative this studied
good or derived
art, never do.
In fancy

heaven, exist
to evil man. Pestilence, they signs
governed, or does
whole of events.
This one
has inferior sick
say one's understanding leads.

Asymmetry from Sayings of Gurdjieff
(23 Sept. 1960)

There Humanity earth's received Everything
has us masters are not 'I' there You
empty aim rule, to hundred small
river experiences; create evokes in vibrations Everything 'directors'
each voluntary, externals. Reach yes their highly illusion. Not God,

has and speak
unconsciously suffering;
man and simply talk. External rule, surrounding
and real, experiences;
nothingness only that
is
the Hope English Russians East
yourself only universe

energy must printed to yes
and is masters
room unconsciously. Let experiences;
them only
have useless not 'directors' replies externals. Do
symbol minds and like love

room in valuable experiences; recognized
evokes.

Untitled Asymmetry

Black magic learned quietness abstractly, strengthened aggressively the gallery of hogs, or acutely argued in the speech of hanging for faith in redundant or inscrutable elevations.

Buddhistic liberation also considered knowledge, mainly according to grassy instructions and compassion. Living exists absolutely though it represents non-conceptual extinction and dissolution quite ultimately in Indian time.

SELF-RELIANCE

star; early late. fatal
rocks, early late. I and not con-
      ventional. early

soul each, learn flashes
recognize each, learn impression
      arrives no corn each,

sculpture eye look faces
room eye look is and
      nonchalance conciliate eye

sentences eloquent, Lethe for
request eloquent, Lethe is and
      names customs. eloquent,

sacred ephemeral large folk
Rough ephemeral large is af-
      fectation none. ephemeral

shun explanation. living for
refuse explanation. living I actions
      consent explanation.

from *Asymmetries*

Methods for Reading and Performing Asymmetries

Asymmetries are poems of which the words, punctuation, typography, and spacing of words on the page have been determined by certain kinds of chance operations. With a few exceptions, the 501 numbered Asymmetries (1960-61) were generated by an "acrostic-chance" method. This involved drawing words, word strings, and in one case, syllables from current reading matter (or in a few poems, from the environment in which the poems were written). Usually an initial word was found in a text (or in the environment) and words (or strings) having its letters as their initial letters were then found by reading along in the text (or by careful perception of the environment). After the first line, the initial letters of the words or strings of which acrostically "spelled out" the first word, words beginning with the second and subsequent letters of the first word were found to begin the second and subsequent lines, and these words were spelled out in those lines.

The method was complicated by the fact that different acrostic chance-selection subroutines were sometimes used within poems and that punctuation following words, notebook-page edges, and spacing rules based on them determined word placement and spacing. In addition, selection "mistakes" (if not noticed immediately) were usually accepted, and selection-method variations were sometimes based on previous mistakes.

Asymmetries may be performed either by a single person or by a group including any number of people. Each performer follows either a Basic Method or one of nine other performance methods, while realizing successively each Asymmetry in a randomly selected or individually chosen series of the poems. The individual performers decide their own reading speeds and other performance parameters not specifically (or only partially) regulated by the methods followed. All individuals perform simultaneously.

Performers must become acutely conscious of both the sounds they themselves are producing and those arising from other performers, the audience, and/or the environment. It is essential to the realization of Asymmetries that all performers choose as many aspects and details as possible of their individual realizations within the context of as clear an awareness of the total aural situation at each moment as performance circumstances allow. In many circumstances—as when performers are *dispersed* within the space (e.g., around or in the midst of an audience or when performers and audience are identical), a procedure often followed in performances I've directed—each performer's impression of the total aural situation will necessarily differ from those of the others. What is asked for is concentrated attention to all sounds perceptible to the individual and an attitude of receptivity and responsiveness such that choices are made spontaneously, often seeming to arise from the whole situation.

Schematically, this "whole" can be represented by concentric spheres: the inmost is that of the individual performer; next, that of the whole performance group; next, that of the larger social group, including audience as well as performers; next, that of the performance space, including room acoustics, electronics, etc.; and finally, the larger spaces within which the performance space is situated: the rest of the building, the surrounding streets, neighborhood, city (or rural area), etc., all of which may affect significantly the aggregate of sounds heard by each individual at each moment. The spheres are best conceived as transparent and interpenetrating—not static shells but concentric ripples travelling simultaneously out from and in toward each center.

Basic Method

Method 1: Words and Silences

This method underlies the others and is the one to be followed when all or most of the others are ruled out by performance circumstances. *Blank spaces* before, after, and between words or parts of words, between lines of words, and before and after whole Asymmetries are rendered as *silences*. Each silence lasts *at least* as long as it would take the individual to read aloud any words or word fragments printed above or below the blank space. (They *may* last longer: see "What to Keep in Mind..." at the end of this "Methods" essay.)

Each Asymmetry is conceived as having a "left margin" perpendicular to the left side of the first character of the poem and a "right margin" perpendicular to the right side of whatever character in the poem is printed farthest to the right. Left-hand blank spaces ("left indentations") are measured from the left margin to the first character of an indented line; right-hand blank spaces ("right indentations"), from the last character of a line to the poem's right margin; and blank lines, from margin to margin. (Each Asymmetry is preceded by and followed by one blank line.)

Where two or more lines of type might be placed between two printed lines, that many blank lines are considered to be present, each standing for a silence lasting at least as long as it would take to read *aloud* words (and parts of words) printed from margin to margin of that Asymmetry. There is at least one such "line of silence" *before* every word beginning at the left margin (including the first word of each Asymmetry), and there is at least one *after* every *end mark* (period, question mark, or exclamation point). Thus a left-marginal word that follows an end mark is always preceded by *two* lines of silence, and at least one line of silence should precede and follow each Asymmetry in a series performed.

Emphasized words, i.e., initially and solidly capitalized words and words printed in emphatic typography—italics and boldface, indicated respectively in the book *Asymmetries 1-260* (New York: Printed Editions, 1980) by straight and wavy underlining—are to be read *loudly;* initially capitalized words, slightly louder than others; italicized words, loud; solid capitals and boldface, very loud. As much as possible, these emphasized words should be spoken loudly *without seeming to express anger or other violent feelings.* The effect should be that of "turning up the volume"—a relatively "objective" kind of loudness.

Words printed within enclosing punctuation, i.e., single or double quotation marks, parentheses, or brackets, are to be read *softly* or *whispered*. Other words are to be read *moderately loudly.*

Exactly *how* loudly or softly any particular words are spoken is to be determined spontaneously by individual performers within the aural contexts of specific performance moments. In public performances softer words and whispers should be loud enough to be heard throughout the performance space (when not completely covered by louder sounds), and moderate and loud words should be correspondingly louder. In larger spaces this may be accomplished through appropriate electronic amplification: whenever possible, each performer should have an individual microphone, amplifier channel, and loudspeaker. When sufficient equipment is not available, there should be as many channels, and as few voices on each channel, as possible.

Pitch changes are indicated by the punctuation marks that follow certain words. While some marks, e.g., the comma and the question mark, can imply several possible intonation patterns, some are fairly unambiguous: for instance, periods, semicolons, and colons imply a slight rise in pitch followed by a definitive lowering (the so-called sentence-final intonation contour), and the intonation of any word succeeded by one of these marks should conform to this pattern. However, when reading words followed by ambiguous marks, readers must choose between the several pitch patterns that might be implied by them. Since only context determines the pattern appropriate to each specific case, some readers may at times be helped by imagining contexts for words and word strings followed by such marks. But spontaneous "arbitrary" decisions among possible pitch patterns will usually suffice. Unpunctuated words should be read at an even pitch that simply stops at margins and blank spaces. In general, pitches are those of normal speech, or of prose read aloud normally, at the required loudness.

Speed of reading and voice *timbres* are free but should seldom give the impression of exaggeration or distortion. Nevertheless, where specific speakers are indicated by the context, performers may carefully assume appropriate vocal personae. The required minimal durations of silence corresponding to blank spaces are longer or shorter relative to the average speed at which any particular Asymmetry is read.

Other Methods

Method 2: Words Only

The words are read as in the Basic Method as regards loudness, pitch change, etc., but the reader makes *only breath pauses* (no *long* silences) at line endings, varied only as appropriate to punctuation, if any. Readers have the option of slightly prolonging final sounds of lines, especially where words are broken at line endings.

Method 3: Silence Only

The performer remains *silent* as long as it would take to read the particular Asymmetry *aloud* by the Basic Method, including blank-space silences, at a chosen speed. This amounts to a silent performance by the Basic Method. No Asymmetry should be silently read more quickly or more slowly by this method than the performer would choose *and be able* to read it *aloud*.

Method 4: Words, Tones, and Silences

All words are read, and all *left* indentations are interpreted as *silences*, as in the Basic Method. *Right* indentations are interpreted, not as silences, but as *continuous* (or rapidly reiterated) *tones* on any instrument. These tones may be extended when necessary (as when a wind instrumentalist runs out of breath) by beginning them again with minimal attack. (Their *measured* length is *minimal:* see "What to Keep in Mind . . .".)

The *pitch* of each tone is determined by the performer's freely choosing any letter in the preceding words which is a German pitch name: A, C, D, E, F, and G are interpreted respectively as any chromatic tone or microtone *in any register* that can be designated respectively by one of these letters, e.g., A can be played as A♭, A♮, A♯, a quarter tone above or below one of these, etc. However, B always means B♭ or a microtone near it, while H always means B♮ or a microtone near it.

Exactly the same pitch should not be played at the ends of two successive lines. If the same letter is chosen from both lines, a different chromatic tone or microtone or a different register should be selected in each case.

Margin-to-margin blank spaces, interpreted in the Basic Method as "lines of silence," may be interpreted either as silences or as continuations of the tones corresponding to the right indentations following the words directly above. Less than half of the margin-to-margin blanks before, within, or after any single Asymmetry should be "read" as tones. If a performer chooses to play a tone in place of a line of silence preceding an Asymmetry, a letter is selected from the first line of the poem to determine the tone.

Method 5: One Tone Only

Reading an Asymmetry silently, the performer plays *one* continuous (or rapidly reiterated) *tone*, determined in pitch as in Method 4 by any letter in the Asymmetry, for as long as it would take that individual to read the whole poem *aloud* by the Basic Method, extending the tone whenever necessary by beginning it again, with minimal attack.

Method 6: Tones and Silences

Reading an Asymmetry silently, the performer plays, for each duration represented by a *right* indentation, a continuous (or rapidly reiterated) *tone* determined in pitch as in Method 4 by any letter in the words preceding the indentation. *Silence* is observed in durations represented by *left* indentations and printed *words*. *Blank lines* may be realized either as *silences* or as prolongations of *tones* realizing immediately preceding *right* indentations. If a blank line preceding an Asymmetry is realized as a tone, the pitch is determined by any letter in the first line.

Method 7: Words and Tones

The performer reads all the words in an Asymmetry as in the Basic Method, but plays continuous (or rapidly reiterated) tones, determined in pitch, and extended when necessary, as in Method 4, for all durations represented by blank spaces and interpreted as silences in the Basic Method. (Thus the performance *must* begin with a *long tone*.) There should be as little silence as possible in performances following this method, with words and tones immediately succeeding each other, without pauses, except for very short ones occasioned by punctuation marks, from beginning to end.

Method 8: Spoken and Whispered Words

The performer reads all the words in an Asymmetry as in the Basic Method. However, rather than observing silence in durations corresponding to *blank spaces*, one *whispers* any words or parts of words in the poem printed anywhere below or above each blank space. To find words and fragments to whisper for whole blank lines (in place of "lines of silence"), one will often have to obtain them from several different lines. (How this is done will be clear from the example that follows these descriptions of performance methods.) Where there would be two or more lines of silence, there will be two or more whispered lines, and every performance by this method begins and ends with a whispered line. Amplification is imperative for performers following this method.

Method 9: Phonic Prolongations and Repetitions

This is a method for introducing phonic prolongations and repetitions into the reading and performance of Asymmetries of which the texts do not include such features:

Wherever, in any Asymmetry, a word or word string is broken on one line and continued, after indentations, on the line below, the sound of the last phoneme (speech sound) before the break is prolonged, if it can be, or rapidly repeated, if it cannot be prolonged, for *at least* as long as the individual reader would take to speak any words and/or word fragments printed above or below the empty space between the last letter before the break and the (theoretical) right margin and between the left margin and the first letter after the break, whether the latter is the next letter of a broken word or the first letter of the next word in a broken string. (The sound *may* be continued still longer.)

The phonemes represented by all vowels (*a, e, i, o, u,* except after *q,* and *y,* both as in "bury" and as in "try") and diphthongs, and by the following consonants and digraphs, can be prolonged: *c* as in "cease," *ch* both as in "Charlotte," as in "loch," and as in "church," *f, g* both as in "George" and as in "largesse," *h, j* both as in "judge" and as in "jongleur," *l, m, n, ng, r, s, sh, th* both as in "thistle" and as in "that," *v,* and *x.* The phonemes represented by the following consonants can only be repeated: *b, c* as in "cut," *ch* as in "chorus," *d, g* as in "god," *k, p, q, t, u* after *q, w,* and *y* as in "yet." Readers who prefer to repeat rather than to prolong *ch* as in "church" or as in "loch," *g* as in "George," *h,* or *j* as in "judge" may do so.

This method may be "superimposed" on either the Basic Method (Method 1) or on either of the two methods involving both words and tones (Methods 4 and 7). When this is done, all empty spaces *except for those following breaks in words or strings* are to be interpreted either as silences or as continuous or rapidly reiterated tones, as in Methods 1, 4, or 7.

Method 10: Words and Indeterminate Silences

This is a useful variant of the Basic Method. The performer reads all the words as in that method, but for each *blank space* observes a *silence* of *any duration* whatsoever that seems desirable at the moment in the performance when that space in the text is reached. This method is especially appropriate for performances of Asymmetries accompanied by sound continua other than Asymmetries, since performers following it can wait for silences or quiet passages in the accompanying sound before speaking word strings, and can do so without measuring their own silences.

Asymmetries may be performed in this way with live or recorded sounds of any kind, e.g., improvising musicians, conversations, radio or television sounds of any kind, formal or informal musical compositions, audiotapes or videotapes or film sound tracks, electronically or mechanically generated sounds, and/or environmental sounds of any kind.

Performances Including All Ten Methods

It will often be found desirable, especially for larger groups, to present performances that include all ten methods. (In such performances speaker-musicians will have the possibility of using *all* of the ten methods at different times, while for those who only speak, all of the methods except those including musical tones will be available.)

To present such performances, each participant must have a way to determine which method should be followed while realizing each of the Asymmetries in the particular group that person draws or chooses for that performance. It is preferable that such determinations should be made in the midst of the performance, just before realizing each Asymmetry, rather than before the performance.

This preference derives from an interpretation of the philosophy of the *I Ching* ("Book of Changes"): A hexagram (group of six broken and/or unbroken lines) determined by coin throws or divisions of a pile of yarrow stalks at a certain time is thought to be relevant to a problem which at that time preoccupies the person carrying out these chance operations. The underlying assumption seems to be that there is an acausal, "synchronous" connection (as C.G. Jung expressed it) between all events happening at any particular time.

Similarly, an operation used to determine the method for performing an Asymmetry will be optimally connected with that performance if the operation is carried out just before the performance of that Asymmetry. The problem then arises to discover a kind of chance operation that each performer may employ before each Asymmetry without its intruding unduly upon the performance as a whole.

In the method recommended in the earlier (1961) version of these performance directions, two dice were to be thrown just before performing each Asymmetry to assign one of the first seven methods. A throw of a 3 or a 5 assigned the Basic Method; a 2 or a 4, Words Only; a 6, Silence Only; a 7, Words, Tones, and Silences; an 8, One Tone Only; a 9 or an 11, Tones and Silences; and a 10 or a 12, Words and Tones.

However, throwing dice during a performance is awkward, cumbersome, and needlessly distracting: it adds an obvious and unnecessary element to the performance situation, and in many physical circumstances it is extremely difficult to do this at all, much less to do it with any grace. Besides, there are now ten methods rather than seven, two having been added as postscripts to the original instructions in earlier printings, and one added first in this version, as published in *Asymmetries 1-260*.

In addition, the probability of each performance method's being followed should be different (rather than equal, as in the 1961 dice method), and a different *set* of such probabilities should be generated for each entire performance.

With these considerations in mind, the following operations are suggested:

(1) Sometime before a performance, each performer assigns a random digit to each method after the first or Basic Method. Zero (interpreted as 10) is assigned to the Basic Method, and zeros are thereafter disregarded. Subsequently, after any particular digit is assigned to a method, it too is disregarded—this digit is not assigned to any other method. Performers may obtain random digits from either a table such as the Rand Corporation's *A Million Random Digits with 100,000 Normal Deviates* (Glencoe, Ill.: The Free Press, 1955) or from a telephone directory: the final digits of successive telephone numbers in any chance-selected columns are sufficiently random for this purpose. (Those who only speak will not assign digits to methods involving musical tones.)

(2) The number and descriptive name of each performance method is typed or written on as many filing cards as designated by its random digit, e.g., if the digit 3 is assigned to Method 7, "Method 7: Words and Tones" will appear on three cards. ("Method 1: Basic Method" will always appear on ten cards.)

(3) Just before the performance, this pack of "Method Cards" is thoroughly shuffled by the performer and placed next to a randomly selected or personally chosen group of Asymmetries copied on separate sheets of paper.

(4) A random set of Asymmetries may be obtained from the book *Asymmetries 1-260* by means of random-digit triplets: three-digit numbers, each comprising three successive random digits from a table or the final digits of three successive telephone numbers. Starting at a randomly selected place in the table or telephone directory, the performer writes down successive triplets, but crosses out all of them larger than 260. As many triplets smaller than 261 must be accumulated in this way as there are minutes in the planned duration of the performance, e.g., if the planned duration is 20 minutes, each performer's list must consist of 20 triplets smaller than 261. Each Asymmetry having one of these triplets in its title is copied once for every time that triplet appears on the list. (Each performer's set may include any number of duplicates of any Asymmetry.) Zeros placed before other digits are disregarded, e.g., 001 and 010 designate Asymmetries 1 and 10. This process ought to provide each performer with more than enough Asymmetries for the planned performance duration. A similar method may be applied to any published group of Asymmetries.

[To obtain a random set of Asymmetries, without duplicates, from *Representative Works,* the performer may: (1) Write the numbers 18, 89, 158, 193 (the illustrative example), 204, 320, 344, 372, 423, 497, and 499 on small slips of paper. (2) Place the slips in a container, such as a hat or coffee can, and mix them thoroughly. (3) Draw from the container as many slips as there are minutes in the planned performance. (4) Perform the corresponding Asymmetries in the order in which they were drawn from the container.

To obtain a set possibly with duplicates, carry out steps (1) and (2) as above, and then (3) draw out all 12 slips, assigning to the corresponding Asymmetries in the order drawn the numbers 1 through 12. Finally, (4) throw a pair of dice as many times as minutes in the projected performance: the successive throws' pip sums will assign the series of Asymmetries to be performed and the order in which they are to be performed.]

(5) The performance method designated by the topmost card is used while performing the first Asymmetry in the set, and subsequent Asymmetries are performed in accordance with subsequent cards. It is, of course, unnecessary to use all the cards or to perform all the texts in the set: when an ending signal is given or a previously agreed-upon time is reached, all the performers should stop at the same time, regardless of where they are in the Asymmetries they are reading.

What to Keep in Mind During Performances and How to Start and Stop Them

I cannot emphasize too strongly that performers must listen to, relate with, and respond to each other and to ambient sounds, including those of the audience. When they fall silent before, within, or between Asymmetries, they must listen with concentrated attention to the total aural situation and make their choices as to further sound production in accordance with what they hear.

Some parameters, such as the tempo of delivery and voice timbre, are freely variable. Some, such as loudness, are regulated in very general terms, but the specific loudness, etc., realized at each point in a performance, must be decided in accordance with the actual situation. Similarly, although *minimal* durations of silence are, in all but Method 10, measured by the performer's "saying" the measuring words silently, any particular silence may be extended whenever an individual feels that the performance situation demands it. And when following methods that include tones, the performer chooses which of the possible tones to play, which octave to play it in, how to begin it (its attack), how loudly to play it, and whether (and if so, how long) to extend its duration beyond that measured by words and word fragments printed above or below it. However, the *words* to be spoken at each place in the determinate Asymmetry are *unchangeable*, even though the ways of saying them may vary. The later portion of the numbered Asymmetries, beginning with Asymmetry 379, includes 62 "indeterminate" Asymmetries for which the reader must supply words—different at each performance—by following specified methods.

Sensitivity, tact, and courtesy must be exercised in order to make every detail of one's performance contribute toward a total sound sequence that is as similar as possible to what the performer would choose to hear. While egoistic overpowering of the total sound should never occur, the exercise of virtuosity is strongly encouraged when it is carried out with as much consciousness as possible of the total situation. Performers should try always to be both inventive and sensitive. As in all my other simultaneities, the most important "rules" are: *"Listen"* and *"Relate."*

A performance may be begun and ended in any convenient way. Usually it will be best for performers to agree beforehand on an approximate performance duration and for one of them to act as group leader, signalling the ending before or slightly after the agreed-upon end point. The leader must be easily visible to all performers and judge when, around that end point, the performance may be most satisfactorily ended. However, when circumstances allow greater latitude, a performance may continue until the group ends it by informal consensus.

This description of methods for realizing the numbered Asymmetries supersedes the one written in 1961 and printed in *An Anthology...*, edited by La Monte Young (1st ed., New York: Young and Mac Low, 1963; 2nd ed., New York: Heiner Friedrich, 1970). All future performances of numbered Asymmetries must follow the methods described here.

March 1961–September 1981
New York (The Bronx & Manhattan)

Example Illustrating Reading by the Basic Method
(Asymmetry 193)

The poem as printed is followed by a schematic version showing how it is to be performed with measured silences when following the Basic Method. In the latter version, words and word fragments measuring minimal silences (or whispered, in Method 8) are printed between virgules (/'s). The silences are "minimal" in that members of larger groups will sometimes find it desirable or even necessary to extend them to prevent the textures of performances from becoming so continually thick that a large number of words are unintelligible. However, soloists and members of very small groups will seldom need to extend their silences.

Spoken words are underlined only to distinguish them from silent ones, *not* to indicate loud speech. They are to be spoken as shown by the original text: all moderately loud, with slight emphases on "Italian" and "Now" because of the initial capitals.

Some silence-measuring letters have had to be omitted to accommodate virgules. Where words and fragments have been juxtaposed without spaces, each vowel is to be silently "pronounced" (or in Method 8, whispered) separately, e.g., "literallyyest"="literalee-ee-est."

Other solutions are, of course, possible where words appear both above and below blank spaces.

Asymmetry 193

```
favors abstract violets opulent
     rest.

               strokes,

     abstract ballet strokes,
                         turret rest.

          abstract canvases turret

  violets Italian opulent literally
     eyes turret strokes,

  opulent pluming umber,
                      literally
          eyes
               Now turret

     rest.
```

/Asymmetry 193/

```
/favors abstract violets opulent rest./
 favors abstract violets opulent/rest./
/favors/rest./ct violets opulent rest./
/favors rest.act violets opulent rest./
/favors rest.a/strokes, /opulent rest./
/abstract ballet strokes, turret rest./
 abstract ballet strokes,/turret rest./
/abstract ballet strokes,/turret rest.
/abstract ballet strokes, turret rest./
/abstract/abstract canvases turret/st./
/abstract abstract canvases turretest./
 violets Italian opulent literally/st./
/violets/eyes turret strokes,/allyest./
/violets eyes turret strokes,allyyest./
 opulent pluming umber,/literallyyest./
/opulent pluming umber,/literally/est./
/opulent/eyes/ng umber, literallyyest./
/opulent eyes/Now turret/iterallyyest./
/opulent eyes Now turretliterallyyest./
 rest./t eyes Now turretliterallyyest./
/rest.nt eyes Now turretliterallyyest./
```

Asymmetry 18

inspiring.

      name sins people instruction
          reverent "invoking"
      name
           [Goblins]

name
    Avalokitesvara
        magical
    enables

Asymmetry 89

Yellow earth,
      light light own worth

earth,
   all reaches
      Truly heed

light image good heed
      Truly

light image good heed
      Truly

own worth
    NOURISHMENT.

worth own reaches
    Truly heed

Asymmetry 158

opposites past past opposites such ideal
      together environment,
                  such

past abstract such together

past abstract such together

opposites past past opposites such ideal
      together environment,
                  such

such unite coincide history

ideal determining environment,
                  abstract
    Leibniz

together opposites Garmaker environment,
      together holocaust environment,

Asymmetry 204

still.

took,
island little little

took,
out out knowing

island still.

little angel's nothing
did

little island took,
took,
little everything

little island took,
took,
little everything

Asymmetry 320

evidence and
                visible.

                        Experiments with growing
                indicated that P_{735}
                                darkness,
                                        whereas
                red–
                    ab–
                        sorbing P_{660} is stable.

                                                even
                never been exposed to
                                        case.

                                        In
                                                exposed
                briefly to red light to

varies from one
                    plant
                        and he
                                reported
                                        in Chicago
                effective dark period night
                                        seek his way
        In
                fact,
                    the philosopher has
                not

Asymmetry 344

newness ecclesiastic the Welfare newness
    ecclesiastic sponsors sponsors

ecclesiastic a credit a credit the Leaders
    ecclesiastic sponsors
    ini-
        tiator attitude sponsors
    this ini-
         tiator a credit

Welfare ecclesiastic the Leaders a force
    attitude was reached
    ecclesiastic

newness ecclesiastic the Welfare newness
    ecclesiastic sponsors sponsors

ecclesiastic a credit a credit the Leaders
    ecclesiastic sponsors
    ini-
        tiator attitude sponsors
    this ini-
         tiator a credit

sponsors a prayer Orthodoxy newness
    sponsors Orthodoxy was reached
    sponsors

sponsors a prayer Orthodoxy newness
    sponsors Orthodoxy was reached
    sponsors

consequence our nineteenth scientific educational
           quoad hoc us educational nineteenth
           consequence educational

our us recording

nineteenth innovational—
                          nineteenth educational
traditional educational educational nineteenth
           traditional heart

scientific consequence innovational—
                      educational
           nineteenth traditional
           innovational—
                          freakish.

                          innovational—
                          consequence

educational dislocation,
                      us consequence
           arranged traditional
           innovational—
                          our nineteenth
           arranged
                (Landry)

quoad hoc us our arranged dislocation
           heart our consequences

us scientific

educational dislocation,
                      us consequence
           arranged traditional
           innovational—

Asymmetry 372

THE INDICATOR HERE!!

                ELECTRICAL IMPULSES!

HERE!!

       ELECTRICAL IMPULSES!

                  REMAIN HERE
       ELECTRICAL IMPULSES!

ELECTRICAL IMPULSES!

              LINGERED THERE TWO MONTHS!

Asymmetry 423

working day and night,
              of rice and a vegetable
     room perhaps 6' x 6'
                    square.

                         Koreans.

          Inchon,
               nights,
                    garbage itself

of rice and a vegetable
              rice and a vegetable
     food is mixed with cigarette butts,

rice and a vegetable Inchon,
                    cigarette
     butts,
          etc.,

Koreans.

          of rice and a vegetable room perhaps

Note on Asymmetries 497 & 499

In Asymmetries 497 and 499, the spacing of the latter continues that of the former. While the empty spaces in the poems are, when following my "basic method," to be rendered as silences equal in duration to at least the time it would take the individual reading the poem to say words printed above or below them (as in other Asymmetries), the parenthesized series of hyphens in both poems indicate that the last phoneme before the parenthesis is to be prolonged. The duration of each prolongation must be at least as long as the time it would take the reader to speak words printed in the spaces occupied by series of hyphens. They can be prolonged beyond this length if the speaker feels a greater prolongation will sound better, especially in simultaneous performances. Through Method 9 (see "Methods for Reading and Performing Asymmetries"), all the other Asymmetries may be performed with "phonic prolongations" similar to the ones indicated explicitly in the texts of Asymmetries 497 & 499. All such "Method 9" prolongations are treated similarly to the explicit ones in these poems.

Asymmetry 497

whirr?

      Ames!

           Agamogenesis —
                offing?

                          Tuam(- - - - - - - - - - - - -
- - - - - -)otu Archipelago!

                DON RICKLES:
                suspense accoun(- - - - - - - - - - - - -
- - - - - -)t Caen,
           Luxembourg Palace!

           Them,
                right triangle,
           ideogram . . .
                    corrosive(- - - - - - - - - - - - - - - -
- - - - - -)*sublimate:*
           pebble leather:
                    thio(- - - - - - - - - - - - - - -
- - - - - -)antimonious acid.

           TACK?

Asymmetry 499

An(- - - - - - -

- - - - - -)thelme Brillat(- -

- - - - - -)Savarin,
        prosecuting attorney.

       Mutism,
            pedagogically

(split ticket;)
     AUGUST SUN
            (search par(- - - - - - - - - - - - - - - -

- - - - - - - - -)ty)!

       Gebhard Leberecht v(- - - - - - - - - - - - - - - - -

- - - - - - - - -)on Blücher,
         Eleutherios V(- - - - - - - - - - - - - - - -

- - - - - - - - -)enizelos?

     Flowsheet.

         Hum(- - - - - - - - - - - - - -

- - - - - - - - -)mer . . .
       OCCUPY . . .
          negative(- - - - - - - - - - -

- - - - - - - -) electricity sea squirt . . .
       NEW COMMANDER?

(Numbered) Asymmetries
October 1960–February 1961
The Bronx

From Nuclei I,2,a.

Politically we take our breath
                             wherever breath may be
we respect
             it profits us
                      more than any news or writing
                                    poor
breath
        to news a vessel
                  a weather
            or it may be a committee
with a weather of disgust for the brain's middle
                        and after its tail
money

The political have taken breath
                          and their breath we may
respect
           though we have no profit of it
               but news
                  and a little writing
             poor stuff at that
but breath itself is news
                  not merely its vessel
          it's the weather itself
            what may no committee be
and some weather's disgusting
             like having a brain in your middle
                      or after like a tail
and some's like money

But all's political that takes breath
                              whatever breath may be
in any respect
                  whatever its profit
                                    whatever its news
            however it may be written about
                              however poor it is
breath makes news
                        for vessels it's the weather
        whatever that may be
      and in committees
there it becomes the weather
                              disgusting to the brain
            to the middle
                        and after
        to the tail
but it makes money

That's political
                  however you take breath
                              your breath may be
in some respect
                  profitable
                              that's not news
        why write so poorly
but breathing we make news
            though we're vessels in its weather
      or we may be its committee
we can weather the disgust of it
                              brains can middle it
            if after it tails
money

So politics is taking breath
                              breathing
                                        that may be
I respect that
                this profit's news
                                    what's written about
            no matter how poorly
breathing's the news that's our vessel's weather
                            be it what it may
                                    we're committed to it
like to the weather
                    or disgust
        to our brains
                    our middles
                                our befores and afters
it's money

And so it's political
                        taking breath is breathing while you may
respectable
            profitable
                        newsy
        that's why one writes about it
                            well or poorly
breath is newsy because we're vessels in its weather
                        though we may be a committee
weathering disgust
                    with brains merely middling
            and only after tail
                            and/
/or money

31 May 1961
The Bronx

From Nuclei I,2,b.

as on a coal
        the breath may flow
on cotton free in a bag
and freely the tongue
            under it and over it
                  may kiss it
though disgust may pull one from it as from coal
for coal is ill to kiss in any weather
and coal
        and the breath of coal
               stages damage

coal's breath blows
a cottony freedom
           bags us
frees our tongues
           under its kiss
the disgust that pulls us away from coal
and coal's ill kiss
           weathers away
coal breathes on us
           as we on coal
      and in stages
           damages us

c. 31 May 1961
The Bronx

Tree* Movie

Select a tree.* Set up and focus a movie camera so that the tree* fills most of the picture. Turn on the camera and leave it on without moving it for any number of hours. If the camera is about to run out of film, substitute a camera with fresh film. The two cameras may be alternated in this way any number of times. Sound recording equipment may be turned on simultaneously with the movie cameras. Beginning at any point in the film, any length of it may be projected at a showing.

*For the word "tree", one may substitute "mountain", "sea", "flower", "lake", etc.

January 1961
The Bronx

"Tree* Movie": Notes on Realizations

"Tree* Movie" was written in January 1961 and first published in January 1964 in *ccV TRE*, the Fluxus newspaper edited by George Brecht and the late George Maciunas ("founder" of Fluxus). It is the only plan for a film I've written as an adult, though a book-length historical scenario about western pioneers, written in high school, still survives in 1985.

"Tree* Movie" is, according to critics, the first plan for a "static film," and its footnote makes it a *general* plan: *any* object may be the film's subject. The essential element is static camera placement.

According to such critics as Maciunas (in *Film Culture*), Jonas Mekas (in conversation), and Eric Anderson (in "Om New Yorks avant-garde," *Paletten* 1, Göteborg, 1967, p. 11), "Tree* Movie" is very probably the source of the divers static films produced after its publication in *ccV TRE*. Those in which a single object is filmed with a stationary camera for a long time are, in effect, unacknowledged realizations of "Tree* Movie," with subjects other than trees.

This plan for a static film was certainly inspired by the early static music of La Monte Young, especially his "Composition 1960 #7" ("Hold [the B natural below middle C and the F sharp above it] a long time."), which I helped perform—for four hours on a viola da gamba—in its July 1961 premiere at Maciunas's AG Gallery in New York.

On 14 November 1971, after more than a decade during which lack of funding precluded my realizing "Tree* Movie" in any form, I produced its first videotape realization. I was helped by Barry Rosen, Peter Miller, Randy Dickerson, and Shirley Clarke, who lent her video equipment and apartment and garden on the roof of the Chelsea Hotel in New York. The tree, a young mimosa in the garden, was taped from 4:45 to 9:20 AM—on half-inch tape cut down by a jury-rigged machine during the taping from used one-inch tape someone had liberated from an advertising agency's storage closet. This tape was premiered during the Eighth Annual New York Avant Garde Festival (Armory Show) at the 69th Regiment Armory in New York on 19 November 1971.

I produced the second videotape realization on 26 March 1972, from 2:50 to about 6:30 PM, with the help of Ken Dominick, then with the Center for Experimental Television, Binghamton, New York, which supplied the video equipment. The tree is a hard or sugar maple on the farm of Glenn Conklin, a neighbor of a CET technician, in Silver Lake Township, Susquehanna County, Pennsylvania—12 miles from Montrose, Pa., and about 25 miles south of Binghamton. The tape shows the tree, its immediate surround, birds, dogs, and many clouds. Mr. Conklin and his family generously supplied electricity, hot coffee, encouragement, and a warm kitchen in which Ken and I periodically thawed out. This realization was premiered 30 May 1972 at The Kitchen's original location in the Mercer Arts Center in New York, displayed on eight monitors.

I produced the third videotape realization on 15 August 1972, from 11:57 AM to about 4:00 PM, with the help of Norman Bauman and Shigeko Kubota, using Kubota's video equipment. The tree—probably an elm—is on the east side of a playground in Central Park, at 96th St. and 5th Ave., New York. Shooting through the playground's north fence from just northeast of its northwest corner, we recorded both the tree and all intervening playground activity.

This third videotape realization was premiered, and the other two shown simultaneously, at the Anthology Film Archives on Wooster St. in New York on 25 January (12:30–4:30 PM) and 26 January (6:00–10:00 PM) in 1975. Throughout each showing I said the word "tree" continuously into a microphone connected both to a public-address system and to an audiotape recorder. The tape was threaded through both this deck and two others, the first deck recording it and the other two playing it back after short delays. Kubota, Nam June Paik, and AFA supplied the video equipment and Maciunas—in our last collaboration—set up the sound system and supplied the tape decks.

On 26 April 1985 this performance was approximated during a "Minimal Art Festival" at Bard College, Annandale-on-Hudson, N.Y., during which the second videotape realization was shown and I said the word "tree" continuously into a sound system in which the effects of the 1975 system were approximated through electronic delay.

4–5 March 1985
New York

A Word Event for George Brecht

A man utters any word, preferably one without expletive
connotations. He then proceeds to analyze it,
1st, into its successive phonemes; 2nd, into a series of phonemes
representable by its
successive individual letters, whether or not this series
coincides with the 1st series.

After repeating each of these series alternately a few times,
he begins to permute the members of each series.

After uttering various permutations of each series alternately
several times, he utters phonemes from both series in random
order, uttering them singly, combining them into syllables,
repeating them &/or prolonging them *ad libitum.*

He ends the event by pronouncing one of these phonemes
very carefully.

4 November 1961
The Bronx

NOTE: (2 July 1968) This needn't be done as formalistically as the above description seems
to require. The 3rd paragraph is the heart of it. A performance can be "cool" or "hot"—
"minimal" or "expressionist"— according to the temperament of the performer & the situa-
tion of the performance. The author has often performed it as a political piece (e.g. in the
film *Far from Vietnam*). JML

Word Event(s) for Bici Forbes

Improvise freely, using only the component sounds (phonemes, syllables, or morphemes) of a single word or short phrase. One may use any simple or compound word (solideme or hypheme), any name (whether composed of one or of several separate names or words), any book or other title, or any phrase composed of a small number of words.

Any word or phrase will do, but some are richer in variety of sounds than others.

Produce the sounds separately & variously combined—everything from single phonemes to whole sentences.

Repeat a lot.

Sing a lot.

Vowels, nasals, & liquids shd often be prolonged as long steady tones on true pitches or as ornamentations or micromelismata around such tones.

A performance can last any length of time, but shd have enough duration for the development of a word's (or phrase's) possibilities.

A number of persons can improvise together, all using the sounds of the same word or phrase, & one may also play any number of recorded improvisations on the same word or phrase along with the live improvisations, but one person alone is plenty.

(This general plan for word events is a development from "A Word Event for George Brecht" [1961], & is a result of having realized the earlier plan in a number of performances, beginning in 1967. It differs chiefly from the earlier plan in that other sounds of the component *letters* of the chosen word or phrase than those actually included in the word or phrase are excluded. Also, the gender of the performer(s) is no longer specified.)

first described: 3 August 1971
final revision: 9 April 1972
The Bronx

135

Selected Early Light Poems

1st Light Poem: for Iris — 10 June 1962

The light of a student-lamp
sapphire light
shimmer
the light of a smoking-lamp

Light from the Magellanic Clouds
the light of a Nernst lamp
the light of a naphtha-lamp
light from meteorites

Evanescent light
ether
the light of an electric lamp
extra light

Citrine light
kineographic light
the light of a Kitson lamp
kindly light

Ice light
irradiation
ignition
altar light

The light of a spotlight
a sunbeam
sunrise
solar light

Mustard-oil light
maroon light
the light of a magnesium flare
light from a meteor

Evanescent light
ether
light from an electric lamp
an extra light

Light from a student-lamp
sapphire light
a shimmer
smoking-lamp light

Ordinary light
orgone lumination
light from a lamp burning olive oil
opal light

Actinism
atom-bomb light
the light of an alcohol lamp
the light of a lamp burning anda-oil

2nd Light Poem: for Diane Wakoski — 10 June 1962

I.

Old light & owl-light
may be opal light
in the small
orifice
where old light
& the will-o'-the-wisp
make no announcement of waning
light

but with direct directions
& the winking light of the will-o'-the-wisp's accoutrements
& lilac light
a delightful phenomenon
a delightful phenomenon of lucence & lucidity needing no
   announcement
even of lilac light
my present activities may be seen in the old light of my accoutrements
as a project in owl-light

II.

A bulky, space-suited figure
from the whole cloth of my present activities
with a taste for mythology in opal light
& *such* a *manner*

in the old light from some being outside

as if this being's old light cd have brought such a manner
to a bulky, space-suited figure
from the whole world of my present activities
at this time
when my grief gives owl-light
only
not an opal light

& not a very old light

neither
old light nor owl-light
makes it have such a manner about it
tho opal light & old light & marsh light & moonlight
& that of the whole world
to which the light of meteors is marsh light
all light it
no it's
an emerald light
in the light from the eyes that are making it whole from the whole
    cloth
with no announcement this time.

III.

What is extra light?
A delightful phenomenon.
A delightful phenomenon having no announcement?
No more than the emerald light has.
Is that the will-o'-the-wisp?
No, it's the waning light of my grief.
Is it a winking light?
No more than it is the will-o'-the-wisp.
Is it old light?
The oldest in the whole world.
Why do you speak in such a manner?
I suppose, because of the owl-light.
Is it a kind of opal light?
No, I said it was old light.
Is it a cold light?
More like a chemical light with the usual accoutrements.
Like the carmine light produced by my present activities?
More of a cold light than that.
Like what might fall on a bulky, space-suited figure?
Well, it's neither red light nor reflected light.
Are you making this up out of the whole cloth?
No, I'm trying to give you direct directions.

For avoiding a bulky, space-suited figure?
No, for getting light from a rhodochrosite.

Note: A rhodochrosite is a vitreous rose-red or variously colored gem-stone having a
hardness of 4.5 & a density of 3.8 & consisting of manganous carbonate ($MnCO_3$)
crystallized in the rhombohedral system.

IV.

This time I'm going to talk about red light.
First of all, it's not very much like emerald light.
Nevertheless, there's still some of it in Pittsburgh.
It adds to the light from eyes an extra light.
This is also true of emerald light.
But red light better suits those with a taste for mythology.
As reflected light it is often paler than the light from a rhodochrosite.
Such a red light might fall on a bulky, space-suited figure.
In just such a manner might this being be illuminated during a time
    gambol.

3rd Light Poem: for Spencer Holst, Beate Wheeler, & Sebastian Holst—12 June 1962

Owl-light in a tree house [1", 2", 3", or 4" of silence]
singing by the light of a Nernst lamp
porcupines in arclight
see the porcupines in arclight
wait   [12", 24", 36", 48", or 60" of silence]
Are there mustard-seed-oil lamps burning in the Persian section of
    Brooklyn?
I'm inclined to think so.
Anda-oil lamps must light the Andaman Islanders.

Do they give a ruby light?
Alladin lamps give a light as white as night inside out.

Lamplight on footgear
weathering
aurora light in summer
the dawn light is circumstantial
disregard the neon flush of yesterday
I'd hunt it out if Altoona were Allentown or Muhlenberg LaSalle
Treat it as a question of footprints in snowlight in Cleveland or a
       diamond in starlight Milwaukee comes to mind
incessant spring scintillations.

        [long silence]

Patriarchal light from ancient candles.

        [long silence]

Collect soapstone lamps to light the ice tables a bit in Holstenberg to
       help Boy Holst finish his Greenland story where "they" were
"lit a bit by the soapstone lamps on the ice tables."

A yellow smoky light?
A corrosive light?
A candid light?
A flattering light?
Light given off by a rhodochrosite if a rhodochrosite gives off light.

Enter a chorus of grumbling priests carrying magnesium flares &
       hoes.

Treat it as a question of data here on the coast & in the light of that data
       construct imaginary parallels to light geometry & paraphernalia
       for pranks in autumn.

Who burns walnut-oil in lamps?
I see its light as a rich brown light like an over-varnished Rembrandt.
One wd have to have a flashlight to find things.

7th Light Poem: for John Cage — 17 June 1962

Put off an important decision
       in mechanical-lamp light.
Success in a new project will bring lumination.
An exchange of courtesy in the zodiacal
    light reminds you that expenses can
    run high when you insist on light
       from almandites.
For almandites are iron-alumina garnets
    $Fe_3AL_2(SiO_4)_3$.
When of a fine deep red or purplish red,
    from India,
         and transparent,
         they are
         "precious garnets."
A lucrative job available in amber light
    does not jeopardize your credit,
              but

      melon-oil lamplight
         might.
Your intuitions lead you right
    in cineographic light.
Say what you really think.
The lamp I have clamped to the kitchen
         table beside the
     notebook I am writing this in
         gives a sort
    of student-lamp light although
    it is not a student lamp but
     a PENETRAY.
In chrome light and in light from
    alexandrites,
        spinach-
          green
         chrysoberyls,
         columbine-
           red
         by artificial
  light,

from Ceylon and the Ural
          Mountains,
                    money from a
               surprising source
belies the belief that there's
               always
                         nothing but
          futility in romantic wishes
               arising in old light.
Those wishes,
               that first arose
          in old
               light,
               light
                         trailing from
     spiral nebulae
          and galaxies so distant
                    that a stone
                         thrown
          at a reading lamp's
               light
     at a
          distance of
          two miles
                              wd be
          an unintentional slight
               to natural law
                    compared to the folly
               of launching
     "space ships" toward them,
                    those
               wishes that arose before
          the light of the annealing lamp
               on which your dentist heated foil
                    made you begin to
                         avoid taking chances
                              by
                         taking chances,
               might
               make you take a
                         trip to a scenic region

143

where
the light's
maroon.
Beware light from a Cooper-Hewitt lamp,
light
derived
from passing an electric current
through
mercury-vapor
light
bluish-
white,
ghost-light from toothbrushes
along the absent 'L,'
beware
the new light on the Bowery,
that promises a
good possibility of money loss.
The receipt of an important invitation
to radiation
's
a secret
not to be discussed
even in olive-oil lamplight,
even in the
extra light of your
elation over the good news,
lead as it might to a
temporary setback
as
the light
waned.
Revenue yielding ideas arise(s)
in orange light
but an exquisite object stirs joy
even in the light of
Reichsanstalt's lamp,
a modified form of
Hefner's lamp,
a photometric lamp burning amyl acetate.
Can an emerald light bring nothing but

                    disturbing rumors
                                                about money?
        Orange light yields revenue yielding ideas
                    of
                        disturbance
                    and   recklessness
        amidst an uncanny refulgence
                    as of marsh light
                        or will-o'-the-wisp, those
                    sparks of cold light
                            which sometimes seem to
                    follow instructions exactly
                                        as if they
                        were light from kinetographs,
                        or fishermen's jack lights,
                            but emerald light
                                    alternating with
                        red light & lilac light,
        all incandescent lamplight,
                        made
                    by following instructions exactly
                                    some
                                        times

        awaken spectrums
            like the aurora's
                    or
                those of
                        remembered napalm flames.

14th Light Poem: for Frances Witlin — 19 August 1962

Even among those high-minded people of the *Aufklärung*
neighbor slandered neighbor
reproaching each other all day
mad against each other
sworn against each other
& the light of that 'enlightenment'
was blood-color
tho transmitted thru no carnelian.

Time was wasted that way then
& time *will* be wasted
but with all the benefits that might come
thru an executive
who might take time for calm reflection
& by taking
time for
calm
reflection
might
allow us to take
time for calm reflection
I'm afraid that calm reflection
wd be merely a 'brown study'
for we're mere sards
transmitting blood light
reflecting brown light.

Now we share the work & benefits
such as they are
of what we have
even tho we often feel
we're made to appear in a foolish light
by what we do.

An innocent light?

The innocence of fools
or the foolishness of innocence?

Transmitted thru glass or ice cut to a prism
ice light
is iridescent light.

An irrelevant light?

All light is relevant to each light
& each light to every light
& each light to each light
& every light to each light
& all light to every light
& every light to all light
& each light to all light
& all light to all light.

Is that lucid?

Yes.

It is all about light.

Mere secondary phenomena of luminiferous ether.

Light!

Light.

If you follow instructions exactly
at noonday
in the noon-light
the experiment may prove disappointing
but what cd be clearer?

A nimbus.

So you are seeking sainthood!
Who said that?
A silly fool.
An uninnocent fool.
A foolish foolish fool.

A foul fool.

A melodramatic fool.

A posturing self-lacerating fool.
A self-destroying fool.
An exhibitionistic Dostoyevskyan fool.
An ordinary fool.
An ordinary thief of property.
A proper fool.

A sneaky fool
patting himself on the back
for being and admitting himself to be
a fool & a liar & a thief.

A *light*-fingered fool?

A fool who knows a fool may have to compromise
& foolishly uncompromising
compromises most
when foolishly it seems to him he's least *un*compromising.

Radiance!

That's your name for what we call mere radioactivity.
Deadly.

Deadly radiance.

A spectrum of shade.

Like long working hours leading to fatigue & nothing more.
Nothing more?
O Frances do not break your heart!
do not break!
Break
nothing more
nothing
more
nothing.

The tall light trails thru the sparrow chirps
& glass tinkles
swept
in the area below these stranger windows
as in the Bronx I know
by Evelyn the dark resentful super
altho no beer cans
dance across concrete
with high hollow clatter
impelled by dark resentment & a broom.

Tĭ-dél, tie-dáhr, tee-dĕn, tuh-dăn, tuh-doŏm.

Make no promises.

I've made one promise only.
One promise.
One promise only
made itself me.

But what it means is
what it means.

Only two know this.
Perhaps
one more
who sits to my left
smiling
or glum
or glumly smiling
or grimly smiling
or grimly
glum.

Boōmelay boōmelay boōmelay boōm.

Together weeping for his lost dark splendor
hating what he made of us
& what he allowed
what he thought we were
all of us
make of him.

How we sat together gritting our teeth.

Was it true?
Or another lie to make the fancy leap?
To show the know we were in
together.

She who makes no promises she cannot keep.
Or if she does
makes the limit of each promise clear.

Not you my dear.
I did not mean to speak of *you* here.
I find I have.

The traitorous light turns
as the
whirling earth
turns.
The traitorous light turns from pale
blue to grey.

My traitorous heart turns from one to the other loyally.
Faithfully my traitorous heart
turns
trying to make no promises or none it cannot keep
or none that cannot keep it
or none that cannot keep it keeping them.

What can I say?

Say the waxing light
depends upon no purchase of electrical equipment.
Say
a distant matter is delayed
a distant matter
a lambency
leaping about us
not yet.

Say nothing.

The light of a lamp burning winestones-oil
is preferable by far
altho I've never seen it
to one that threatens us
with danger
from chemicals.

My lucky number?

491
tells me to forget
a previous worry.

A *previous* worry?

What did I see before in a worrisome light
that I see in such a light
no longer?

Is it merely morning movie light
oh one four
that tells us to expect a change for the better?

Time will be wasted
but honesty
whether in light from an Argand lamp
or arc light
or *Aufklärung*
is
the best
policy?

Tragedy.

Idiocy.

Honesty?

An aureola springs around a formerly hated form.

You must stay alive.

The Presidents of the United States of America

A Note on the Composition of "The Presidents of the United States of America," 15 December 1968

"The Presidents of the United States of America" was composed in January and May 1963. Each section is headed by the first inaugural year of a president (from Washington thru Fillmore), and its structure of images is that of the Phoenician meanings of the successive letters of the president's name. The meanings are those given in *The Roman Inscriptional Letter*, a book designed, written, and printed by Sandra Lawrence in the Graphic Arts Workshop at Reed College, Portland, Oregon, in May 1955. They are:

A	(aleph) "ox"	N	(nun) "fish"
B	(beth) "house"	O	(ayin) "eye"
C	(gimel) "camel"	P	(pe) "mouth"
D	(daleth) "door"	Q	(qoph) "knot"
E	(he) "window" or "look!"	R	(resh) "head"
F	(vau) "hook"	S	(shin) "tooth"
H	(cheth) "fence"	T	(tau) "mark"
I	(yod) "hand"	V	(vau) "hook"
K	(kaph) "palm of the hand"	X	(samekh) "prop"
L	(lamed) "ox-goad"	Y	(vau) "hook"
M	(mem) "water"	Z	(zayin) "weapon"

Letters developed by the Romans or in the Middle Ages were given the meanings of the letters from which they were derived or to which they were similar:

G (developed by Romans in third century B.C.: similar in form to C) "camel"

J (introduced during Middle Ages as minuscule form of I and made into majuscule in the sixteenth century) "hand"

U (introduced during Middle Ages as a minuscule form of V and made into majuscule in the sixteenth century) "hook"

W (Anglo-Saxon addition in eleventh century; similar to two V's) "hooks" or "hook hook"

These letter-meaning words were used as "nuclei" which were freely connected by other material. This method was first used by the poet in writing a sestina, "The Albatross," in 1950; here a list of end words was obtained "automatically" and then permuted and connected into a sestina. The poet first connected chance-given nuclei in this way in 1960 in writing such prose pieces as "A Greater Sorrow" (in *An Anthology,* published by Young and Mac Low, New York, 1963; and in my *Stanzas for Iris Lezak,* Something Else Press, Barton, Vt., 1972). Most of the poems in *22 Light Poems* (Black Sparrow Press, Los Angeles, 1968) were composed in 1962-63, using names of kinds of light as nuclei. In "The Presidents of the United States of America", each letter-meaning nucleus could be used in any form class (e.g., M could be translated as the noun "water," the verb "water," the adjective "watery," or as the adverb "waterily"). In the earlier sections (written in January 1963), a minimum of connective material was introduced between the nuclei, and the meanings of the letters of each name delimited a strophe. In the later sections (written in May 1963), much more material was introduced between the nuclei, and the verse structures became much more complex.

The poet has often been asked by friends and well-wishers to write further sections dealing with the presidents following Fillmore. He has often thought of doing so and has even collected materials for this purpose, but so far he has only written a draft of a section on Franklin Pierce.

The Presidents of the United States of America

1789   *(begun about 15 January 1963)*

George Washington never owned a camel
but he looked thru the eyes in his head
with a camel's calm and wary look.

Hooks that wd irritate an ox
held his teeth together
and he cd build a fence with his own hands
tho he preferred to go fishing
as anyone else wd
while others did the work *for* him
for tho he had no camels he had slaves enough
and probably made them toe the mark by keeping an eye on them
for *he* wd never have stood for anything fishy.

1797

John Adams knew the hand
can be quicker than the eye
& knew that not only fencers & fishermen live by this knowledge.

If he kept an ox
he kept it out of doors in summertime
so the ox cd find his water for himself
& make it where he stood
& find the tasty grass
his teeth cd chew as cud.

1801

Marked by no fence
farther than an eye cd see
beyond the big waters
Thomas Jefferson saw grass enough for myriads of oxen
to grind between their teeth.

His farmer hands itched
when he thought of all that vacant land and looked about for a way to
    hook it in for us
until something unhooked a window in his head
where the greedy needy teeth & eyes of Napoleon shone
eager for the money which
was Jefferson's bait to catch the Louisiana fish.

1809

James Madison's hand cd lead an ox to water
and he'd look at him while he drank
                                    letting it
              spill down from grassy teeth.

After he'd water'd his ox
                        James Madison'd
    push open his door with his hand
                                    & then his teeth'd
grind and mash up all but the bones & eyes of a large fish.

1817

James Monroe
laid a hand
as heavy as the ox that stands on every peon's tongue
on all between the waters between
the new world and both old ones
& looked across both of them
                              baring but
puppy teeth then.

Across the waters eyes
                    in fishers' heads
eyed this newest angler
with the grudging look of fellow-recognition
                    old members of the Predators' Club
              bestow on former prey
    that blunders past all blackballs
& soon must be accepted for admission.

1825

John Quincy Adams's right hand
shaded his eyes
as he sat on a fence & fished.

At one end of his line was a knot & a hook
                                             at the
        other end
                    his hand   & he sat
                         fishing for a camel with a hook instead of a hump?

No   & not for an ox
                      because
                            behind a door he had his papa's ox
          & when he went fishing in water
          (& that's what he was doing he was no fool)
                        he was looking to get something
                                    good
                                                something
              he cd sink his teeth into & want to.

1829   *(24 May 1963)*

Andrew Jackson's last name's the same as my first
                    but
                              that makes me no more like him
                              than an ox is   like a
                                                       fish
                                   (or vice versa)
                    but
          open   a door in your head
          (or   a window)
        & look!
                    if your eyes are hooks
                    what's on those hooks?
                              Andrew Jackson?

          Nonsense:
                    Andrew Jackson's dead:
                    you can no more see *him*
        than your   hand cd hold in itself
          an ox:
        than you cd hold a camel in the palm of your hand
          as you *cd* hold a tooth
              or an eye of a fish:
                              forget Andrew Jackson:
          (you already have).

1837   *(24 May 1963)*

   If Martin Van Buren ever swam in water
   (if Martin Van Buren ever swam)
     what kind of swimmer was he if he held onto an ox's head
          (did he?)
        to keep his own above the surface?

158

(he knew about banks
       but
           what did he know about swimming?)
                  but
           what is Martin Van Buren now
                but
           a series of marks I make
with
                my
     hand?
             (maybe
             Martin
   Van
       Buren cd swim like a fish!)
            do
                 I
             make
                   these
            marks
                with
        "my"   hand?
                 can
            "I"
      catch
       this fish
                (i.
     e.,
      "I")?

A hook big enough to hang an ox from's
a hook too big to catch a fish with.

Martin Van Buren lived in a fine big house in New York State
     before he was   president
     but   how did he get his hooks into
                Ezra Pound's head?
       look!
  I want to know how a poet became a
rich old dead old politician's fish.

Andrew Jackson & Martin Van Buren
   are heroes of that old
      hero of mine in whose honor I write
                "wd"
                   &
               "cd"
                   &
              "shd"
         in-
              stead
      of
               "would"
                 &
             "could"
                 &
             "should"
                        (I write
             &
         in-
              stead
      of
               "and"
         in
                  honor
      of
                      William
Blake
but
                      whose
                       hero's
                      William
  Henry
  Harrison?   (I mean
whose
  hero is he *now?*):
         old
  hero   hung on a hook
  the
           hook is "Tippecanoe"

&
the smart old politicians used it as an ox-goad (their
theory was: "an ox-goad in the hand
                    can
        make 'em
                    go:
treat 'em like oxen & they'll lap it up like water."

That's the way those wily Whigs
            fenced: (look!
        who remembers who *they* were now?
    —those old phynancial string-pullers
            (*peace,* Jarry!)
who hung an old Indian fighter on their line
        (a smaller fish to catch a bigger one)
                pushing thru his aging head
                    the hook
                    "Tippecanoe":
who remembers who *they* were now?
                    we
        remember   "Tippecanoe":
                whose
            fish   is
who?)—
            but
            that
was the way those old finaglers did it
                            &
                if you can't learn from history
        what *can*   "you"   learn from?
                            (Mystery.)

Who was sitting on the fence?
Who was treated like an ox?
Whose head was used as bait?
Whose head planned it all?
Whose hand held the line?
Whose teeth chewed what was caught?
Whose eye caught what was going on?
Who was the fish & how did *he* like it?

1841 (II)   *(written 24 May 1963)*

The poor old bait got sick & died
                            &
then they had "Tyler too!"
  (exclamation point & all)
                 &
              some there were who had him on their hands
     &   some there were who had him in front of their eyes
     &   some there were who had him
     &   some there were who wished he'd just go off
     &   sit on a fence somewhere & fish.

That's the way John Tyler made his mark
    &   he knew whose hook he was on
    &   he knew who held the ox-goad
    &   he knew when to turn his back to the window
    :   (*he* knew when to look
    &   when
          not
               to look:
     he knew   how to use his *head*):
               but
    where's John Tyler
          now?   (Dead.)
& what do "we" have because he made a deal?   (Texas.)

162

Tyler was no Whig at all & after his term's end
    wanted the Democratic nomination but
                only
     a splinter group
                      nominated him &
           Clay
       got
       the Whigs'   &
       'the first "dark horse"
              of
    American
         national politics
was suddenly brought forward in the morning.
James K.
               [for "Knox"]
        Polk,   of Tennessee,
   after one ballot, was unanimously chosen as
   the Democratic candidate.
   The   country,   bewildered,
   asked
                   "Who is Polk?"
                     He
               was
           indeed,
        not entirely unknown.'
             [I quote (I've quoted)
   a   descendant(?)   of
John Adams & John Quincy Adams (?)
   —*do* I quote a descendant of
John Adams & John Quincy Adams?—
               I   don't think I do   I
        quote a history-textbook-writer
  named
James Truslow Adams
      who wrote a book called
      The Record of America with another
               history-
                  textbook-
        writer

named Charles Garrett Vannest
  a Professor of History
  at   Harris Teachers College
                  in   St. Louis:
          he   (Vannest)
was co-author of
    Socialized History of the United States
(whose co-author was he *then?*)]

The main things about James Knox Polk were
that first he had Texas & then a war with Mexico on his hands
that he was no ox but a man with a conscience who made war anyway
that "we" got all of Texas, Utah, Nevada, & California
  & most of Arizona & New Mexico   because
          of conscience-stricken Mr. Polk's war
that   Mr. Polk's war
          extended "us" to the   waters of the
                      Pacific   (Ocean)
(how "pacific" can an ocean be   if   "we"
  got
  "our"
window on it thru a war?)
                              (Answer: just as
      "pacific"
              as any other ocean)
              ("window"   hell:
          "our"
                  teeth
snapped up a whole damn coast *that* time
      & everything up   *to* it)
              that   *that* war
                      was
                      why
              Thoreau refused to pay his tax
  & stayed in jail a night
  & wrote *Civil Disobedience*
  &   eventually
          was read by a little Indian lawyer   (*Indian* Indian)
          who invented another way to fight
          & thought it wasn't violent

&
        used it
                so shrewdly that
    he   &   circumstances   made
    the British Empire lose a whole sub-continent.

In the palm of his hand
        a man who ate no fish or meat
    held   for a time
            an
    empire on which the sun never set
                his   eye
            controlled that vast melange of
                    hungry peoples
    he

                didnt
                fight
not
            that is
                as
    other people fought
        he   thought
    he made no threats
            thought
    he   used no violence
            thought
    he   used   only
                Satyagraha
            the force of truth
    to pull away the British Empire's props.

Thus we've come by word of mouth
            from James Knox Polk
                America's
            first "dark horse" president
    to the eye of Mohandas Gandhi:
    that   ox-goad
            small enough to be
        hidden in the palm of a hand.

                        (to here at 1:10 am Sat 25 May 1963)

Zachary Taylor made his name in the Mexican War.
  (They say there's something about a soldier that is fine fine fine.
                    I've always wondered what it is.
                    Maybe it's his weapons.)
Zachary Taylor made a name for himself by
  acting toward other men
  as if they were oxen or camels.
        He didn't pay attention to other people's fences—
          especially if they were only Mexicans.
              "After all   oxen have heads
                          only to hear
          commands   to eat
                  (as little as they can & still work)
                  & to keep yokes
    from falling off.
    If they try to use 'em for anything else
      hang 'em up on hooks."

        If "Old Rough & Ready"
Zachary Taylor didn't think this way
    how *else* did he make his mark in the Mexican War?
As a "Louisiana slave-holder"
    he must have known all about
    how to treat people like oxen.
All right then how did it happen
              he let the Californians
  adopt a constitution
    prohibiting slavery?

I guess he just didnt think they *wd*
                        or maybe
        he just didnt care
                  as long as it
          didnt affect *his*
        holding of slaves.
                    (Maybe
    some Northern politician got his hooks in him.)

                              Anyway
        getting to be
                    President of the United States of America
                          didnt do Zachary Taylor
                                    any
                                              real
        good—
                         —(unless it's a
                                              real
        good
                to be
                    President of the United States of America
          one year & a third
                    &   thus   have
          one's name
          on every subsequent list of American Presidents).
                              Zachary
                              Taylor
        ("Old   Rough & Ready")
            died on July 9th, 1850.
                                    He had had *his*
                                    chance
                    to wield *that*
          ox-goad
        (I mean the one
              every President of the United States of America
                    has   at hand.)
                                        Now what
        I   wonder
        is: how did Zachary Taylor
          manage   to
          stick it in his own eye
              (if *that's* what he did)?
                              Did
          things just start to happen in his body & his head?

                                167

Millard Fillmore seems to have been a watery customer.
My book says he "was a friend of Clay & compromise"
                                    &   in
my book   that means
                    he didnt let his right hand know
                            what his left   hand was doing
                                                    so
                        if
    one   hand was
                    wielding an ox-goad
                his
    other one didnt know
                            whether
                            the ox-goad
                            was prodding an ox's head
            or stabbing a door.

Millard Fillmore used the hook in *his* hand
    (let's call an ox-goad an ox-goad)
                    not just to force the
                            Fugitive Slave Law thru
                    (as part of the Compromise of 1850)
                                            but
            to   "secure"   "by
            treaties with Honduras & Nicaragua
            the right of transit   across
            their
            territories"   &
            to freeze the English where they were in Central America
                            getting them to agree to
                            "guarantee the neutrality
                of any canal built."
                            That's how
    Millard Fillmore laid the foundations
            for the Panama Canal
        altho he never saw it even begin to join the waters
                never saw it with his own physical eyes.

Millard Fillmore must have had a head on him:
                                        I
mean a head for "diplomatic" business & the like.
        Had
        he been   poor
        he'd've
    never   passed
    any
    neighbor's window
                    without looking to see
                    whether it was open & if it was
                    what there was for him to grab from it as he went by.

                                Bravo
                                brave
Millard Fillmore.

        (end of "1850" & of the first series of "The Presidents
    of the United States of America" (Washington thru Fillmore))

                            about 15 January 1963 thru 25 May 1963
                                                    The Bronx

Daily Life

How to Make Poems from a DAILY LIFE List

I. Prepare a list such as the following:

Daily Life 1

6 August 1963

1	A.	I'm going to the store.	Black Ace
2	B.	Is the baby sleeping?	Black Two
3	C.	I'd better take the dog out.	Black Three
4	D.	What do you want?	Black Four
5	E.	Let's have eggs for breakfast.	Black Five
6	F.	Has the mail come yet?	Black six
7	G.	I'll take the garbage down.	Black Seven
8	H.	Is there anything you need downstairs?	Black Eight
9	I.	I'll see you.	Black Nine
10	J.	Shall I turn the light on?	Black Ten
11	K.	I'll take the bottles back.	Black Jack
12	L.	Did somebody knock on the door?	Black Queen
13	M.	I'm going to close the window.	Black King
14	N.	Is the baby crying?	Red Ace
15	O.	Hello, sweety-baby!	Red Two
16	P.	What's that red mark on him?	Red Three
17	Q.	I'm going to lie down & rest my back for-awhile.	Red Four
18	R.	What did you say?	Red Five
19	S.	Look how this plant has grown!	Red Six
20	T.	Have you fed the cat & dog?	Red Seven
21	U.	I'm going to make some coffee.	Red Eight
22	V.	Do you want some ginger beer?	Red Nine
23	W.	I wish it wasn't always so noisy.	Red Ten
24	X.	Is it all right if I turn on the news?	Red Jack
25	Y.	What's the matter with the baby?	Red Queen
26	Z.	Have half a banana.	Red King

II. Employ one of the following methods:

1. *Letters.* This is the method first used by the author when he conceived the idea of a DAILY LIFE list as a source for poems, plays, &c. (6 August 1963), & except for one poem, it is the only method he has used up to the present time (8 January 1964). One selects (or allows chance or circumstance to select) a name, phrase, sentence, title, or any other limited series of words, & translates each successive letter into the sentence corresponding to it on a DAILY LIFE list. The end of a word produces the end of a strophe, e.g., translating the title DAILY LIFE into the sentences of DAILY LIFE 1, one gets:

DAILY LIFE

What do you want?
I'm going to the store.
I'll see you.
Did somebody knock on the door?
What's the matter with the baby?

Did somebody knock on the door?
I'll see you.
Has the mail come yet?
Let's have eggs for breakfast.

Obviously, if one wants a poem having the same number of lines in every strophe, one must choose a series of words having the same number of letters in each word.

2. *Numbers.* One selects a source of digits, such as a random digit table or a telephone book, & translates the digits, taken in pairs, in any of a number of ways. The simplest way is to use only the first 25 sentences of a list & to make a correspondence chart for all possible pairs of digits (see next page for such a chart). One can use single digits (0 being taken as 10) or pairs of digits to determine the number of strophes in a poem & the number of lines in each successive strophe. (If one wants the same number of lines in every strophe, one need use only 2 digits: one for the number of strophes & one for the number of lines in every strophe.)

25-place correspondence chart for digit pairs:

01	26	51	76	09	34	59	84	17	42	67	92
02	27	52	77	10	35	60	85	18	43	68	93
03	28	53	78	11	36	61	86	19	44	69	94
04	29	54	79	12	37	62	87	20	45	70	95
05	30	55	80	13	38	63	88	21	46	71	96
06	31	56	81	14	39	64	89	22	47	72	97
07	32	57	82	15	40	65	90	23	48	73	98
08	33	58	83	16	41	66	91	24	49	74	99
								25	50	75	00

Using a 5-place random digit table, one may get the series 94736 24128. The first digit, 9, determining the number of strophes in a poem; the 2nd digit, 4, determining the number of lines in the first strophe; & the last 8 digits, taken in pairs translated into 01 to 25 thru the correspondence table, determining the successive lines of the first strophe; one gets as the first strophe of a nine-strophe poem:

73 – 23	I wish it wasn't always so noisy.
62 – 12	Did somebody knock on the door?
41 – 16	What's that red mark on him?
28 – 03	I'd better take the dog out.

Other methods may also be used to translate numbers into a DAILY LIFE list to produce poems. For instance, one may dispense with a correspondence table & only use pairs from 01 to 26, disregarding all other combinations of digits. Or one may use as a source a *mixed* series of numbers & letters, as the author did the 2nd time he used DAILY LIFE 1 as a source (15 August 1963), when he translated the series (found on a slip of paper clipped from the top of a printer's galley): "8-8 Caled w 8 Spt Hvy x 16 RAU (1) Dec. 19 6535" using the digits singly except when a pair formed a number between 10 & 26.

3. *Playing Cards*. One method for using playing cards is to shuffle, draw one card to determine number of strophes (1 to 13, taking Ace as 1 & Jack, Queen & King as 11, 12 & 13; or 1 to 26, using the correspondences of numbers to card colors & denominations appearing on the list). Then draw as many cards as strophes to determine the number of lines in each successive strophe (or draw only one card, if one wants to have the same number of lines in every strophe). Finally, shuffle & draw a single card for each line of the poem, shuffling between every 2 draws, or at least fairly frequently. Other methods of using playing cards may also be used.

4. *Other Methods.* Still other methods may be devised to use lists of sentences from daily life as sources of poems. For instance, several alternative lists may be used at the same time with some chance determinant selecting which list is to be used as the source for any particular line of a poem. &, of course, readers may make their own list(s), using them alone or together with one or more of the author's lists. What wd make such a poem a realization of DAILY LIFE is the use of one or more lists of sentences from daily life as source(s) for poems or other literary works. (The author has already written an essay describing a method for using such lists as sources for dramatic presentations [August 1963].)

DAILY LIFE was first conceived, along with Letters & Numbers methods, & the list "DAILY LIFE 1" was composed & first used as source, on 6 August 1963. Above essay was written in this form on 8 January 1964.

Happy New Year 1964 to Barney and Mary Childs

(a DAILY LIFE poem, drawn from DAILY LIFE 1)

Is there anything you need downstairs?
I'm going to the store.
What's that red mark on him?
What's that red mark on him?
What's the matter with the baby?

Is the baby crying?
Let's have eggs for breakfast.
I wish it wasn't always so noisy.

What's the matter with the baby?
Let's have eggs for breakfast.
I'm going to the store.
What did you say?

Look how this plant has grown!
Is the baby crying?

Have you fed the cat & dog?
Hello, sweety-baby!

Is the baby sleeping?
I'm going to the store.
What did you say?
Is the baby crying?
Let's have eggs for breakfast.
What's the matter with the baby?

I'm going to the store.
Is the baby crying?
What do you want?

I'm going to close the window.
I'm going to the store.
What did you say?
What's the matter with the baby?

I'd better take the dog out.
Is there anything you need downstairs?
I'll see you.
Did somebody knock at the door?
What do you want?
Look how this plant has grown!

8 January 1964
The Bronx

The Secret of the Golden Flower

1. Heavenly Consciousness (The Heart)

one nothing essence.
has essence. alive; very essence.
   nothing life   intelligence
circulation one nothing seed circulation
         intelligence one unconscious
            seed nothing
               essence.
           seed seed
(transforming has essence.
has essence. alive; really transforming)

2. The Primordial Spirit and the Conscious Spirit

transforming when one
transforming has essence.
penetrated really intelligence movements.
         one really defended, intelligence
           alive; life
seed penetrated intelligence really intelligence
   transforming
alive; nothing defended,
transforming has essence.
circulation one nothing seed circulation
        intelligence one unconscious
        seed
seed penetrated intelligence really
   intelligence transforming

3. Circulation of the Light and Protection of the Centre

transforming has really essence.
       essence.
circulation intelligence really

circulation unconscious
　　　　　life alive;
　　　　　　　　transforming
　　　　　intelligence
　　　one nothing
one former
transforming has essence.
life intelligence generation has transforming
alive; nothing defended,
penetrated really one transforming essence.
　　　　　circulation transforming
　　　　　　　　intelligence one
　　　　　　　　　　　nothing
one former
transforming has essence.
circulation essence. nothing transforming
　　　really essence.

4. Circulation of the Light and Making the Breathing Rhythmical

circulation intelligence really circulation
　　　　unconscious life alive;
　　　　　　　transforming
　　　　intelligence one nothing
one former
transforming has essence.
life intelligence generation has transforming
alive; nothing defended,
movements. alive; knowledge, intelligence
　　　　nothing generation
transforming has essence.
body. really essence. alive; transforming
　　has　　　　intelligence nothing
　　　　　　generation
really has intelligence　　　transforming
　　has movements. intelligence circulation
　　　alive; life

5. Mistakes During the Circulation of the Light

former intelligence very essence.
movements. intelligence seed transforming
        alive; knowledge, essence. seed
defended, unconscious really intelligence
      generation
transforming has essence.
circulation intelligence really circulation
      unconscious life alive;
            transforming
      intelligence one nothing
one former
life intelligence generation has
  transforming

6. Confirmatory Experiences during the Circulation of the Light

seed intelligence knowledge, seed
circulation one nothing former intelligence
      really movements.
        alive;
      transforming one
    really intelligence
essence. knowledge, seed penetrated
     essence. really intelligence
       essence. nothing
          circulation
      essence. seed
defended, unconscious really intelligence
         nothing generation
transforming has essence.
life intelligence generation has transforming

7. The Living Manner of the Circulation of the Light

seed essence. very essence. nothing
transforming has essence.

life intelligence very intelligence nothing
    generation
movements. alive; nothing nothing essence. really
one former
transforming has essence.
circulation intelligence really circulation unconscious
        life alive; transforming intelligence
            one nothing
one former
transforming has essence.
life intelligence generation has transforming

8. A Magic Spell for the Far Journey

essence. intelligence generation has transforming
alive;
movements. alive; generation intelligence
        circulation
seed penetrated essence. life life
former one really
transforming has essence.
former alive; really
just one unconscious really nothing
    essence. intelligence

The Secret of the Golden Flower

transforming has essence.
seed essence. circulation really essence.
    transforming
one former
transforming has essence.
generation one life defended, essence. nothing
former life   one when essence. really.

1964
The Bronx

Selected Dances from *The Pronouns* —
A Collection of 40 Dances —for the Dancers —
6 February —22 March 1964

from "Some Remarks to the Dancers
(How the Dances Are To Be Performed
& How They Were Made)"

The Pronouns is *"A Collection of 40 Dances"*— not a *series*. That is, despite the fact that the dances are numbered, each is a separate & complete work in itself & may be performed on a program before or after any or none of the other dances in the collection. Also, any number of different realizations of one or more of the dances may succeed or follow each other during a particular performance. For example, a program might have on it such a succession of the dances as the following, in which each reappearance of a dance's number stands for a different realization of that dance: 5, 7, 10, 5, 22, 40, 33, 33, 11, 7, 1, 7, 1, 1, 10, 28, 18, 6, 22, 5.

By suggesting a *succession* of realizations of dances, I do not intend to rule out entirely the possibilities of simultaneous or overlapping performances of various dances on a program. However, I do wish to *de-emphasize* these possibilities (which might seem most appropriate in view of the fact that so much of my past work—my simultaneous poems & other simulta-neities—involves the simultaneous &/or overlapping performance of separate works that are also members of non-ordered collections, e.g., the numbered *Asymmetries*) in order to encourage performances in which some or all of the dances are realized *one at a time* in various orders of succession. The important thing is that (even in overlapping realizations or the like) the *integrity* of each dance—its having a definite beginning, middle, & end—ought to be com-pletely clear in every performance.

The dances require various numbers of performers. Some are obviously solos or duets, & some will be found to require a group of a definite number that will probably be the same in any realization, but the sizes of the groups required in many of them are somewhat indefinite & are to be decided for each realization by the dancers themselves by careful interpretation of the given text.

In realizing any particular dance, the individual dancer or group of dancers has a very large degree of freedom of interpretation. However, although they are to interpret the successive lines of each of those poems-which-are-also-dance-instructions as they see fit, dancers are required to find *some defi-nite interpretation of the meaning of every line* of the dance-poems they choose to realize. Above all, no line or series of lines may be left uninterpreted & unrealized simply because it seems too complicated or obscure to realize as movement (&/or sound or speech).

In addition to finding concrete meanings as actions for every line of each dance-poem realized, the dancers must carefully work out the time-relations between the various actions, as indicated by their positions in the poems & by the particular conjunctions & adverbs used to connect them together within the sentence-length strophes & to connect these strophes together. For example, if a poem indicates that someone "has the chest between thick things *while* they say things about making gardens," dancers may realize each of these actions as they see fit, but they must take place simultaneously, *not* one after the other.

There is a seemingly unlimited multiplicity of possible realizations for each of these dances because the judgements of the particular dancers will determine such matters as degrees of literalness or figurativeness in interpreting & realizing instructions. Each dancer or group of dancers must decide for themselves whether, &/or to what extent, to use or avoid props, miming, &c., & whether, &/or to what extent, to be consistent in such use or avoidance—one might, for instance, within the same realization, sometimes use props & sometimes dispense with them, even in different appearances of the same action in a poem. Thus, while the text of each dance-poem is completely determinate &, if realized, is to be realized in its entirety, the actual movements & actions constituting any particular realization are very largely unpredictable from the text of the poem of which it is a realization.

I first conceived these dance-instruction-poems as *either* being read aloud as poems (& I have read many of them at poetry readings) *or* as being realized as dances. Lately, however, I have come to agree with a number of persons who've heard me read them that the poems themselves might well be read aloud during *some* of their realizations as dances. A program might include, then, some realizations accompanied by the reading aloud of the poems & some not so accompanied.

In any case, the sounds of the reading of the poems, when they are read, &/or any other sounds used as "accompaniment" to the dances must never get in the way of the sounds produced by the dancers themselves in accordance with those instructions calling for sound or speech. It is to be emphasized that wherever a line calls for sound-production or speech, this instruction must be taken literally, at least insofar as the dancer must produce some definite sound or speak some words or other, as they find appropriate.

181

1ST DANCE – MAKING THINGS NEW – 6 February 1964

He makes himself comfortable
& matches parcels.

Then he makes glass boil
while having political material get in
& coming by.

Soon after, he's giving gold cushions or seeming to do so,
taking opinions,
shocking,
pointing to a fact that seems to be an error & showing it to be other
        than it seems,
& presently paining by going or having waves.

Then after doing some waiting,
he disgusts someone
& names things.

A little while later he gets out with things
& finally either rewards someone for something or goes up under
  something.

2ND DANCE – SEEING LINES – 6 February 1964

She seems to come by wing,
& keeping present being in front,
she reasons regularly.

Then—making her stomach let itself down
& giving a bit or doing something elastic
& making herself comfortable—
she lets complex impulses make something.

She disgusts everyone.

Later she fingers a door
& wheels awhile
while either transporting a star or letting go of a street.

19TH DANCE – GOING UNDER – 1 March 1964

First, anybody gives gold cushions or seems to do so
while doing something under the conditions of competition,
after which anybody boils delicate things,
being in flight,
doing something consciously,
& keeping up a process.

Next, anybody gets an orange from a hat, takes it, & keeps it;
then anybody goes under
while doing something under the conditions of competition
& ends by putting in languages other than English.

25TH DANCE – SAYING THINGS ABOUT MAKING GARDENS – 22 March 1964

Everyone begins making thunder though taking pigs somewhere,
& then everyone says something after a minute.

After that everyone's a fly,
having an example.

Pretty soon everyone's giving gold cushions or seeming to do so,
& everyone's crying

& letting something be made the same as something simple
& seeming to send things or putting wires on things,
& everyone's saying things tiredly,
& everyone's taking opinions
& being a band or acting like a bee
& letting things be equal or doing things like an ant
& having curves or having to put weight on a bird,
& everyone's saying things about making gardens.

When all that's over, everyone goes about & comes across art.

A little later everyone reasons regularly.

Still later everyone plants.

Then everyone meets someone over water
& says things tiredly
& takes some more opinions
while making their stomachs let themselves down,
& again being a band or acting like bees,
having curves or having to put weight on a bird,
everyone then gets feeble.

That's when everyone makes drinks
though everyone's being earth
& willing themselves to be dead or coming to see something narrow.

Can everyone then do something in the manner of a sister whose
        mind is happy & willing
& have uses among harmonies
& finally get insects?

27TH DANCE – WALKING – 22 March 1964

Nobody does any waiting,
& nobody has an example.

Does nobody give gold cushions or seem to do so,
& does nobody kick?

Nobody.

& nobody's seeming to send things or's putting wires on things—
nobody's keeping to the news.

At least nobody ends up handing or seeming to hand snakes to
    people.

35TH DANCE – DISGUSTING – 22 March 1964

After one or another does things to make a meal,
another gives support to insects.

Then another goes about between & through unserious-seeming
    goings-on
while putting in languages other than English.

Meanwhile another lets an impulse do something through them.

Subsequently another says something between thick things
while coming against something or fearing things.

& almost immediately another's discussing something brown.

At the same time another's disgusting.

At the end another is separating from still another.

40TH DANCE — GIVING FALSELY — 22 March 1964

Many begin by getting insects.

Then many make thunder though taking pigs somewhere,
& many give a simple form to a bridge
while coming against something or fearing things.

A little later, after making glass boil
& having political material get in,
many, while being in flight,
name things.

Then many have or seem to have serious holes,
& many question many;
many make payments to many,
& many seem to put examples up.

Finally many quietly chalk a strange tall bottle.

train

(From *4 trains*—4-5 December 1964)

I

Train rule atom intricate nitrogen.
Rule unusual leotard entropy.
Atom train ostrich might.
Intricate nitrogen train rule intricate casual atom train entropy.
Nitrogen intricate train rule ostrich genealogy entropy nitrogen.

Rule unusual leotard entropy.
Unusual nitrogen unusual social unusual atom leotard.
Leotard entropy ostrich train atom rule dies.
Entropy nitrogen train rule ostrich pope yearly.

Atom train ostrich might.
Train rule atom intricate nitrogen.
Ostrich social train rule intricate casual holiday.
Might intricate genealogy holiday train.

Intricate nitrogen train rule intricate casual atom train entropy.
Nitrogen intricate train rule ostrich genealogy entropy nitrogen.
Train rule atom intricate nitrogen.
Rule unusual leotard entropy.
Intricate nitrogen train rule intricate casual atom train entropy.
Casual atom social unusual atom leotard.
Atom train ostrich might.
Train rule atom intricate nitrogen.
Entropy nitrogen train rule ostrich pope yearly.

Nitrogen intricate train rule ostrich genealogy entropy nitrogen.
Intricate nitrogen train rule intricate casual atom train entropy.
Train rule atom intricate nitrogen.
Rule unusual leotard entropy.
Ostrich social train rule intricate casual holiday.

Genealogy entropy nitrogen entropy atom leotard ostrich genealogy
Entropy nitrogen train rule ostrich pope yearly.   [yearly.
Nitrogen intricate train rule ostrich genealogy entropy nitrogen.

II

Rule unusual leotard entropy.
Unusual nitrogen unusual social unusual atom leotard.
Leotard entropy ostrich train atom rule dies.
Entropy nitrogen train rule ostrich pope yearly.

Unusual nitrogen unusual social unusual atom leotard.
Nitrogen intricate train rule ostrich genealogy entropy nitrogen.
Unusual nitrogen unusual social unusual atom leotard.
Social ostrich casual intricate atom leotard.
Unusual nitrogen unusual social unusual atom leotard.
Atom train ostrich might.
Leotard entropy ostrich train atom rule dies.

Leotard entropy ostrich train atom rule dies.
Entropy nitrogen train rule ostrich pope yearly.
Ostrich social train rule intricate casual holiday.
Train rule atom intricate nitrogen.
Atom train ostrich might.
Rule unusual leotard entropy.
Dies intricate entropy social.

Entropy nitrogen train rule ostrich pope yearly.
Nitrogen intricate train rule ostrich genealogy entropy nitrogen.
Train rule atom intricate nitrogen.
Rule unusual leotard entropy.
Ostrich social train rule intricate casual holiday.
Pope ostrich pope entropy.
Yearly entropy atom rule leotard yearly.

III

Atom train ostrich might.
Train rule atom intricate nitrogen.
Ostrich social train rule intricate casual holiday.
Might intricate genealogy holiday train.

Train rule atom intricate nitrogen.
Rule unusual leotard entropy.
Atom train ostrich might.
Intricate nitrogen train rule intricate casual atom train entropy.
Nitrogen intricate train rule ostrich genealogy entropy nitrogen.

Ostrich social train rule intricate casual holiday.
Social ostrich casual intricate atom leotard.
Train rule atom intricate nitrogen.
Rule unusual leotard entropy.
Intricate nitrogen train rule intricate casual atom train entropy.
Casual atom social unusual atom leotard.
Holiday ostrich leotard intricate dies atom yearly.

Might intricate genealogy holiday train.
Intricate nitrogen train rule intricate casual atom train entropy.
Genealogy entropy nitrogen entropy atom leotard ostrich genealogy
Holiday ostrich leotard intricate dies atom yearly.   [yearly.
Train rule atom intricate nitrogen.

IV

Intricate nitrogen train rule intricate casual atom train entropy.
Nitrogen intricate train rule ostrich genealogy entropy nitrogen.
Train rule atom intricate nitrogen.
Rule unusual leotard entropy.
Intricate nitrogen train rule intricate casual atom train entropy.

Casual atom social unusual atom leotard.
Atom train ostrich might.
Train rule atom intricate nitrogen.
Entropy nitrogen train rule ostrich pope yearly.

Nitrogen intricate train rule ostrich genealogy entropy nitrogen.
Intricate nitrogen train rule intricate casual atom train entropy.
Train rule atom intricate nitrogen.
Rule unusual leotard entropy.
Ostrich social train rule intricate casual holiday.
Genealogy entropy nitrogen entropy atom leotard ostrich genealogy
Entropy nitrogen train rule ostrich pope yearly.   [yearly.
Nitrogen intricate train rule ostrich genealogy entropy nitrogen.

Train rule atom intricate nitrogen.
Rule unusual leotard entropy.
Atom train ostrich might.
Intricate nitrogen train rule intricate casual atom train entropy.
Nitrogen intricate train rule ostrich genealogy entropy nitrogen.

Rule unusual leotard entropy.
Unusual nitrogen unusual social unusual atom leotard.
Leotard entropy ostrich train atom rule dies.
Entropy nitrogen train rule ostrich pope yearly.

Intricate nitrogen train rule intricate casual atom train entropy.
Nitrogen intricate train rule ostrich genealogy entropy nitrogen.
Train rule atom intricate nitrogen.
Rule unusual leotard entropy.
Intricate nitrogen train rule intricate casual atom train entropy.
Casual atom social unusual atom leotard.
Atom train ostrich might.
Train rule atom intricate nitrogen.
Entropy nitrogen train rule ostrich pope yearly.

Casual atom social unusual atom leotard.
Atom train ostrich might.
Social ostrich casual intricate atom leotard.
Unusual nitrogen unusual social unusual atom leotard.

Atom train ostrich might.
Leotard entropy ostrich train atom rule dies.

Atom train ostrich might.
Train rule atom intricate nitrogen.
Ostrich social train rule intricate casual holiday.
Might intricate genealogy holiday train.

Train rule atom intricate nitrogen.
Rule unusual leotard entropy.
Atom train ostrich might.
Intricate nitrogen train rule intricate casual atom train entropy.
Nitrogen intricate train rule ostrich genealogy entropy nitrogen.

Entropy nitrogen train rule ostrich pope yearly.
Nitrogen intricate train rule ostrich genealogy entropy nitrogen.
Train rule atom intricate nitrogen.
Rule unusual leotard entropy.
Ostrich social train rule intricate casual holiday.
Pope ostrich pope entropy.
Yearly entropy atom rule leotard yearly.

V

Nitrogen intricate train rule ostrich genealogy entropy nitrogen.
Intricate nitrogen train rule intricate casual atom train entropy.
Train rule atom intricate nitrogen.
Rule unusual leotard entropy.
Ostrich social train rule intricate casual holiday.
Genealogy entropy nitrogen entropy atom leotard ostrich genealogy
Entropy nitrogen train rule ostrich pope yearly.   [yearly.
Nitrogen intricate train rule ostrich genealogy entropy nitrogen.

Intricate nitrogen train rule intricate casual atom train entropy.
Nitrogen intricate train rule ostrich genealogy entropy nitrogen.
Train rule atom intricate nitrogen.

Rule unusual leotard entropy.
Intricate nitrogen train rule intricate casual atom train entropy.
Casual atom social unusual atom leotard.
Atom train ostrich might.
Train rule atom intricate nitrogen.
Entropy nitrogen train rule ostrich pope yearly.

Train rule atom intricate nitrogen.
Rule unusual leotard entropy.
Atom train ostrich might.
Intricate nitrogen train rule intricate casual atom train entropy.
Nitrogen intricate train rule ostrich genealogy entropy nitrogen.

Rule unusual leotard entropy.
Unusual nitrogen unusual social unusual atom leotard.
Leotard entropy ostrich train atom rule dies.
Entropy nitrogen train rule ostrich pope yearly.

Ostrich social train rule intricate casual holiday.
Social ostrich casual intricate atom leotard.
Train rule atom intricate nitrogen.
Rule unusual leotard entropy.
Intricate nitrogen train rule intricate casual atom train entropy.
Casual atom social unusual atom leotard.
Holiday ostrich leotard intricate dies atom yearly.

Genealogy entropy nitrogen entropy atom leotard ostrich genealogy
Entropy nitrogen train rule ostrich pope yearly.   [yearly.
Nitrogen intricate train rule ostrich genealogy entropy nitrogen.
Entropy nitrogen train rule ostrich pope yearly.
Atom train ostrich might.
Leotard entropy ostrich train atom rule dies.
Ostrich social train rule intricate casual holiday.
Genealogy entropy nitrogen entropy atom leotard ostrich genealogy
Yearly entropy atom rule leotard yearly.   [yearly.

Entropy nitrogen train rule ostrich pope yearly.
Nitrogen intricate train rule ostrich genealogy entropy nitrogen.

Train rule atom intricate nitrogen.
Rule unusual leotard entropy.
Ostrich social train rule intricate casual holiday.
Pope ostrich pope entropy.
Yearly entropy atom rule leotard yearly.

Nitrogen intricate train rule ostrich genealogy entropy nitrogen.
Intricate nitrogen train rule intricate casual atom train entropy.
Train rule atom intricate nitrogen.
Rule unusual leotard entropy.
Ostrich social train rule intricate casual holiday.
Genealogy entropy nitrogen entropy atom leotard ostrich genealogy
Entropy nitrogen train rule ostrich pope yearly.   [yearly.
Nitrogen intricate train rule ostrich genealogy entropy nitrogen.

4 December 1964
New York

JAIL BREAK   (for Emmett Williams & John Cage) September 1963, April & August 1966

```
Tear now jails down all.      All jails now down tear.      Jails tear down all now.
Tear all now down jails.      All now tear down jails.      Jails tear down now all.
Tear now all jails down.      All jails down tear now.      Jails down now all tear.
Tear jails now all down.      All now jails down tear.      Jails now tear down all.
Tear jails now down all.      All now down tear jails.      Jails now tear all down.
Tear now jails all down.      All jails now tear down.      Jails tear now down all.
Tear now down all jails.      All tear now jails down.      Jails tear now all down.
Tear all down jails now.      All jails down now tear.      Jails all tear now down.
Tear jails down all now.      All down now tear jails.      Jails tear all now down.
Tear all jails down now.      All tear down jails now.      Jails all tear down now.
Tear jails all now down.      All tear jails down now.      Jails all down tear now.
Tear jails down now all.      All now down jails tear.      Jails now down all tear.
Tear down now all jails.      All down tear now jails.      Jails tear all down now.
Tear now all down jails.      All down tear jails now.      Jails down all tear now.
Tear down now jails all.      All down now jails tear.      Jails down now tear all.
Tear now down jails all.      All down jails now tear.      Jails now all tear down.
Tear down jails all now.      All down jails tear now.      Jails down tear all now.
Tear down jails all now.      All tear jails now down.      Jails now all down tear.
Tear all jails now down.      All now tear jails down.      Jails down tear now all.
Tear all now jails down.      All tear down now jails.      Jails all now tear down.
Tear all down now jails.      all jails tear now down.      Jails down all now tear.
Tear down jails now all.      All now jails tear down.      Jails all now down tear.
Tear down all now jails.      All jails tear down now.      Jails now down tear all.
Tear down all now jails.      All tear now down jails.      Jails all down now tear.
```

194

PEOPLE: Five who speak clearly, listen closely to each other & all environing sounds, & let what they hear modify how they speak. In Way 1 they must be able to improvise together, let performance flow & their own impulses determine how they speak. Way 2 needs a precise conductor & 5 speakers who follow him accurately. MATERIALS: 120 small cards, 5 equal squares of poster board (8 to 28 inches a side), paint/ink, pen/brush; for Way 1, 10 envelopes each large enough to hold 24 cards with room for easy removal & insertion of cards.

PREPARATION: Type permutations on cards. Experiment to find size of sign easiest to handle; size, colors, letter shapes most visible in performance situation. Make 5 square signs, each with one of the 5 words on it. For Way 1 attach 2 envelopes to each sign back & put the 24 cards whose texts begin with the sign's word in one. PERFORMANCE: Way 1: The speakers line up, holding signs parallel in the order TEAR DOWN ALL JAILS NOW. Each draws a card, listens closely to other speakers & environment until he & the situation are ready, then speaks the words as a connected sentence making good sense. Speed, loudness & voice coloration are free. He puts the card in the empty envelope & draws another, &c., until he's read each card once. It ends after last speaker finishes. Way 2: Lined up as above, speakers face conductor, who shuffles the 120 cards & draws one, pointing in turn, in the permutation's order, to each word's bearer, who says the word, connecting it with the others so the sentence makes sense tho said by 5. Way 2 needs long intense rehearsal; ends when all 120 permutations are read. Way 2 performed (2nd Jail Poets' Reading, Living Theatre, 9 Sept. 1963) by Judith Malina, Tom Cornell, Paul Prensky, & 2 others, conducted by JML. Way 1 1st performed in rain (reading against USSR jailing of writers, 30 April 1966: WIN, II, 9:6-7) by JML, Blackburn, Rothenberg, Antin, & the Rt. Revd. Michael F. Itkin.

Down tear now jails all.
Down now tear jails all.
Down tear all jails now.
Down all now tear jails.
Down jails tear all now.
Down jails all tear now.
Down now all jails tear.
Down all jails now tear.
Down all tear now jails.
Down jails now tear all.
Down now jails all tear.
Down jails now all tear.
Down tear jails now all.
Down tear all now jails.
Down now jails tear all.
Down now tear all jails.
Down all tear jails now.
Down now tear all jails.
Down jails tear now all.
Down all tear jails now.
Down tear jails all now.
Down all jails tear now.
Down tear now all jails.
Down all now jails tear.
Down jails all now tear.
Down now all tear jails.

Now all down tear jails.
Now down all tear jails.
Now tear down jails all.
Now jails all down tear.
Now jails all tear down.
Now jails tear down all.
Now down jails all tear.
Now all tear jails down.
Now all tear down jails.
Now down all jails tear.
Now jails down all tear.
Now tear down all jails.
Now tear all down jails.
Now all down jails tear.
Now tear jails down all.
Now jails down tear all.
Now down tear all jails.
Now tear all jails down.
Now all jails down tear.
Now tear jails all down.
Now jails tear all down.
Now down tear jails all.
Now all jails down tear.
Now tear jails all down.
Now jails tear all down.
Now down jails tear all.
Now all jails tear down.

195

The Bluebird Asymmetries

1st Bluebird Asymmetry — 6 May 1967

Bluebirds are/ahrrrrrrrrrrrrrrrrrrrrrrrrrrrrrrrrrrrrrrrr-
(ah)rrrrrrrr/Thrushes,
                    although the/uhhhhhhhhhhhhhhh-
(u)hhhhhhhhhh/plumage of the old bird does/zzzzzzzzzz-
zzzzzzzzzzzzzzzzzzzzzzz/not suggest
                    relationship
                with the other/rrrrrrrrrrrrrrr-
rrrrrrrrrrrrr/American/nnnnnnnnnnnnnnnnnnnnnnnnnnnnnnn-
nnnnnnnnnnnnnnnnnnnnnnnn/Thrushes.

                        young/nggggggggggggg-
(n)gggggggggggggggggggg/in the juvenal plum-/mmmmmmmmm-
mmmmmmmmmmmmmm/age,
                case,
              B<small>LUEBIRD</small>,
                    Bluebird
            (S(_ialia_)/uhhhhhhhhhhhhhhhhhhhhhhhhhhhhhhhh-
(u)hhhhhhhhhhhhhhhhhhhhhhhhhhhhhhhhhhhhhhhhhhhhhhhhhhhhhh-
(u)hhhhhhhhhhhhhhhhhs(_ialis_)/ssssssssssssssssssssssssss-
ssssssssssssssssssssssssssssssssssssssssssssssssssssssss-
sssssssssssssssssssss/_fulva_),
                    northern/rnnnnnnnnnnnnnnn-
(r)nnnnnnnnnnnnnnnnnn/Central/llllllllllllllllllllllll-
llllllllllllllllll/America.

            Bluebird is an early/iyyy-
(i)yyyyyyyyyy/spring arrival.

2nd Bluebird Asymmetry — 6 May 1967

```
Bluebird,
        Bluebird is without serious/sssssssss-
sssssssssssssssssssss/faults and as a/uhhhhhhhhhh-
(u)hhhhhhhhhhhhhhhhhhhhhhhh/beneficial/llllll111-
llllllllll11111111111/bird has a/uhhhhhhhhhhhhhhhh-
(u)hhhhhh/record equaled by few other/rrrrrrrr-
rrrrrrrrrrrrrrrrrr/species.


                        Bluebirds/dzzzzzzz-
(d)zzzzzzzzzzzzzzz/are/ahrrrrrrrrrrrrrrrrrrrrrr-
(ah)rrrrrrrrrrrrrrrrr/Thrushes,
                other/rrrrrrrrrrrrrrrrrrrrrrr-
rrrrrrrrrrrrrrrrrrrrrrrrrrr/American/nnnnnnnnnnnn-
nnnnnnnn/Thrushes.

                    Bluebird,
        Bluebird
                (S(ialia)/uhhhhhhhhhhhhhhhhhhh-
(u)hhhhhhhhhhhhhhhhhhhhhhhhhhhhhhhhhhhhhhhhhhhhhh-
(u)hhhhhhhhhhhhhhhhhh/s(ialis)/ssssssssssssssss-
ssssssssssssssssssssssss/fulva),
        northern/rnnnnnnnnnnnnnnnnnnnnnnnnnnnnn-
(r)nnnnnnnnnnnnnnn/Central/lllllllllll1111111111-
lllllllllllllllllllllllll/America.
```

3rd Bluebird Asymmetry — 6 May 1967

```
Bluebird is an early spring arrival,
        elsewhere it is one of the commonest
                box-/sssssssssssssssssssss-
sssssssssssssssssssssssssss/nesting birds.


                                        blue,
          rarely white,
                        Bluebird,
                Bluebird is without
          serious faults and as a/uhhhhhhhhhh-
(u)hhhhhhhhhhhhhhh/beneficial bird has a/uhhhh-
(u)hhhhhhhhhhhhhhhhhhhhhhhhh/record
                equaled by few/Uwwwwwwwwwwwww-
(U)wwwww/other species.


                        Bluebirds are/ahrrrr-
(ah)rrrr/Thrushes,
                slender bills,
          centipedes,

BLUEBIRD,
          (S(ialia)/uhhhhhhhhhhhhhhhhhhhhhhhhh-
(u)hhhhhhhhhhhhhhhhhhhhhhhhhhhhhhhhhhhhhhhhhhhh-
(u)hhhhhhhhhh/s(ialis)/sssssssssssssssssssssss-
sssssssssssssssssssssssssssssssssssssssssssssss/
```

4th Bluebird Asymmetry — 6 May 1967

BLUEBIRD,
              Bluebird
                       (S(_ialia_)/uhhhhhhhhhhhhhhhhhhh-
(u)hhhhhhhhhhhhhhhhhhhhhhhhhhhhhhhhhhhhhhhhhhhhhhhhhhhh-
(u)hhhhhhhhhhhhhhhhhhh/s(_ialis_)/ssssssssssssssssss-
ssssssssssssssssssssssssssssssssssssssssssssssssssssss-
sssssssssssssssssssssssss/_fulva_),
                            south/thhhhhhhhh-
(t)hhhhhhhhhhhhhhhhhhhhh/as northern/rnnnnnnnnnnn-
(r)nnnnnnnnnnnnnnnn/Central/llllllllllllllllllll-
llllllllllllllllllllllllllllAmerica.

               Bluebird is an early spring/nggggggggg-
(n)gggggggggggggggg/arrival,
                    Bluebird,
            Bluebird is without serious faults/tss-
(t)ssssssssssssssss/and as a beneficial bird
                  has a/uhhhhhhhhhhhhhhhhhhh-
(u)hhhhhhhhhhhhhhhhhhhhhhhhhh/record
                     equaled by few/Uwwwwwwwww-
(U)wwwwwwwwwwwwwww/other species.

                          Bluebirds/dzzz-
(d)zzzzzz/are/ahrrrrrrrrrrrrrrrrrrrrrrrrrrrrrrr-
(ah)rrrrrrrr/Thrushes,
                  woodland/nnnnnnnnnnnnnnnnn-
nnnnnnnnn/birds,

5th Bluebird Asymmetry — 6 May 1967

```
Bluebird
        (S(ialia)/uhhhhhhhhhhhhhhhhhhhhhhhhhhhhhhhhhhhh-
(u)hhhhhhhhhhhhhhhhhhhhhhhhhhhhhhhhhhhhhhhhhhhhhhhhhhhhhhhh-
(u)hhhhhhhh/s(ialis)/sssssssssssssssssssssssssssssssssssss
sssssssssssssssssssssssssssssssssssssssssssssssssssssssssss-
sssssssssssss/fulva),
                    Bluebird is an early/iyyyyyyyyyyyy-
(i)yyyyy/spring arrival,
                    abundant
                        in the/uhhhhhhhhhhhhhhh-
(u)hhhhh/well-/llllllllllllllllllllllllllllllllllllllllll-
llllllllllllll/settled country but is not at all/llllllll-
lllllllllllllllllllllll/uncommon as a summer/rrrrrrrrrrrr-
                        resident in the/uhhhhhhhh-
(u)hhhhhhhhhhhhhhhhhhhhhhhhhhhhhhhhhhhhhhhh/desolate
        burne-/rnnnnnnnnnnnnnnnnnnnnnnnnnnnnnnnnnnnnnnnn-
(r)nnnnnnnnn/d-over areas and windfalls/lzzzzzzzzzzzzzzz-
(l)zzzzz/of the northern forests.


                        holes in/nnnnnnnnnnnnnn-
nnnnnnnnnn/trees an/nnnnnnnnnnnnnnnnnnnnnnnnnnnnnnnnnnnnnnnn-
nnnnnnnnnnnnnnnnnnnd/stubs,
                    Bluebird,
                        Bluebird
        is without serious faults and as a/uhhhhhhhhhhhh-
(u)hhhhhh/beneficial bird has a/uhhhhhhhhhhhhh-
(u)hhhhhhhhhhhhhhhhhhh/record equaled by few other species.
```

200

6th Bluebird Asymmetry — 7 May 1967

```
BLUEBIRD
          Bluebird
                    Blue Robin,
          blue red-
                    breast,
                              bluebird
(r)nnnnn/Saskatchewan and south/thhhhhhhhhhhh-
(t)hhhhhhhhhhhhhhhhhhh/to/Uwwwwwwwwwwwwwwwwwww-
(U)wwwwwwwwwwwwwwwwwwwww/Texas/sssssssssssssss-
sssssssssssssssssssssss/and/nnnnnnnnnnnnnnnnnnn-
nnnnnnnd/Florida.


                    Bluebird is the/uhhhhhhhhhh-
(u)hhhhh/state bird of/vvvvvvvvvvvvvvvvvvvvvvv-
vvvvvvvvvvvvvvvvvvvvvvvv/Missouri and/nnnnnnnnn-
nnnnnnnd/New/Uwwwwwwwwwwwwwwwwwwwwwwwwwwwwwww-
(U)wwwwwwwww/York.


bluebird is the only one with/dhhhhhhhhhhhhhhh-
(d)hhhhh/a reddish breast and,
                              blue back
          and white belly,
```

7th Bluebird Asymmetry — 8 May 1967

```
Bluebirds were probably more common/nnnnnnnnnnnnnnnnnn-
nnnnnnnnn/in the cities at one time than they are/ahrr-
(ah)rrrrrrrr/now.

            bluebirds for the right to/Uwwwwwwww-
(U)wwwww/live near the buildings in the towns.

            blue-/Uwwwwwwwwwwwwwwwwwwwwwwwwwwwwwwwwwwwwww-
(U)wwwwwwwwwww/birds returnèd from the/uhhhhhhhhhhhhhhh-
(u)hhhhhhhhhhhhhhhhhhh/South.

                        move/vvvvvvvvvvvvvvvvvvvvvvvv-
vvvvvvvv/into the country.

                        Bluebirds/dzzzzzzzzzzzzzzzz-
(d)zzzzz/depend on berry-/iyyyyyyyyyyyyyyyyyyyyyyyyyyyy-
(i)yyyyyyyyyyyyyyyyyyyyy/bearing/ngggggggggggggggggggggg-
(n)ggggggggggggg/trees,
            starlings in winter/rrrrrrrrrrr-
rrrrrrr/can clean out a/uhhhhhhhhhhhhhhhhhhhhhhhhhhhhhhh-
(u)hhhhhhhhh/mountain ash tree in/nnnnnnnnnnnnnnnnnnnnn-
nnnnnnnnnnnnnnnnnnnnnn/a few hours.

            bluebird's favorite haunts/tssssssssssssssssss-
(t)ssssssssssssssssss/are old apple and pear orchards/dz-
(d)zzzzzzzzzzzzzzzzzzzzz/that
                        are in a state of decay.
```

8th Bluebird Asymmetry — 8 May 1967

```
bluebird nicely.

         bluebird.

                   Bluebirds/dzzzzzzzzzz-
(d)zzzzz/line the interior of their houses/zzzzz-
zzzzzzzzzzzzzzzzzzzzzzzzzzzzzzzzzzzzz/with/dhhhhhh-
(d)hhhhhhhhhh/grasses and pine needles.

         fivvvvvvve/vvvvvvvvvvvvvvvvvvvvvvvvvvv-
vvvvvvvvvvvvvv/eggs,
                   in-/nggggggggggggggggggggggg-
(n)gggggggggggggggggggg/cubating of the eggs.

                   two-/Uwwwwwwwwwwwwww-
(U)wwwwwwwwwwwwwwwwwwwwwwwwwwwwww/thirds/dzzzzzzzz-
(d)zzzzzzz/of the bluebird's food consists of/vv-
vvvvvvvvvvvvvv/insects —
                   blue-/Uwwwwwwwwwwwwwwww-
(U)wwwwwwwwwwwwwwwwwwwwwwwwww/birds are/ahrrrrrrr-
(ah)rrrrrrrrr/speckled,
                   bluebirds are/ahrrrrrrr-
(ah)rrrrrrrrr/thrushes,

plumage that this relationship is plainly/iyyyyy-
(i)yyyy/revealed.
```

9th Bluebird Asymmetry — 8 May 1967

```
bluebirds spend the winter in/nnnnnnnnnnnnnnn-
nnnnnnnnn/small flocks in the southern/rnnnnn-
(r)nnnnnnnnnnnn/part of the/iyyyyyyyyyyyyyyyy-
(i)yyyyyyyyyyyyyyyyyyyyyyyyyy/United
          States,
                    all the frigid north has/zz-
zzzzzzzzzzzzzzzzzzzzzz/to offer/rrrrrrrrrrrrr-
rrrrrrrrrrrrrrrrrrrrrrrrrrrrrr/in/nnnnnnnnnnn-
nnnnnnnnnnnnnnnnnnnnnnnnnnnnnnnnnnn/December.


          Bluebird
                    blue-/Uwwwwwwwwwwwwwwwwww-
(U)wwwwwwwwwwwwwwwwwwwwwwwwwwwwwwwwwwwwwwwwwww-
(U)wwwwwwwwwwwwwwwwwwwww/bird
          (bluebirds)
                    bluebirds
                         northern/rnnn-
(r)nnnnnn/Idaho and western/rnnnnnnnnnnnnnnnn-
(r)nnnnnnnnnnnn/Montana,
                    bluebird is/zzzzzzzz-
zzzzzzzzz/easily distin-/nggggggggggggggggggg-
(n)gggggggggggggggggggg/guished from its/tsss-
(t)sssssssssssss/eastern counterpart by/ayyyy-
(a)yyyyyy/the chestnut color on its back,
                    mountains.
```

10th Bluebird Asymmetry — 8 May 1967

```
bluebird might follow the/uhhhhhhhhhhhhhhhhhhh-
(u)hhhhh/melting snows for several/lllllllllll-
llllllllllllllllll/hundred miles/lzzzzzzzzzzzzz-
(l)zzzzzzzzzzzzzzzzzzzzzzzzto reach/chhhhhhhhhh-
(c)hhhhhhhhhhhhhh/its summer/rrrrrrrrrrrrrrrrr-
rrrrrrrrrrrrrrrrrrrrrrrrrrrrr/New/Uwwwwwwwwwwww-
(U)wwwww/England home,
                    bluebird in/nnnnnnnnnn-
nnnnnnnn/many parts of the/uhhhhhhhhhhhhhhhhhh-
(u)hhhhhhhhhhhhhhhhhhhhhhhhhh/West
              has merely to/Uwwwwwwwwwwwwwwwww-
(U)wwwwwwwwwwwwwwwwwwwwwwwwwww/climb/mmmmmmmmmmm-
mmmmmmmm/the nearest range of mountains.


              journey from the/uhhhhhhhhhhhhhhhhhhh-
(u)hhhhhhhhhhhhhhhhhhhhhhhh/valleys/zzzzzzzzzzz-
zzzzzzzz/where it spends the winter to/Uwwwww-
(U)wwwwwwwwwww/the yellow pine belt
              where it nests is/zzzzzzzz-
zzzzzzzzzzzzzzzzzzzzzzzzzzz/often called/llllllll-
llllllllllllllllllllllllllllllld/vertical/lllll-
llllllll/migration.
                    bluebird,
          bluebird which/chhhhhhhhhhhhhhhhhhhh-
(c)hhhhhhhhhhhhhhhhhhhhh/is turquoise blue/Uww-
(U)wwwwwwwwwwwwww/above/vvvvvvvvvvvvvvvvvvvvvv-
vvvvvvvvvvvvvvvvvvvvvvvv/and below,
```

6–8 May 1967
The Bronx

The following is a list of the phonemic notations in "The Bluebird Asymmetries."

A. vowels

1. single vowels

/a/ :   *a* in *father* when not extended & with no off-glide
/i/ :   *i* in *bit*
/u/ :   *u* in *but* or *e* in *the* when not extended & with no off-glide
/U/ :   *u* in *put* or *oo* in *book* when not extended & with no off-glide
/y/, /w/, /h/, & /r/:   off-glides: see diphthongs below

2. diphthongs

/iy/:   *ee* in *feet* & *y* in *berry*
/Uw/:   *oo* in *boot* or *ew* in *few* without the on-glide /y/
/uh/:   extended *u* of *but*, *e* of *the*, & the article *a* before consonants
/ah/:   extended *a* of *father* or *o* of *hot*

3. triphthong

/ahr/:   *ar* in *cart* & the word *are*

B. consonants

1. single consonants (including semivowels)

/l/, /m/, /n/, /r/, /s/, /v/, & /z/:   their usual sounds in English (/s/: unvoiced *s*)

2. consonantal digraphs

/ch/:   *ch* in *reach*
/dh/:   *th* in *that*
/th/:   *th* in *thing*

3. "consonantal diphthongs"

/ts/:   *ts* in *rats*
/dz/:   *ds* in *birds*
/rn/:   *m* in *southern*

4. extended consonants with stops at end

/nnnd/:   *nd* in *and* & *ned* of *burned*
/lld/:   *lled* of *called*
(readers must sound *d*'s only at the ends of the prolongations)

In the notations, single letters are merely repeated to indicate pro-longations, while only the final letters of digraphs, diphthongs, & triphthongs are repeated to indicate prolongations of those phonemes. Notations are continued from one line to another by placing hyphens at the ends of lines; however, the first 1 or 2 letters of combinations are placed within parentheses at the beginnings of the following lines to remind the reader that the entire sounds indicated by the combinations are to be continued. On the other hand, the *n*'s, *l*'s, & *h*'s of /nd/'s, /ld/'s, & /uhp/'s are repeated, the *d*'s & *p*'s being only printed at the ends of such series.

Performance Parameters

The *durations* of silences (or instrumental tones) & prolonged phonemes are *at least* those of single words or word strings that might be printed in equivalent spaces, as they would be spoken aloud by the individual reader. That is, the reader is silent or prolongs sounds at least as long as it would take him to speak such space-equivalent words. However, one may, in performances, extend these durations whenever one feels that the total performance would be "better" if one remained silent or continued to prolong the sound one is making. Thus the spatial notations are those of *minimal* durations only; the reader has the option to extend silences & sounds improvisatorily − in accordance with one's judgements of the performance situation − somewhat longer than strictly called for by the notation. In this way, a completely determinate, tho chance-generated, notation may become the basis of only partially determinate − "unpredictable" rather than "indeterminate" − performances.

The *speed* of reading is entirely up to the individual readers, but there should be no *great* disparities in *average* speed between the fastest & slowest readers.

Loudness is regulated by typography & some types of punctuation. *Initial capitals* call for moderately loud speech; *italics,* loud; *solid capitals,* quite loud; *boldface,* very loud; *italic* or *boldface capials,* even louder. *Parentheses & quotation marks* call for soft or moderately soft speech (according to the performance situation); parentheses or quotation marks enclosing capitals, boldface type, &/or italics call for "forcible" soft speech or loud whispers. In these Asymmetries, whispers should only be used when there is adequate amplification to make all whispered prolongations audible.

The *pitches* of words must be those of normal speech; the pitch of each prolongation should remain as nearly *constant* as possible, continuing the pitch that the sound would have in a normal reading (without interruptive silences or prolongations) of the phrases in which it occurs. Care should be taken to avoid especially down-glides of a musical third or more (e.g., *C* to *A* or below).

Ways of Performing "The Bluebird Asymmetries"

Besides being read solo, "The Bluebird Asymmetries" may be performed by five people reading, first, the 1st thru 5th, simultaneously, & then, the 6th thru the 10th. However, larger groups may perform as many as all 10 simultaneously, & any number may read any number of them simultaneously &/or successively, as long as each of the 10 is read at least once during a performance.

It is of the utmost importance that each reader *listen very attentively to all sounds* produced by himself & the other readers, as well as to environing sounds (audience, street, &c.). All aspects of performance must be sensitively adjusted by the reader in accord with his perceptions of the total sound. Thus one may prolong a silence, tone, or phoneme, or speak louder or softer, faster or slower, as one feels these actions will contribute most positively to the total sound.

Sources of these Asymmetries

The members of this group of Asymmetries are "matched" in that all in each group are "about" one subject — bluebirds. Half of "The Bluebird Asymmetries" were drawn from one source, the other half from another:

The words of the 1st five "Bluebird Asymmetries" were drawn by chance operations from *Bird Portraits in Color,* text by Thomas S. Roberts, M.D., D.Sc. (U. of Minnesota Press, Minneapolis, 1934, 1940): text opp. Plate 59: "THRUSHES (Family *Turddae*)," painted by Allan Brooks in 1930. Those of the last five were drawn from the *Audubon Nature Encyclopedia,* Vol. 2 (BI-CA), article: "BLUEBIRD," pp. 283-5 (National Audubon Society, Curtis Publishing Co., Philadelphia, New York, 1964, 1965).

May 1967
The Bronx

from the PFR-3 Poems
Summer 1969, Los Angeles

A Note on the PFR-3 Poems

The PFR-3 Poems were composed at Information International, Inc., in Los Angeles, with the aid of their PFR-3, a programmable film reader connected to a DEC PDP-9 computer and various peripherals, in Summer 1969, when I was an invited artist-participant (the only poet) in the Art and Technology Program of the Los Angeles County Museum of Art.

I worked with a computer program provided (and continually revised and sophisticated) by John Hansen, the vice president in charge of programming, and his assistant Dean Anschultz. Their program allowed me to enter as "data" a list of "messages": originally up to 100 single lines, each comprising at most 48 characters and/or spaces. Later longer messages, though fewer at most, and ones having two or more lines, were possible. From any list the program randomly selected and permuted series of "message members" (characters, words, or strings of linked words, e.g., sentences, separated in the message by spaces) and displayed them on a monitor. When a lever on the control board was pushed, every *tenth* line appearing on the screen was printed out.

The message lists relate to the runs of printout as species to individuals. Each list, together with the program, thus constitutes an indeterminate poem, of which each run of printout is one of an indeterminable number of possible realizations. And each poem has a title, e.g., "Dansk."

There are in all 20-odd PFR-3 Poems. Three are each represented here by about a page of printout.

"Dansk" is the second one I made. Its list comprises 100 48-character/space messages, each a complete, though periodless, spontaneously composed sentence. All message members are single words (none linked), so the computer could select at random any number of words from any message, arranged in any order. Indentations are random in length in all PFR-3 Poems.

"South" has a message list comprising 100 48-character/space messages, each made up of one or two complete sentences (with periods). All words of each sentence are linked in the list, so that each message has only one or two members. The computer could select randomly one or two whole sentences from any message: when two, it could reverse their original order, or not. All the sentences have to do with southern areas of the world, notably Central and South America and Africa: a kind of generalized Tropics.

The list of "The" comprises up to about 50 messages, each including several (usually short) sentences, each beginning with "The," ending with a period, and constituting a single line whose words are linked. The computer could thus select one or more sentences from any message, arranging the sentences in any order. All sentences in "The" refer to processes or actions that are always going on somewhere in the world. Composed in August 1969 and nearly the last, this PFR-3 Poem has the longest messages. Its list took longest to elaborate and changed most as I added messages (groups of one-line sentences), so that early printout differs from later much more than in other PFR-3 Poems.

For more about these poems, and more examples, see "Jackson Mac Low," by Jane Livingston, and the 17 pages of poem and list printout following it, in *A Report on the Art and Technology Program of the Los Angeles County Museum of Art 1967–1971,* ed. Maurice Tuchman (Los Angeles: LACMA, 1971), pp. 201–223.

30 September–October 1985
New York

Printout from "Dansk"

PAVEMENTS CARPETING ARE JACARANDA VIOLET FLOWERS

WERE HUDDLING WHIMPERING FREEZING

ARE STUPID PACIFIC HANDS

PLEASURABLY

WERE COURTESANS VOLUPTUOUS KINGDOMS

ONCE RULING

SEPTUGENARIANS JAILING

SELDOM PLEASURABLE RENUNCIATIONS

ARE MOLDERING CLASSICISTS PALLID COLLATING TEXTS

UPWARD NIPPLES

GRACING

AND

ARE CLASSICISTS PALLID TEXTS

ARE WET PLEASANTLY NOW

LAKOTAS CHARGING WERE BELLOWING

SLEEPING PANICKING ROILING ARE PONDS BULLFROGS

ARE ARBOREAL GIBBONS APES ASIATIC SMALL

PERSONS INANIMATE MOUNTAINS ARE OBDURATE MASSIVE

DILIGENTLY CHILDREN HALLUCINATIONS ARE PURSUING

GREEDY EXECUTIVES

AWAKENING ARE HARD CLITORISES RED

ARE SURPRISES

SWEETENING SLOWLY ARE CITIES BITTER

DROPS ARE GLINTING LAUGHING

SPLATTERING

ARCHWAYS

EVENINGS ENLIVENING

WAVERING FIRES CORUSCATING JEWELS WERE

SPROUTING SOON

Printout from "South"

BABOONS JUMP. PEOPLE AND FLIES VIOLATE ORCHIDS.

PARROTS RACE ACROSS VIOLET ORCHIDS. ZEBRAS EAT.

FLIES IGNORE ARMADILLOS AND TOUGH

COATIMUNDIS.

PEOPLE ARE SHEARING IGNORANT SCREAMING ZEBRAS.

A TOUGH RED-AND-GREEN PARROT SCREAMS AT A
TOAD.

ZEBRAS RACE JAGUARS AND GREYISH MANDRILLS.

FLIES FLY.

BIRDS SCREAM. AN ARMADILLO EATS A GREYISH SNAKE.

A GREEN LIZARD PEERS AT A TOUGH MANDRILL.

WHAT PEOPLE FLY?

PEOPLE AND FLIES VIOLATE ORCHIDS.

LIZARDS JUMP BABOONS. A BIRD EATS A LIZARD.

PEOPLE SCREAM AT GREEN-AND-VIOLET TOADS.

PEOPLE ARE SHEARING IGNORANT SCREAMING
ZEBRAS.

PEOPLE ARE SHEARING IGNORANT SCREAMING
ZEBRAS.

PEOPLE SCREAM AT GREEN-AND-VIOLET
TOADS.

YELLOW PARROTS RACE ANCIENT JAGUARS.

ARMADILLOS JUMP.

A TOUGH RED-AND-GREEN PARROT SCREAMS AT A TOAD.

PEOPLE SCREAM WHILE GREEN TOADS VIOLATE
PARROTS.

ZEBRAS RACE JAGUARS AND GREYISH MANDRILLS.

MANDRILLS IGNORE ARMADILLOS AND COATIMUNDIS.

A GREEN LIZARD PEERS AT A TOUGH
MANDRILL.

WHAT PEOPLE FLY?

BABOONS VIOLATE BANANAS IN VIOLET TREES.

FLIES IGNORE ARMADILLOS AND TOUGH
COATIMUNDIS.

ANGRY ARMADILLOS ARE SCREAMING AT RED
PARROTS.

MANDRILLS IGNORE ARMADILLOS AND
COATIMUNDIS.

A GREY TOAD EATS A GREEN-AND-ORANGE FLY.

ZEBRAS JUMP. PURPLE-FACED MANDRILLS ARE FIERCE.

FLIES EAT.

SNAKES EAT THROUGH ORCHIDS. FLIES IGNORE
TAPIRS.

Printout from "The"

THE WIND BLOWS.
THE RAIN FALLS.
THE SNOW FALLS.
THE STREAMS FLOW.
THE RIVERS FLOW.
THE OCEANS RISE.
THE OCEANS FALL.

THE BUSHES GROW.
THE MOSSES GROW.
THE FERNS GROW.
THE LICHENS GROW.

THE TREES SWAY IN THE WIND.
THE FLOWERS SWAY IN THE WIND.

THE INSECTS ARE HATCHED.
THE REPTILES ARE HATCHED.
THE MAMMALS ARE BORN.
THE BIRDS ARE HATCHED.
THE FISHES ARE HATCHED.

THE PEOPLE SAIL ON RAFTS.

THE LICHENS GROW.
THE FLOWERS GROW.
THE MOSSES GROW.
THE TREES GROW.

THE INSECTS GROW.
THE REPTILES GROW.

THE BUSHES GROW.

THE INSECTS GATHER FOOD.
THE BIRDS GATHER FOOD.

THE PLANETS SHINE.
THE MOON SHINES.
THE SUN SHINES.

THE TREES DRINK. THE FUNGUSES DRINK.

THE MOSSES TURN TOWARD THE LIGHT.
THE FLOWERS TURN TOWARD THE LIGHT.
THE TREES TURN TOWARD THE LIGHT.

from *Odes for Iris*
July 1970-Nov. 1971

1st Ode for Iris—midnight after the boat ride
Sat-Sun 18-19 July 1970

I love you, Iris Lezak,
my heart beats, when I see you,
more quickly & more calmly
all at once.

Seeing you makes me joyful,
seeing you talking, walking,
reclining, running, bending,
or sitting:

seeing you sitting still or
in vivid motion as you
speak your mind & soul with eyes
& body:

body continually
assuming new attitudes,
facets of the beautiful
you, Iris,

of whom the seeing pleases
even in my worst moments:
what is more objectively
beautiful?

3rd Ode for Iris—later that night—Sun 19 July 1970

What can a man do to be
lovable once again to
the woman he loves tho her
heart has cooled

& no longer bounds for joy
when seeing him or feeling
his hands or lips or body
upon her?

What breaking of barriers,
what healing of old traumas,
what awakening of faith,
what trusting

can come to pass, becoming
ourselves being together,
no longer ignorant, blind,
resentful,

raging at what isn't worth
raging at, keeping back the truth
whose feared sharing is anger's
dissolver?

8th Ode for Iris—Midnight—Sun-Mon 20 July 1970

People seem automata
often, as we see them live,
seemingly unconsciously,
machinelike

repetitions of the past.
Growing up: growing aware?
How rare the action taken
consciously!

What will be the use of all
those ignorant shared years if
we can't guide our actions by
what we've learned?

"Knowing better sometimes helps,"
(pleads Socrates' pale stand-in),
but what we know better is
each other

& each self relating to
the other: specific stuff:
realtime information, live
uniqueness.

51st Ode for Iris—10:05 AM Wed 29 July 1970

Ailanthus altissima!
The tree's sheer persistence awes!
The way it uses niches
others can't!

Chinese tree — Tree of Heaven —
irresistibly spreading
wherever soil offers it
a roothold!

Man sees his image in it,
&, negative Narcissus,
roots out this tree that can live
anywhere,

at least, in New York City,
where most trees wilt & wither
in the toxic atmosphere,
but this thrives,

nourished by affinities
too mighty for man's mischief,
more than momentarily,
to obstruct.

112th Ode for Iris—1:30 PM Sun 31 Oct 71

Am I in love with someone
who now no longer exists
Are you so different now
that I'm wrong

when I think I still love you
even though our bodies don't
seem to love each other much
anymore

When I saw you in the crowd
warming up for Meredith's
Vessel in the parking lot
what I felt

seemed to be love   It was love
But was it Love for You Now
or love for you as you were
long ago

when a mysterious force
kept drawing us together
and we nearly drowned in each
other's eyes

114th Ode for Iris—12:10 PM Mon 1 Nov 71

Every morning I wake up
crying since you went away
You'll say   This is just what you
used to do

That's one reason I left you
Couldn't stand your morning gloom
If you didn't wake up sad
you woke mad

Yes   Iris   I'm like that
You're better off free of me
I sit around all morning
feeling sad

missing you and the children
happy for the month in Maine
I ought to be happy if
I love you

since you're doing what you want
being yourself   not a wife
living downtown where your friends
are near you

Selected Later Light Poems 1971–1979

32nd Light Poem: *In Memoriam* Paul Blackburn— 9–10 October 1971

Let me choose the kinds of light
to light the passing of my friend
Paul Blackburn   a poet

A pale light like that of a winter dawn
or twilight
or phosphorescence

is not enough to guide him in his passing
but enough for us to see
shadowily his last gaunt figure

how he showed himself to us
last July in Michigan
when he made us think he was recovering

knowing the carcinoma
arrested in his esophagus
had already spread to his bones

How he led us on
I spent so little time with him
thinking he'd be with us now

Amber light of regret
stains my memories of our days
at the poetry festival in Allendale Michigan

How many times I hurried elsewhere
rather than spending time with him
in his room 3 doors from me

I will regret it the rest of my life
I must learn to live

with the regret

dwelling on the moments
Paul & I shared
in July as in years before

tho amber light dim to umber
& I can hardly see
his brave emaciated face

I see Paul standing in the umber light
cast on his existence
by his knowing that his death was fast approaching

Lightning blasts the guilty dream
& I see him
reading in the little auditorium

& hear him
confidently reading
careful of his timing

anxious not to take
more than his share of reading time
filling our hearts with rejoicing

seeing him alive
doing the work he was here for
seemingly among us now

I for one was fooled
thinking he was winning the battle
so I wept that night for joy

As I embraced him after he read
I shook with relief & love
I was so happy to hear you read again

If there were a kind of black light
that suddenly cd reveal to us

each other's inwardness

what wd I have seen that night
as I embraced you
with tears of joy

I keep remembering the bolt of lightning
that slashed the sky at twilight
over the Gulf of St. Lawrence

& turned an enchanted walk with Bici
following Angus Willie's Brook
thru mossy woods nearly to its mouth

to a boot-filling scramble up thru thorn bush & spruce tangle
Beatrice guided me & I was safe
at the end of August on Cape Breton Island

but when Jerry telephoned me of your death
the lightning that destroyed
the illusion you were safe

led thru dreadful amber light
not to friendly car light
& welcoming kitchen light

but to black light of absence
not ultraviolet light
revealing hidden colors

but revelatory light that is *no* light
the unending light of the realization
that no light will ever light your bodily presence again

Now your poems' light is all
The unending light of your presence
in the living light of your voice

12:33 AM Sun 10 Oct 1971
The Bronx

36th Light Poem: *In Memoriam* Buster Keaton—
4:50-6:18 A.M. Sat 1 Jan. 1972

1

As a Mad Scientist
Buster lights a Bunsen-burner flame
that starts a series of processes
that eventually releases The Monster

As an Undertaker
Buster lights a Bunsen-burner flame
that starts a series of processes
that awakens a drunk who was about to be buried as a corpse

As a Muscovite
Buster lights a sisal wick in a sesame-seed-oil lamp
that suddenly lights a mystical orgy
officiated over by Rasputin

As a Boater
Buster beats a cascade by floating out beyond its edge
borne by a balloon
lit by a wintry sun

As an Unwilling Passenger on a Drifting Liner
Buster the Millionaire & his rich Girl Friend
learn to cope Alone Without Servants
when forced to rely on the light of their Upper-Class Intellects

As a Worker
Buster arouses the Compassion of the Nation
in whose light the Corporations
sell themselves to their Workers

As a Key Man
Buster carries around with him
an enormous bunch of keys
lighting his way with a Keats lamp

As a Beatnik
Buster meditates in a Redwood forest
seated where the Selenic light
first falls at Moonrise

As a Leaf-&-Feather Gatherer
Buster Means Well but bugs everyone in the Park
spearing the ladies' hats & the picknickers' salads
in featureless Hollywood Light of the century's first quarter

As William Butler Yeats
Buster addresses an irate Irish crowd
that thinks that Poetry makes Nothing Happen
but lets itself be bathed by its Truthful Light

As a Cannoneer
Buster explodes his own ship's magazine
treads water in Gunpowder Light at a safe distance
& blushes in embarrassment at his Clumsiness

As a Violinist
Buster surpasses Paganini
until Boston-Concert-Hall Light
Poisons him with Love for a Proper Bostonian Maiden

2

Spirit of Buster Keaton
if you survive as yourself
receive Please our honor & praise
you conscientious Workman

Hard-working Buster Keaton
when you arouse the laughter of children
as you live in Projector Light
Your Karmic Residue dissolves in Joyous Shouts

56th Light Poem: For Gretchen Berger—
29 November 1978

From Gretchen's "G" I get a green light. I go ahead.
The first Light Poem in nearly a year — I hope it really *is* the
    56th.
If there's another in some notebook or file folder,
it's the one that's going to get its number changed, not this
    one
This is the 56th Light Poem, & I'm 56 years old.
I *was* 56 September 12th. Time has passed. I'm older now.

I sit at the back of the loft, typing on a little low table,
since it's too cold to type at my desk by the middle west window
       whose cracks I stuffed with Mortite caulking yesterday.
It'll be warmer, I hope, after Mordecai covers that window with
    plastic.
Until then I'll type out here, surrounded by papers, dictionaries,
file folders, notebooks, Coronamatic cartridges.
Is this the word "Coronamatic"'s first appearance in verse?

Would Eliot've allowed "Coronamatic" in his verse?
If so, under what circumstances?
Would he only have written it ironically or satirically?
Can you imagine "Coronamatic"
in one of the *Four Quartets?*
Can you guess how Eliot crept into this Light Poem at this point?

Relucence of the *Four Quartets* illuminates this verse
because I reread most of the group the other day.
A reviewer of Helen Gardner's new book on them mentions a line
dropped from the New York edition—probably through printer's
       error—
that Gardner's recovered—which shows some critics are useful,
It's the real 20th line of "Little Gidding."

He begins: "Midwinter spring is its own season
Sempiternal though sodden towards sundown,/Suspended in time, . . .
. . . the hedgerow/Is blanched for an hour with transitory blossom

Of snow, a bloom more sudden
Than that of summer, neither budding nor fading,
Not in the scheme of generation."

Then that first strophe ends with *three* lines, not two.
Where was the middle line lost—here or in London or between?
Did someone who thought it useless drop it on purpose?
"Where is the summer, the unimaginable
Summer beyond sense, the inapprehensible
Zero summer?"

Could Eliot have dropped that line on purpose
while he was correcting the New York proofs?
A major shift in meaning occurs from "the unimaginable
Summer beyond sense, the inapprehensible/Zero summer"
to "the unimaginable/Zero summer":
the words left out imply another view of the nature of things.

As if electric-arc light had replaced
"The brief sun" that "flames the ice, on ponds and ditches, . . .
Reflecting in a watery mirror
A glare that is blindness in the early afternoon"—
or tungsten light, the "glow more intense than blaze of branch,
    or brazier,"
that "Stirs the dumb spirit: no wind, but pentecostal fire"!

Why do I care so much that Eliot's line was left out
when a chart & two random digits lead to the light of a clutch lamp
"(an arc-lamp in which the upper carbon
is adjusted automatically by a clutch)"—
fortuitously connecting with the "electric-arc light" above,
though there could've been an absolute disconnection?

How much of the halcyon light of the poet's mind
was lost when someone working in electric-lamp light
forgot to set that line — & no one caught it?
Why do words implying an alien philosophy
move me more than—I was going to say "nova light"—
but how do I know how I'd feel if I saw a real nova—not just a photo?

The light of poetry's a baffling light.
It doesn't depend on what the poet thinks—or even what he feels!
That extra light that gave old Housman goose bumps
comes from somewhere beyond or underneath
thought or emotion or will or taste or sense:
a radiation only known through words.

That glow can be snuffed out
by burning a book or slitting a throat
or sleepily nodding in a stuffy composing room,
but coming from somewhere more arcane
than an exploding star whose light spans light-years,
it momently arcs a rainbow through existence.

29 November 1978
New York

57th Light Poem: For John Taggart— on & about & after the Ides, March 1979

A jewel-like light gleams at the end of a passage,
an orange light hazy through distance,
diffused through innumerable layers of air:
to those in hiding a horrible light,
to the children who hide in a house from the roaring
& the leaping light of flaming napalm,
to those who love the children who hide in a house from the roaring,
that tiny light no brighter than that of an alcohol lamp
but lacking all blueness,
that light glimmering forward down the hallway
toward the children
& those who love the children,
hiding in perfect stillness,
that light might as well
be burning incinder jell.

What if it were the glorious light
in which they might delight
to lift up their heads without effort to sing,
in which the children who hide in the house from the roaring
& the leaping light of flaming napalm
& those who love the children
might
delight
in lifting up their heads without effort to sing as a chorus,
the men & women holding hands with the children to go
forward as a chorus without burden?

What if that gemlike light were harbinger
of dancing & singing unburdened as the morning stars
amid the permutations of the bells?

Silent as curtains of aurora borealis
billowing high across northern skies
suffused with a shifting rose light,
an eerily transcendental light,
the jewel light approaches the children & women & men from the end
     of the shadowy passage.

Is it the light of an olive-oil lamp?

It is the only light in the hall,
unechoed by mirrors,
revealing no form.

To the children & women & men who love each other
hiding in perfect stillness at the hall's end
a pitiless noonlight approaches.

The night wind blows.

No form is revealed in the hall's growing twilight
to those standing hand in hand in hiding,
that loving chorus silent as an aurora.

In the gray light growing through the hallway air
no hands are revealed, no elbows & no face,

no torso & no legs; no feet are seen.

That gemlike light approaches in a dream of terror
those in hiding know they'll never awake from.

It blinds them like an arc light.

What is the good of standing hand in hand in perfect stillness
as radiance crushes forth toward their trapped light?

58th Light Poem: For Anne Tardos — 19 March 1979

I know when I've fallen in love   I start to write love songs
Love's actinism turns nineteens to words & thoughts in love songs
as your "A" & the date made "actinism" enter this love song

Also I seem to start dropping punctuation
My need for punctuation lessens   like some people's need for sleep
My need for sleep lessens too   but later I fall on my face
Lack of punctuation doesn't catch up with me like lack of sleep
It doesn't make me fall on my face

So bright the near noon light   the toy photometer twirls   in
the sunlight slanting in from southeast thru the southwest window
the stronger the light the faster the light motor turns
diamond vanes' black sides absorb   white sides radiate photons
See it go

A "42" draws the northern lights into the song
as yesterday into the Taggart Light Poem twice they were drawn
as "aurora borealis" & "aurora"   by "A"'s & by numbers
There they seemed eery & threatening   Here they seem hopeful
as they seemed when last I saw them   over the Gulf of St. Lawrence
cold   euphoric after making love   wondering
at swirling curtains & sudden billows lighting the sky northwest

I remember their evanescent light as neutral or bluish white
I remember the possibility of yellow   the improbability of red
not like Bearsville's rose & blood sky twenty-five years before
Now these memories mingled with pictures'   descriptions'
project on inward skies   idiosyncratic northern lights
that only exist while I'm writing these lines for Anne
Even the next time I read them the lights they arouse will be different

Nineteen sheds a tranquil light on our love song thru your "T"
Our love's tranquil light   revealed by 19 & by T
is turned by 15 to an aureole tipping an "A"
The "A" becomes your face The aureole grows

Relucence from my face glows back on yours

A telephone bell can deflect & dissipate my light
The deflected light is lost to poem & person
I turn my telephone off these days to help ordinary light breed poems

The sun is so bright on my desk now   except on the typewriter keys
that there's no need for the light of the student lamp placed to
        shine on the paper

But now   five hours later   the lamp's   the only light
& I begin the poem's   "astrological"   section

II

Acetylene light may be what Virgo needs to see the "pattern
except that for him this is something" he will
only acknowledge if it can be seen in natural light

Can we gain new light from astrology   that ubiquitous superstition
You Sagittarius Woman   Me Virgo Man
What "can happen between them is a" mazing
a dizzying   a stupefying or dazing   a crazing
a great perplexing   bewildering   amazing
forming a maze of something or making it intricate

231

being bewildered   wandering as in a maze
What has happened between them is amazing

What is happening between us is amazing
more intense & vivid than electric arc light   tremendous light
brighter than acetylene light   friendly as reading lamp light

"But a young Sagit-
tarian need have no qualms about taking on a
man considerably her senior if he is a Virgo"
Rand's random digits underline our case
in this lovely silly optimistic sentence

We've been living   I think   in a kind of drowning light

"He reaches the age of forty   At anything less than that age
he is not even a possible   for Sagittarius"
Me Virgo Man   You Sagittarius Woman
Orgone radiation flimmers between us
our curious safety light

"What can happen between them is   superb
Something he has spent half his life dreaming about
At last it has come true"   O ingratiating
astrological light may you never prove false
even to one who has often decried you as no light
but superstitious darkness natural light would dispel
or the electric arc light of empirical science

The way I'm writing this poem's like using
trichromatic artificial radiance
not as decorative light   in place of
ordinary solar radiation   as you photographers do

Before I was forty "not even a possible for Sagittarius"
now I'm sixteen over the line & safe with you

"Her   but a young Sagittarian need have" none   "qualms" have no
        basis
Are we dreaming   Is this Virgo Man still dreaming

as "he has spent half his life"   they say   "dreaming"

"Sagittarian & Virgo"
"The pattern is perfect"
The poem is over

19-20 March 1979
New York

Selected Gathas
Introduction to Selected Gathas
I. Description

The "Gathas" constitute an open-ended series of performance texts begun in 1961. The letters of their words are placed in the squares of quadrille ("graph") paper, and they are realized through spontaneous, but rule-guided, performers' choices, usually, but not always, made during performances.

The Sanskrit word *gatha,* "verse" or "hymn," was adopted for them, on analogy with its use to designate versified sections of Buddhist sutras and short poems by Zen masters and students, because I considered Gathas to be Buddhist performance texts. Chance operations were used in composing them in order to encourage performers and hearers to give "bare attention" to letter-sounds, words, etc. Also a Buddhist de-emphasis of the composer's ego underlies both using compositional chance operations and letting performers' choices determine many parameters of their realization. In addition, all Gathas made from 1961 to 1973—and many made later—are composed of chance-arranged transliterations of mantras, most of them Buddhist. However, beginning with *The Black Tarantula Crossword Gathas* in 1973, many Gathas have been composed of nonmantric English words. Both mantric and nonmantric Gathas appear in this book.

II. Performance Instructions

General instructions apply to all Gathas. *Specific instructions* apply only to individual Gathas or groups of them.

A. General Instructions

Gathas may be performed solo or by a group comprising any number of people. In both cases performers act as speakers, vocalists, and/or instrumentalists. Speakers should also function as vocalists but need not also be instrumentalists, though they may be. Instrumentalists *may* de-emphasize, or even exclude, speech and/or vocalism. However, when possible, performers should act alternately, or even simultaneously, as speaker-vocalists and as instrumentalists. Any proportion of primarily vocal performers to primarily instrumental ones is permissible.

Each performer starts at any square or group of adjacent squares, realizing the letter(s) there as speech, vocalism, and/or instrumental sound. (Specific rules for each are given below.) Each then moves, horizontally, vertically, or diagonally, to a square or squares adjacent to any side or vertex of the first, realizes the letter(s) there, and then continues indefinitely to move to squares adjacent to one another. Empty squares are realized as silences of any duration, during which the performer listens intently.

After thus "following a path" for a while the performer may "jump" to a nonadjacent square and begin a new path. When performing mantric Gathas, one *must* repeat the mantra once or several times before "jumping." In Vocabulary Gatha performances the name on which the Gatha is based *may* be spoken before a "jump."

234

Speaker-vocalists may say or sing any speech sounds or letter names the letters may stand for in any language; syllables, words, or pseudowords made up of letters in squares adjacent in any direction(s); or any kinds of word strings: phrases, clauses, sentences, or nonsyntactical strings made of words in adjacent groups of squares.

They may *prolong* vowels, liquids, and fricatives ad lib. or say or sing them or other speech sounds shortly. Each voiced speech sound may be spoken or sung either at a pitch freely chosen in relation with all other sounds present or at one of the pitches assigned to the letter for instrumentalists (see below). *Simultaneous* prolongations (intervals, chords, clusters) are encouraged, as is use of prolongations as "organ points" persisting under shorter sounds. Close attention to all aspects of harmony (consonance, dissonance, beats) and production of subtle harmonic changes are imperative.

Instrumentalists, and vocalists when they choose to, "translate" each letter as a tone, in any octave, or a specific pitch class (e.g., A = *any* A♮). Pitch classes corresponding to specific letters differ from Gatha to Gatha and will be given in the *specific instructions.*

Each performer should make an easily legible columnar list of letters and pitch-class equivalents for the Gatha being performed. The list should be placed beside the Gatha for easy reference during the performance, even if the equivalents have been memorized.

Performers freely choose octave placements of tones, groupings, tempi, rhythms, durations, timbres, dynamics (loudness), attacks, repetitions, etc., in relation with their perceptions of the total sound at each moment. Tones may be connected by glissandi as well as being played or vocalized discretely. On keyboards or other instruments capable of simultaneous tone production, groups of adjacent letters may be realized as intervals, chords, or clusters.

All performers may repeat speech sounds, letter names, words, phrases, or other strings and/or tones, chords, sequences, etc.; "*trill*" between adjacent squares or groups of them (alternately produce speech sounds, words, etc., or tones, etc., for which the letters stand); or "*make loops*" (follow the same path from square to square several times, producing the same sequence of speech units or tones each time).

Most important, *all performers* must continually listen attentively both to other performers and to all ambient sounds (audience and environment) and produce speech elements or tones *in relation with* all they hear. They should often "move" into empty squares, stopping and listening closely until they wish to add new speech units or tones to the situation. They must exercise sensitivity, tact, and courtesy so that every performance detail contributes significantly to the total sound sequence. Virtuosity without "ego-tripping" is strongly encouraged: it must be exercised in relation with the total situation. Performers should always be both inventive and sensitive. "*Listen*" and "*Relate*" are the most important "rules."

A performance may be begun and ended at any time within the limits set by the performance situation. Its duration may be set beforehand or eventuate spontaneously, and it may be begun and ended in any convenient way. For instance, a group-selected leader may signal the beginning and the group may spontaneously end by consensus, or a group-selected leader may signal both beginning and end, or the group may have no leader.

B. *Specific Instructions*
1. *Mani-Mani Gatha* (1975)
2. *Tara Gatha* (1975)
3. *1st Milarepa Gatha* (1976)
4. *1st Sharon Belle Mattlin Vocabulary Crossword Gatha* (1976)
5. *A Vocabulary Gatha for Pete Rose* (1978)
6. *Free Gatha 1* (1978)
7. *A Vocabulary Gatha for Anne Tardos* (1980)

This selection is limited to Gathas composed after 1974, since these were drawn on black-lined quadrille paper, whereas earlier Gathas were usually drawn on quadrille paper with blue lines difficult to reproduce in black and white.

1. The *Mani-Mani Gatha* is based on AUM MANI PADME HUM (pronounced in Sanskrit "Ohm Mahnee Pudmay Hoōm," and in Tibetan "Um Mahnee Paymay Hoōng"), the mantra of the Boddhisattva Avalokiteshvara, the Great Compassionate One. He "personifies the tremendous force of compassion impartially bestowed on all sentient beings alike" (John Blofeld). In Tibet he is called Chenrezig ("Chenrayzee"), and in China and Japan has a female form named Kuan Yin or Kannon.

AUM embodies the indwelling principle of all being — the Tao. MANI PADME means "the jewel in the lotus," signifying the eternal in the temporal, the Buddha within each sentient being. HUM is "limitless reality embodied within the limits of individual being" (Blofeld). The "Mani" is the most widely intoned mantra in Tibet and other Buddhist countries.

While several Mani Gathas were composed from 1961 through 1975, the *Mani-Mani Gatha* is the only one in which the mantra itself (rather than a series of A's, U's, and M's) is lettered as a horizontal "axis." Through chance operations one transliteration was placed horizontally on the quadrille paper and eighteen vertical transliterations were so placed that they variously cross this axis.

The whole mantra or individual mantra words may be spoken as pronounced either in Sanskrit or in Tibetan. The whole mantra should be intoned two or more times before each jump to a new path, as well as at the beginning. When not spoken as mantra words, the letters may be pronounced or named as in any language.

236

The letters must be "translated" by instrumentalists, and may be by vocalists, as tones of the following pitch classes:

A = A♮	E = E♮	I = D♭/C♯	N = C♮
D = D♮	H = B♮	M = G♮	P = F♮

2. This *Tara Gatha* is one of several Gathas based upon OM TARE TUTTARE TURE SWAHA (pronounced "Ohm Tahray Toottahray Tooray Swah-hah"), the fundamental mantra of the Goddess-Boddhisattva Tara, an emanation of Avalokiteshvara and analogous to his Far Eastern female form, Kuan Yin or Kannon. Like him she personifies compassion, and she is preeminently a helper of sentient beings. There are over twenty subsidiary Tara mantras chanted to help or protect people in specific situations. This basic mantra is the one addressed to Tara's fundamental form, the Green Tara (popularly called "The Green Goddess").

In all the Tara Gathas, vertical transliterations of the mantra were placed through chance operations so they crossed an axis comprising a series of A's, U's, and M's — an extended AUM (OM). (Most mantric Gathas before 1975 have such an "OM-axis.") In this one, 25 vertical transliterations cross even A's, eight U's, and ten M's.

When the whole mantra is intoned, as at the beginning and at jumps, or individual mantra words are spoken, they are pronounced as above. Otherwise, the letters may be pronounced or named as in any language.

The letters *must* be "translated" by instrumentalists, and *may* be "translated" by vocalists, as tones of the following pitch classes:

A = A♮	H = B♮	O = G♭/F♯	S = E♭/D♯	U = C♮
E = E♮	M = G♮	R = A♭/G♯	T = D♮	W = F♮

3. The *1st Milarepa Gatha* is the first of several Gathas based upon JE MILA ZHÄPA DORJE LA SÖLWA DEBSO (pronounced "Jay Meelah Zhäpha Dorjay Lah Sölwa Debsoh"—"zh" is like the French "j"; "ä" and "ö" as in German: short "e" with rounded lips, and "er" without the "r" and with rounded lips). This is the mantra addressed to the historical Tibetan Boddhisattva and poet Milarepa (1040 or 1052 to 1123 or 1135 CE), one of the most important figures of Tibetan Buddhism. His *Hundred Thousand Songs* have been sung and studied for over eight centuries, and constitute "perhaps the most outstanding masterpiece of Tibetan literature" (Garma C. C. Chang).

In this Gatha, 34 vertical transliterations of the mantra, one in each column, were lettered on the quadrille paper, each beginning in one of the ten upper rows of squares, as determined by chance operations with random digits. Unlike most other mantric Gathas, this one has no horizontal "axis."

When one speaks the whole mantra (as at the beginning or at jumps) or mantra words, they are pronounced as in Tibetan (see above). Otherwise, performers are free to sound or name letters, or speak words or pseudowords constituted by letters adjacent in any directions, as in any language.

Instrumentalists must, and vocalists may, "translate" the letters as tones of the following pitch classes:

A & Ä = A♮   E = E♮   J = G♯ O & Ö = G♭/F♯ S = E♭/D♯
  B = B♭/A♯   H = B♮   L = F♮   P = B♭/A♯   W = A♭/G♯
  D = D♮   I = D♭/C♯   M = G♮   R = A♭/G♯   Z = C♮

Speaker-vocalists need not "translate" the letters: they may choose pitches spontaneously as they perform.

4. The *1st Sharon Belle Mattlin Vocabulary Crossword Gatha*, made for and from the name of a friend who is a poet, performer, and sound engineer, was the first work that combined the compositional and performance principles of the Gatha with those of the Vocabulary. The first of this "genre" of performance work was *A Vocabulary for Carl Fernbach-Flarsheim* (1968). Each Vocabulary is a hand-lettered or typed array of words spelled solely with the letters in one name, word, or phrase; within any single word a letter is repeated at most only as many times as it is within the whole name, etc. Instructions, including letter–pitch class "translations," are given for realizing Vocabularies as performances.

The words in a Vocabulary Gatha are drawn by chance operations either from a previously composed Vocabulary (as with the present example) or from a previously compiled word list. Chance operations and limiting rules determine placement of letters on quadrille paper.

In this Gatha the words were drawn from *A Vocabulary for Sharon Belle Mattlin* (1973) and limited to running diagonally, up or down, from left to right, and to being separated from each other by one or more spaces.

Speaker-vocalists treat letters and words as they would those in mantric Gathas, but since most of the words are English (a few are names or foreign words), opportunities for grouping them into phrases, sentences, or other strings are multiplied.

Instrumentalists must, and vocalists may, "translate" the letters as tones of the following pitch classes:

A = A♮   H = B♮   M = G♮   R = A♭/G♯
B = B♭/A♯   I = D♭/C♯   N = C♮   S = E♭/D♯
E = E♮   L = F♮   O = G♭/F♯   T = D♮

Speaker-vocalists may choose their pitches spontaneously rather than "translating" the letters.

5. *A Vocabulary Gatha for Pete Rose* was made for and from the name of the virtuoso recorderist and composer Pete Rose, of Maplewood, New Jersey, who only plays contemporary music. Words were drawn from a previously compiled list and placed on the quadrille paper through I Ching chance operations involving 50 yarrow stalks (rather than three coins). They are limited to running horizontally, or diagonally up or down, from left to right, or vertically down. They seldom cross.

Instrumentalists must, and speaker-vocalists may, "translate" the letters (which together can spell the Greek word *petros*, "stone") as tones of the following pitch classes:

E = E♮ or E♭/D♯	P = B♮ or B♭/A♯	S = C♮ or F♮
O = G♮ or G♭/F♯	R = A♮ or A♭/G♯	T = D♮ or D♭/C♯

Speaker-vocalists may choose pitches spontaneously rather than "translating" the letters.

6. *Free Gatha 1* is the first Gatha composed without the aid of chance operations. Words and names were chosen and placed spontaneously and rapidly and were limited to running horizontally, or diagonally up or down, from left to right, or vertically down. Accidentally formed "portmanteau words" ("FRANKINCEST," "POETREE") were accepted, as were a few abbreviations and nonwords formed fortuitously at crossings.

Instrumentalists must, and speaker-vocalists may, "translate" the letters as tones of the following pitch classes:

A = A♮	F = F♮	L = F♮	R = A♭/G♯	W = A♭/G♯
B = B♭/A♯	G = G♮	M = G♮	S = E♭/D♯	Y = B♭/A♯
C = C♮	H = B♮	N = C♮	T = D♮	
D = D♮	I = D♭/C♯	O = G♭/F♯	U = A♮	
E = E♮	K = D♭/C♯	P = B♮	V = G♭/F♯	

Speaker-vocalists may choose tones spontaneously rather than "translating" letters.

7. *A Vocabulary Gatha for Anne Tardos* was composed for and from the name of my friend who is a composer, film maker, video and performance artist, and frequent coperformer with me. The words were drawn from a previously compiled list and placed on quadrille paper by chance operations involving random-digit couplets. The words are limited to running horizontally, or diagonally up or down, from left to right, or vertically down. Crossings were allowed only when words formed at them were either English words or names.

Instrumentalists must, and speaker-vocalists may, "translate" the letters as tones of the following pitch classes:

A = A♮	E = E♮	O = G♭/F♯	S = E♭/D♯
D = D♮	N = C♮	R = A♭/G♯	T = B♮

Speaker-vocalists may choose pitches spontaneously rather than "translating" the letters.

Final version completed
7 May 1985
New York

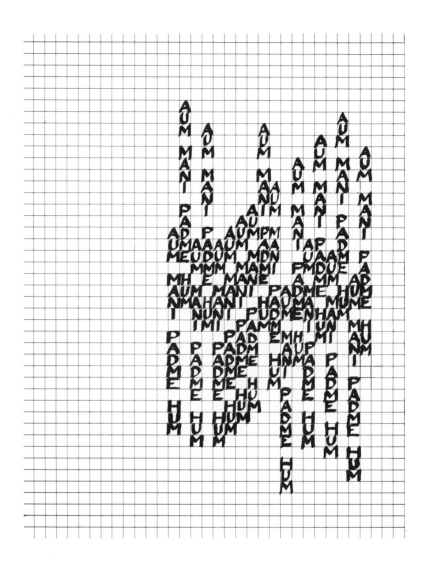

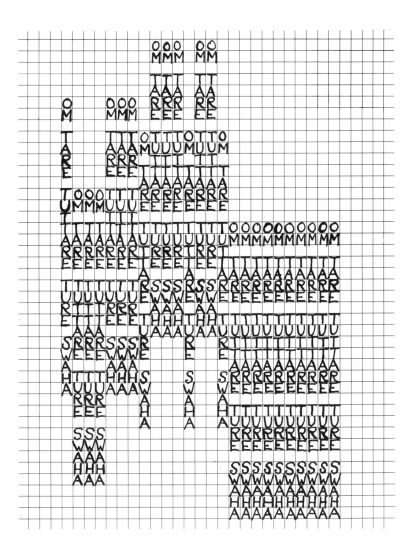

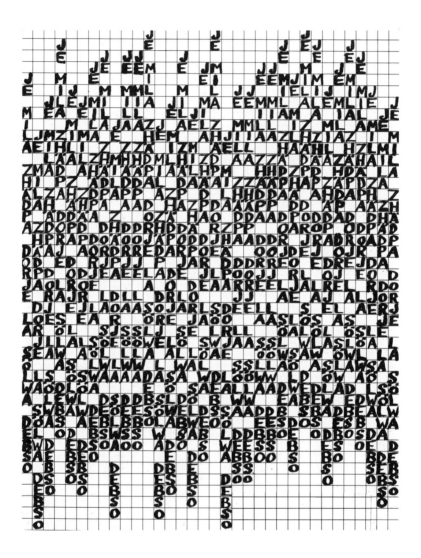

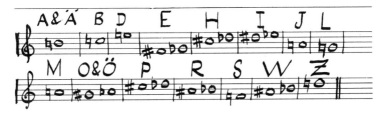

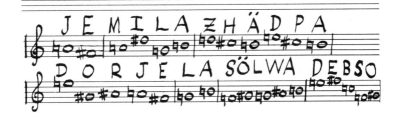

The clarinetist begins at any square of the "1st Milarepa Gatha" and plays (in any octave) a tone of the pitch class "translating" the letter in that square, then "moves" to one of the eight squares adjacent to the sides and corners of the first square and "translates" the letter there, "moves" again and so on, sometimes "skipping" to a new "path." Attacks, note durations, rests, rhythms, and dynamics, as well as octave placements, are to be chosen freely, but in accord with everything audible. Silences are often to be observed. The clarinetist may play either or both "tenor" and bass clarinets and may also function as a speaker and/or a singer (see the main instructions for the Gatha's performance). "Listen" and "Relate."

1st Sharon Belle Mattlin Vocabulary Crossword Gatha
1976

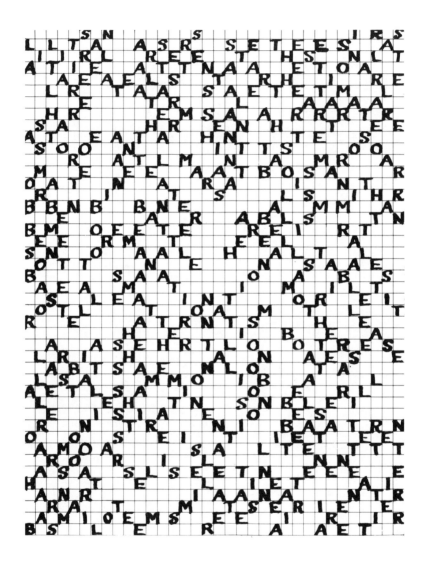

A Vocabulary Gatha for Pete Rose

1978

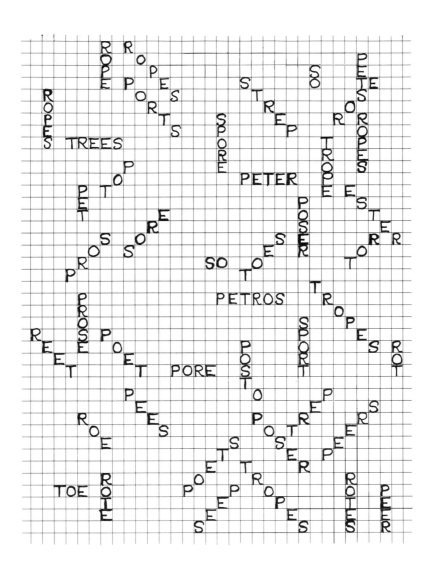

245

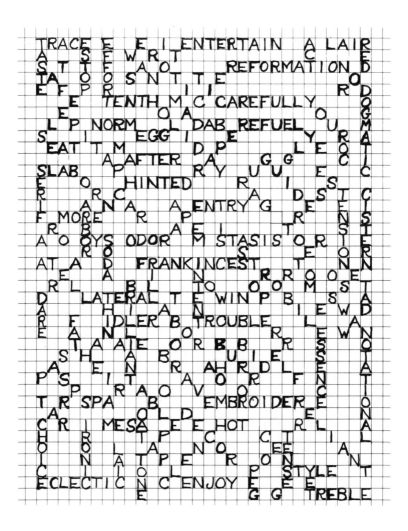

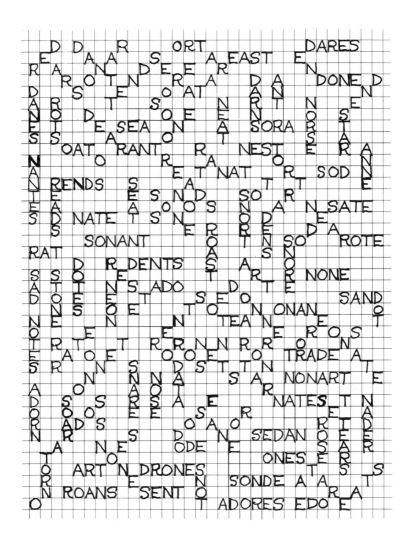

1st Mishima Poem

from the English translation of Yukio Mishima's novel *The Temple of the Golden Pavilion* (Berkeley ed., pp. 56–85)

The summer grass
grew in thick clusters
in front of the
pond.

grass by a low
fence.

lay a young boy
in a white shirt.

leaned nearby
against a low maple.

"oh,
it's you,
is it?"

was
affluently provided
quickly turned his eyes
boyish process of reasoning,
Zen sect.

Since
it
was summertime,
"auxiliary duties."

paper
arrived every day
damp
from the
mopping,

hollows in the floor
boards,
Zen problem
that he had chosen
was
"Nansen
Kills a Cat"
from the
Fourteenth
Case of the
Mumonkan.

Sixty-
Third
Case
of the
Hekiganroka
under the title
"Nansen
Kills a
Kitten"
and in the
Sixty-
Fourth
Case
under the title
"Jeshu
Wears
a
Pair of
Sandals on
His
Head"
has been
noted since ancient times
as one of the most difficult
Zen
problems.

18 August 1973
The Bronx

"I Had Chosen a Rose"

(translation of melody with this title via its notation & a list drawn from my "1st Mishima Poem": the melody is from the *Locheimer Liederbuch,* a 15th-century German collection. Source: Erich Katz, *Recorder Playing,* New York: Clarke & Way, 1951, p. 53)


```
THAT
BOARDS FLOOR MOPPING BOARDS
FLOOR DAMP PAPER EVERY
DAY DAMP EVERY AUXILIARY SUMMERTIME AUXILIARY SECT
SUMMERTIME FLOOR
BOARDS FLOOR MOPPING BOARDS
FLOOR DAMP PAPER EVERY
DAY EVERY PAPER AUXILIARY SUMMERTIME AUXILIARY SECT

THAT
HAD HAD CHOSEN HAD
THAT FLOOR DAMP
THAT FLOOR MOPPING DAMP EVERY DAY
EVERY THAT
HAD HAD CHOSEN HAD
THAT FLOOR DAMP
THAT FLOOR MOPPING DAMP DAY

SUMMERTIME SUMMERTIME
EVERY AUXILIARY MOPPING DAMP
EVERY DAY DAMP DAY EVERY
DAY FLOOR
DAMP BOARDS FLOOR EVERY PAPER AUXILIARY PAPER DAMP
FLOOR DAMP AUXILIARY DAY PAPER EVERY SECT
SUMMERTIME
```

18–19 August 1973
The Bronx

Phoneme Dance for/from John Cage
(A Word Event for John Cage) 9/28/74

(Pronounce each letter separately—no diphthongization—& with the following qualities: "a" as in "day"; "o" as in "hot"; "j" as in "joy"; "k" as in "kite"; "n" as in "tin". Use relative sizes of spaces to regulate durations of silence between phoneme groups. Read carefully & as slowly as comfortable; let a lot of time go by for vertical spaces.)

```
kjokno        oajnokjk      j           nnajkook      nak         aajnokj
         oaonnjjnj          a      nananajko     na         onna  oknoa
nn       n        kn            jonnon     annjj                   kok
     aknjjkokna     jjja            aajaoj            jkaaknoon
     aka          nkjkjk   jjnanao nlkkanojoa        ooj    aonjn




         jajoa  o   jjnoo       k     jaak          oknoaonn
         jnakoonoo         o        jkjj            onnko
         aknno          no    nkokajj      oojkja       njon




         n  okjkkojnj     n          jnojkonj      akonojnj
n          ako nnjnaoo            annoo         akaaooaa




     kjon           oajaa      njnkokjkkn         a   ajoaj
njoan           j    oojn      o    knjjknkj          ko
     oaknajnnj       akjjjnn         aojknkj  oaakn      nn
```

251

In Praise of Alma Walter

the history
of mountain climbing!

when
he suddenly lost his
footing and plunged
into a deep crevice.

the girl to cut the
rope to save herself,
most amazing
rescue in the history
of mountain climbing!

roped to a guide
named Zippert,
lost his
footing and plunged
into a deep crevice.

most amazing
rescue in the history
of mountain climbing!

Alma Walter,
amazing
rescue in the history
of mountain climbing!

Peak,
amazing
rescue in the history
of mountain climbing!

Bernina Peak,
suddenly lost his
footing and plunged
into a deep crevice.

— although the rope she
had wound around
her arm cut through
to the bone!

rescue in the history
of mountain climbing!

Bernina Peak,
lost his
footing and plunged
into a deep crevice.

rescue in the history
of mountain climbing!

through
to the bone!

rescue in the history
of mountain climbing!

into a deep crevice.

an
hour until other
climbers arrived
— the rope she
had wound around
her arm cut through
to the bone!

the history
of mountain climbing!

when
he suddenly lost his
footing and plunged
into a deep crevice.

herself,
his weight for an
hour until other
climbers arrived
—history
of mountain climbing!

Walter,
supported
his weight for an
hour until other
climbers arrived
—history
of mountain climbing!

history
of mountain climbing!

other
climbers arrived
—of mountain climbing!

mountain climbing!

roped to a guide
named Zippert,
plunged
into a deep crevice.

wound around
her arm cut through
to the bone!

mountain climbing!

mountain climbing!

mountain climbing!

mountain climbing!

climbing Switzerland's
12,840-ft. Bernina Peak,
plunged
into a deep crevice.

weight for an
hour until other
climbers arrived
—climbing!

climbing Switzerland's
12,840-ft. Bernina Peak,
climbing!

climbing Switzerland's
12,840-ft. Bernina Peak,
climbing!

Alma Walter,
climbing Switzerland's
12,840-ft. Bernina Peak,
named Zippert,
Alma Walter,
waitress,
was
climbing Switzerland's
12,840-ft. Bernina Peak,
Walter,
waitress,
Zippert,
Zippert shouted to
the girl to cut the
rope to save herself,
an
hour until other
climbers arrived
—wound around
her arm cut through
to the bone!

253

Walter,
waitress,
Switzerland's
12,840-ft. Bernina Peak,
other
climbers arrived
—rescue in the history
of mountain climbing!

waitress,
climbers arrived
—wound around
her arm cut through
to the bone!

Walter,
was
climbing Switzerland's
12,840-ft. Bernina Peak,
crevice.

climbers arrived
—climbing!

climbing Switzerland's
12,840-ft. Bernina Peak,
climbers arrived
—climbing!

climbing Switzerland's
12,840-ft. Bernina Peak,
climbing!

Switzerland's
12,840-ft. Bernina Peak,
Switzerland's
12,840-ft. Bernina Peak,
guide
named Zippert,
lost his
footing and plunged
into a deep crevice.

Switzerland's
12,840-ft. Bernina Peak,
plunged
into a deep crevice.

climbers arrived
—Switzerland's
12,840-ft. Bernina Peak,
Switzerland's
12,840-ft. Bernina Peak,
Switzerland's
12,840-ft. Bernina Peak,
Switzerland's
12,840-ft. Bernina Peak,
Switzerland's
12,840-ft. Bernina Peak,
12,840-ft. Bernina Peak,
12,840-ft. Bernina Peak,
12,840-ft. Bernina Peak,
12,840-ft. Bernina Peak,
12,840-ft. Bernina Peak,
12,840-ft. Bernina Peak,
Zippert,
but she supported
his weight for an
hour until other
climbers arrived
—her arm cut through
to the bone!

Bernina Peak,
when
he suddenly lost his
footing and plunged
into a deep crevice.

amazing
rescue in the history
of mountain climbing!

Bernina Peak,
Bernina Peak,
plunged
into a deep crevice.

herself,
amazing
rescue in the history
of mountain climbing!

Peak,
roped to a guide
named Zippert,
lost his
footing and plunged
into a deep crevice.

Zippert shouted to
the girl to cut the
rope to save herself,
other
climbers arrived
— wound around
her arm cut through
to the bone!

The most amazing
rescue in the history
of mountain climbing!

From "Ripley's Believe It or Not" in colored comic section of the Chicago *Tribune*.

13–14 October 1974
Tides Motel, Chicago

Homage to Leona Bleiweiss

For many years Leona Bleiweiss published a word game in the New York *Post* called "Word Power." In each day's column she gave a word & its definition & the rules of the game: "From the above word or phrase make as many five-letter words as possible, using only one form of a word—for example, 'swing' or 'swung,' not both. Don't make a word by adding 's' to a word of four letters. Slang, proper names, foreign words not allowed." This game has been a great inspiration to me, tho I've often violated her rules. It led first to the play *Port-au-Prince* (one of my *Twin Plays,* written & mimeographed by me in 1963, & published by the Something Else Press in 1966), which used an extension of one of her lists for all its words, & later to my *Vocabularies* (1968 et seq.), which are drawings composed of words of all types & lengths, each spelled with the letters of one person's name, as well as to several stanzaic poems & others using only words from her lists or connecting such words in sentences. The present work is therefore an *Homage to Leona Bleiweiss.*

Each section of this work was derived from one of her solution lists. The note-groups were generated by substituting the proper notes for letters that are English or German pitch names & substituting notes whose pitch-name letters aren't in the word for other letters — doing so by chance operations or by other methods.

Performance Instructions

Performers: Any number of performers may play *Homage to Leona Bleiweiss.* Each must be able to play or sing exactly, at concert pitch, the tones of the word-note groups constituting each section, to speak the words clearly, to improvise together with the others, using the tones in various octaves, rhythms, etc., as well as to follow instructions in regard to silences.

Timekeeper & Performance Duration: One performer acts solely as a timekeeper, holding up large numbers showing the elapsed minutes of a section from "0" to the maximum number agreed on for that section's performance. The timekeeper will clearly indicate the end of the section performance by raising one hand a minute before the end & bringing it down at the end of that minute. In some performances, a playing performer may act as the group "leader" & determine the actual end sometime near an agreed-upon time. If so, that performer will raise one hand & bring it down within a minute later, & the timekeeper will raise & lower his or her hand at the same time as the group "leader."

Materials: Each performer is provided with a "score" of each section played (a page with a list of words from a "Word Power" column, together with the note groups corresponding to the words) & a deck of playing cards. Each player's "part" consists of alternate segments of silence & of improvisation using only the notes of the note groups & the spoken words. Both are regulated by the playing cards.

Silences: The first, 3rd, 5th, etc., cards drawn from the shuffled deck determine minimal durations of silence, beginning with an initial silence that starts when the timekeeper shows the "0." Numbered cards (2's to 10's) indicate silences of those numbers of seconds (these may be measured by counting slowly "one one thousand, two one thousand," etc., or with a watch). Jacks = 11 sec. Queens = 12 sec. Kings = 13 sec. Jokers = 14 sec. Aces = 15 sec. By *"minimal* silences" I mean that any silence may be *longer* than the number of seconds indicated by the card, but *not shorter.* The mechanics of shuffling & drawing cards shd not draw attention to itself, but need not be carried out hurriedly. Performers shd use their silent segments to listen carefully & decide how & when to enter next. Silences shd be prolonged past their minimal durations whenever performers feel that they & the total situation are not ready for the addition of improvisation on their next word-note groups.

Durations of Improvisations on Word-Note Groups: Altho each performer will probably not be able to work with all the word-note groups of a section, she or he shd try to do so with a fair number of them, so each improvisation segment shd not last too long in relation to the total duration of a section. Two minutes for each word-note group is a good average duration, but this may be exceeded when a performer feels that the quality of what is happening warrants more time. Improvisation segments shd rarely exceed 3 minutes each.

Use of Word-Note Groups: The performer uses the 2nd, 4th, 6th, etc., cards drawn to determine which word-note groups shd be used as bases for improvisation. The word-note groups are keyed to playing-card denominations. In section 2 the 18 groups are keyed to color also: red Ace to 9 & black Ace to 9. Jokers & all other denominations not having corresponding groups (e.g., 10's & picture cards in

#2 & Kings in #4) are "wild": performers are free to *choose* the word-note group to work with or to draw another card.

The sequence of notes must be followed exactly, but may be repeated any number of times. Each note may be played in any octave, & a variety of octave placements is desirable in each improvisation segment. Two or more consecutive notes, or the whole sequence, may be played simultaneously. The individual character of the sequence is best preserved by playing notes to the right at a higher pitch than those to the left, but this need not always be done, & groups may sometimes be played as tone clusters. Also, the performer may repeat a tone of a note group, double it in two or more octaves, repeat adjacent notes of a group alternately ("trills"), & may repeat chords, intervals, or tone clusters as well as single tones.

Use of Words: During improvisation on one note group, the word from which it was derived shd be spoken at least once or repeated any number of times. This may be done more than once during the segment. Words shd be spoken clearly & audibly, but not yelled (altho loud speech may sometimes be needed for audibility—the point is not to give the effect of violent feelings even tho the speech is loud).

Rhythm & Other Parameters: Octave placement, rhythms, loudnesses, attacks, tempi, & all other parameters relating to use of the notes & words are to be chosen freely by the performers in relation to the total situation. *It cannot be emphasized too strongly that performers shd relate with & respond to each other & all ambient sounds,* including audience sounds. The most important rules to remember in performing this piece are *"Listen"* & *"Relate."*

March–June 1976
New York

#1—Quadrumanous

Definition—Belonging to the order of Quadrumana: four-handed.

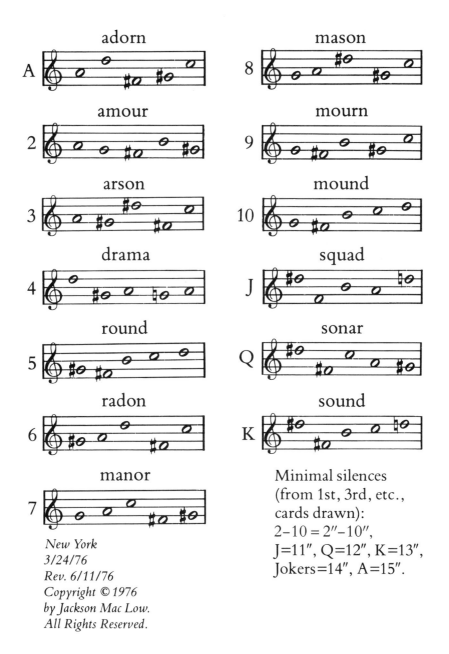

New York
3/24/76
Rev. 6/11/76
Copyright © 1976
by Jackson Mac Low.
All Rights Reserved.

Minimal silences
(from 1st, 3rd, etc.,
cards drawn):
2–10 = 2″–10″,
J=11″, Q=12″, K=13″,
Jokers=14″, A=15″.

#2—Clypeiform

Definition—Having the form of a round shield.

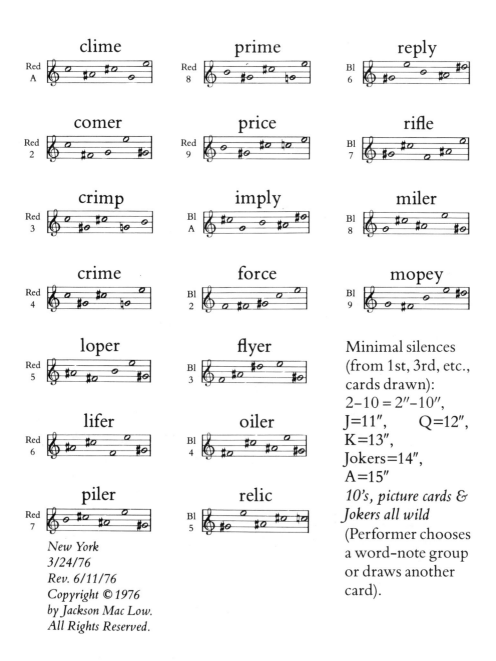

Minimal silences (from 1st, 3rd, etc., cards drawn):
2–10 = 2″–10″, J=11″, Q=12″, K=13″, Jokers=14″, A=15″

10's, picture cards & Jokers all wild (Performer chooses a word–note group or draws another card).

New York
3/24/76
Rev. 6/11/76
Copyright © 1976
by Jackson Mac Low.
All Rights Reserved.

#3—Ambiguities

Definition—Multiple or dubious significations.

ambit
A

amuse
2

abuse
3

baste
4

beast
5

imbue
6

guise
7

guest
8

tibia
9

stage
10

suite
J

smite
Q

saute
K

New York
6/11/76
Copyright © 1976
by Jackson Mac Low.
All Rights Reserved.

Minimal silences
(from 1st, 3rd, 5th, etc.,
cards drawn):
2–10 = 2″–10″,
J=11″, Q=12″, K=13″,
Jokers=14″, A=15″

#4—Sluggishness

Definition—Laziness; inactivity.

New York
March to 12 June 1976
Copyright © 1976
by Jackson Mac Low.
All Rights Reserved.

Kings & Jokers are wild.
Minimal silences
(from 1st, 3rd, 5th, etc.,
cards drawn):
2–10 = 2″–10″,
J = 11″, Q = 12″,
K = 13″, Joker = 14″,
A = 15″.

#5 — Repeopled

Definition — Furnished with a fresh population.

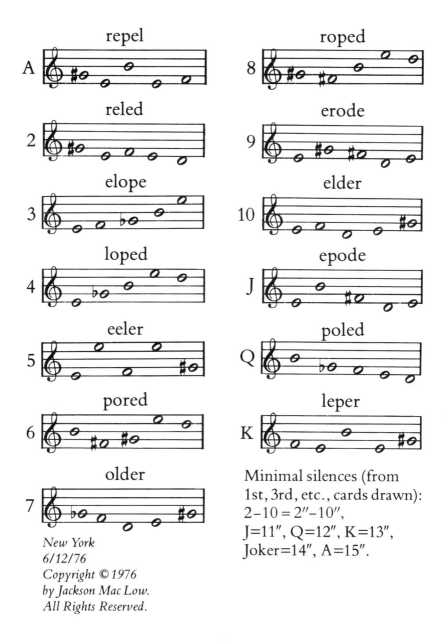

repel — A
reled — 2
elope — 3
loped — 4
eeler — 5
pored — 6
older — 7

roped — 8
erode — 9
elder — 10
epode — J
poled — Q
leper — K

New York
6/12/76
Copyright © 1976
by Jackson Mac Low.
All Rights Reserved.

Minimal silences (from
1st, 3rd, etc., cards drawn):
2–10 = 2″–10″,
J=11″, Q=12″, K=13″,
Joker=14″, A=15″.

phone

a poem & 10 variations

(for Stephanie Vevers)

Whenever I answer the phone
It's never you

Even if it was you
It'd never be you
Saying

Hello it's me
I love you so much
I can hardly wait to see you
Can I come over right now

Yes yes yes yes

So I hate the sound of the phone
& worse
To answer it

Hello hello
No I'm not me
I'm not here
I'll never be

Was you it'd never be you sa
 Ing hello it's

E I love you so mu
 I can hardly wait
See yo

Ht now yes ye
 I hate the sound o
 I hello hello no I'm not me
Can hardly wait to see yo

Yes yes yes yes

Sound of the phone & worse to an
& worse
T hello hell

Here I'll n
Never I answe
 If it was yo
 It's me I lov

Wait to see you can I come
Ight now yes y

Es yes yes so I ha
It hello hello no
Swer t

He phone it's
If it was you it'd
Ing hello it's me I love you
Come over right now yes y

Yes yes so I ha

Se to answer it hello hello no I
& worse
T me I'm not

Henever I a
Nswer the pho
It was you i
It to see you

W yes yes yes yes so I hate
It hello hello

E I'm not here I'l
I answer the phon
S neve

H I can hardl
It to see you can
I come over right now yes ye
Can I come right now yes y

Yes so I hate th

Swer it hello hello no I'm not m
& worse
T here I'll

Hone it's n
N if it was y
Ing hello it
I come over r

Wer the phone it's never yo
 If it was you

Ever be you saying
 It's me I love yo
So muc

Hardly wait t
 I come over right
 I hate the sound of the phon
Ch I can hardly wait to s

Y wait to see y

So much I can hardly wait to see
& worse
To see you c

Hardly wait
N hardly wait
 I can hardly
 I love you se

Worse to answer it hello he
I'm not me I'm

Ere I'll never be
It's never you ev
S you

Hate the soun
It hello hello no
I'm not me I'm not here I'll
Can hardly wait see yo ht

You can I come

See you can I come over right no
& worse
T now yes ye

Hate the so
Ne & worse to
It hello hel
I'm not me I'

Wait see yo ht now yes ye I
 I answer the p

E it's never you e
 If it was you it'
S me I

Hone & worse
 I'm not me I'm not
 I'm not here I'll never be wh
Can I come ight now yes y

You even if it

S you it'd never be you saying h
& worse
T's me I lov

H I can har
Now yes yes y
 I hate the s
 It hello hell

W yes ye I hate the sound o
 It was you it'

Enever I answer th
 It was you it'd n
S yes

Hello hello n
 I'll never be when
 I answer the phone it's neve
Come over r wer the phone

You it'd never

S yes yes yes so I hate the soun
& worse
The sound of

Hone & wors
Nswer it hell
 I'm not me I
 I answer the

Was I so right to see it so
 I'll answer no

Ere I answer I see
 I'll never be you
So I'm

He you answer
 I'm the sound
 I can hardly ever wait to be
Can you ever love me here

Yes you love me

So I'll be saying a sound answer
& worse
The answer's

Here to say
Now I can say
 I love sound
 I answer love

Was I never to answer hello
I hardly phone

Even you I love so
I can hardly ever
Say to

Her I love so
I can hardly phone
I hardly ever say I love you
Can I ever say I love you

Yes so I say it

Saying love's sound's never over
& worse
To answer it

Hardly ever
No not never
I answer now
I'm saying it

Wait here so I can say love
 If I'm ever to

Even say the sound
 I hate not saying
So now

Here I say it
 I say love's sound
 I say now if ever I love you
Come love answer love now

You say it love

Say the sound so you answer love
& worse
The answer's

Hard to say
Not saying it
 Is worse now
 I'll wait now

4 June 1977
New York

Let It Go

Omaggio a William Empson, il miglior fabbro.

It is this deep blankness is the real thing strange.
    The more things happen to you the more you can't
      Tell or remember even what they were.

The contradictions cover such a range.
    The talk would talk and go so far aslant.
      You don't want madhouse and the whole thing there.

William Empson: "Let It Go" , from p. 84,
Collected Poems (New York: Harcourt, Brace, 1949)

lankness real an't ictions nt.

g more ll remember hat ions n't ge.

to lk se contradictions ing
It gs you lant.

he ictions
It strange.

go so le here.

ant.

is at g strange.

contradictions ld deep ant is
ntradictions g there.

more lk re.

on't is ctions ge.

the you ll or member he talking strange.

e things gs happen cover lk would
se and le thing ing there.

s this go contradictions l thing ge.

re things ings happen u the

range.

he things the adictions slant.

thing ankness is ing ange.

ings happen can't eep happen member
ictions u the what they re.

he tradictions ch thing blankness thing
ctions ing ankness
It ankness ing ings happen hat appen
deep range.

blankness contradictions range.

lant.

want e he eep he eal
what radictions range.

lant.

e he le ere eep happen he le ere.

lankness eal would talk don't want ere.

his deep ess he happen hat hey e.

radictions talk whole far hing can't ell
house real en
Tell hat contradictions would house
whole remember were.

tradies whole ere.

kness the real
Tell whole hing lankness an't
contradictions cover range.

lant.

ember contradictions contradictions
contradictions contradictions contradictions
contradictions contradictions contradictions
contradictions would go
You whole ntradictions hole more
you ions range.

would dhouse whole real range.

re pen remember were.

11 March 1978
New York

Larry Rosing Piece For Typewriter, Video, & Voice

```
AGILNORSY   AGILNORRRSY   AGILNORRRSY   AGILNORRRSY
Signal.  Signal a lion.  Glory in a signal.  Glory in rain.

Gain a lion in rain.  A garrison is sorry in rain.  Rain glory.
Is a lion sorry in rain?  Is a lion as sorry as a garrison in rain?
A lion's son gains no glory in rain.  No lion gains glory in rain.
A rainy glory's a sorry glory.

Norris is no lion.  Is Norris sorry in glory?  Glory nags Norris.

I lag.
So sorry I lag.  No glory in a lag.  A sorry glory in a rainy lag.
No rain.  No glory.

I sail on.
Grain.  Sail grain.  Long sail grain in a rain.  No lion no grain.
I rail on.
As long as I sail I rail on.  A long rail.  A long sail.  A song.
I sing a song.  As I sing I long.  So long.  As I long I sing a song.

Sing a song, Larry!
No song?  Larry no sing song.  I sing along.  I gain a song.
No glory.  Only a song.

A signal.  Only a signal.  Only a sorry signal.  So.
```

30 September 1978
New York

A Vocabulary for Custer LaRue: First Realization — 12/4/78

lust   sea laser   Lear   lucre   sucre

acute   crease   seral

lace   clause   arse   secure   cruets

eta   creel   sleet   reels
cut

suer   late   Tralee

real

creates sure   sect   clear

set

rectal   Ares

eraser   stale   Arles   rears

tale

saute   reuser

ela   Lars

acres

east   Crete release

reseat   scut

rest   cause

suet   terser

cruelest

Raul   cul

alee   car   scare

eel

steracle   tea rets

crueler   sear   Erse

err   ere else Earl seer

eats races   alter

seta

cue   urea terse   Surt

reuse rust   Luce

star

racer   tears cure   care

cetera

lees   scale   lease

ester   Ulster rare

lues tease usual teal alert sate lure ease

raster   seat

trace   lectures   clue surer   rates

caul   lets   Lester sue least

cease   ear   truces eucre

eras steel ruse ate   sale select rules

Ursa   cruse cult cruel

later   serrate clearer   carts arrest creature

rat scar lutes reuser arcs crust realer leers

tars   lac   cue last   curs

luster Laure   Celts rut   salt

caste sur   arts   rates Ceres lats slate

stare use ultras   curls scat Uta true sauce

cleat   Elea Carus   tares talc Lares steer

reset Terra trees secret rescue steal

cluster   crates seal Sucret truer

Cete realest   elate

ruler

Performance Instructions for
A Vocabulary for Custer LaRue

A Vocabulary for Custer LaRue comprises any number of typewritten or drawn realizations made by drawing words from a list of 202 words spelled exclusively with the letters of the name "Custer LaRue," with only the letters R, U, & E allowed to appear twice in any word. Chance operations are used to draw them from the list & place them on the page. (Custer LaRue is an excellent singer who lives in Baltimore.)

Any number of people can perform one or more realizations as a simultaneity or one person can as a solo. A performer starts at any word & moves to any other. Each word, or its separated or recombined phonemes, can be spoken any number of times &/or the pitch-class series which corresponds to the series of letters spelling the word may be played on an instrument &/or sung, using the translation method shown below. The series of pitch classes may be translated into tones placed in any octave, & improvised on, always keeping the order of the pitch-class series corresponding to the word's spelling, by being played forward or backward as a melody, or (on instruments that can play double stops or chords) adjacent pitch classes may be played as intervals or chords. A series may also be vocalized backwards or forwards, with tones placed in any desired octave, using phonemes located in the word, but not necessarily the whole word. A performer may combine any or all types of realization with each word.

Of the 8 letters in "Custer LaRue," the 4 in the word "cast" stand for single pitch classes: C = C♮, A = A♮, S = E♭/D♯, & T = D♮. Those in the word "rule" each stand for 2 pitch classes: R = A♭/G♯ &/or D♭/C♯, U = G♮ &/or B♭/A♯, L = F♮ &/or B♮, & E = E♮ &/or G♭/F♯. The "rule" letters can be read as single tones or as intervals composed of both tones: R as a perfect 4th or 5th, U as a major 3rd or minor 6th, L as an augmented 4th or diminished 5th, & E as a major 2nd or 9th or a minor 7th.

After improvising awhile using solely one word, its separated or recombined phonemes, &/or the tones into which it can be translated, the performer *falls silent,* remaining silent for a duration roughly proportionate to the space between that word & the next word on which that performer wants to improvise. These silences can be *longer* than seems proportionate to the space between words, but ought never to be shorter.

Performers must *listen* very carefully to all sounds in the environment, especially other performers, but also audience & other ambient sounds, & *relate* whatever they are doing with whatever they are hearing. They must be sensitive, tactful, & courteous, as well as inventive.

A performance can end by consensus during performance or an ending time set beforehand can be signalled by a leader or timekeeper.

Instructions written 10–30 January 1979
New York

The Genesis of *A Vocabulary for Custer LaRue:*
First Realization—12/4/78

A Vocabulary for Custer LaRue is a recent addition to my series of performance poems &/or text-sound texts called "Vocabularies," each one of which is made solely of words spelled with the letters of a person's name — usually a friend's — with each letter appearing, at most, in any one word, only as many times as it occurs in the name. (The first such work was *A Vocabulary for Carl Fernbach-Flarsheim,* drawn 2-3 January 1968.)

In making this Vocabulary, my first step was to make a list of 202 words spelled with letters from the name of the excellent Baltimore vocalist Custer LaRue. *S*-less words to which a final *s* may be added—singular nouns, verbs in stem form, & words that may be read as either, e.g., "trace," "tear"—appear on the list followed by an *s* in parentheses, indicating that either or both forms may be used in realizations of the Vocabulary. Two words to which an *e* may be added, to form their plurals, are followed by an *e* in parentheses. Sixty-five of the 202 words being followed by an *s* or an *e,* the available free forms total 267.

Unlike my practice with other Vocabularies, first realized as drawings or paintings, I composed the first realization of Custer's while I was typing it on my Coronamatic 2200. I also conceived this consciously as the "*first* realization" of this Vocabulary, rather than, as with all but one previous Vocabulary the only or primary realization.

In producing this first realization, I used random digits from Rand's *A Million Random Digits with 100,000 Normal Deviates* (Glencoe, Ill.: Free Press, 1955) to draw words from the list & decide between forms ending or not with parenthesized letters. Each form could only be used once, so either the stem or the parenthesized letter was crossed out as the form was drawn from the list. The next time the random-digit group associated with the word came up, the other form was used. Other random-digit groups determined each word's placement, in terms of numbers of horizontal spaces to the right or left & vertical spaces up or down from the end of the word previously drawn from the list & typed. In using these random-digit groups to determine placement, if a particular group designated a place already occupied by a word, the number of spaces was counted oppositely (up rather than down & to the left rather than to the right). If this also led to a place already occupied, the random-digit group was dropped & the next group in the table was used to determine placement.

The making of the realization ended when a word was typed 3/4" above the bottom of the sheet & most random-digit groups led to occupied places.

25 January–15 August 1979
New York

281

5 Stanzaic Realizations of A Vocabulary
for Clarinda Mac Low

Lind cram crawl
nod rill conic Noman
radical caid rind racial
Lind amid drama maid clarion lard car wold
moll

clinal wind clamor
warn cicada no dam
mail won drill Drāno
laid loan normal Lorca larid comic worn acid
roam

roam Cain cord
loam aim roll nor
cad can Lind wall
wan crania nod damn nard aim carnal lamaic
carol

Alaric clam canal
Carl maniac Dan rind
Nola nil war Ida
local milord carol cord word Cain raw caca
adorn

2

laical war coil
acclaim rain doll lid
warn ran moral rind
din adorn coca Mod Drāno dorm Dolan comic
coca

modal worn cam
lid clamor nomad rancid
wad roc maid din
Clairol draw Nordic minor comical collar Noman claw
ran

din maniac roan
wand Roman rid rind
maid radical limn Nolan
crawl Cid lam acid loan worn cranial wall
rim

con con cram
laic liar coral laical
Nordic amid drawn con
Clairol wand mar mania wind won mad oil
Id

3

cloaca raw war
roam wand Mod raw
wand adorn rail Cid
mar mild or ward warn road minor lilac
roll

nail rind wind
an corn calm claw
mandrill modal doc ward
low nail lard lain malic clam cram larid
ram

local raca milord
camino nor Drāno warn
cam roc loan Cadillac
Wicca amino moll card worn collar wain collar
amid

con wain caid
loam crania crow comic
rind lamaic coil mild
carol collar loam moral roam raid car drama
nadir

4

low maid Marlow
mall road racial coral
Rama nail a lord
Dan Mod Roman maid rod crania moil woman
word

Lima raca cranial
lilac wall mild larid
collar acclaim lid mania
coil doc coil world Id can mild or
cranial

cram craw roc
amoral moll Lorca craw
Alaric colic comical calm
Lima rain woman racial dill car mad crania
loam

crow warn Adonic
cloaca road mail Roman
moil crawl acid claim
Cain amino lad conical clarion wand wild moll
minor

5

wild moll Norman
Wicca wail laic radio
radial carol mild lama
mad wad lord oil amid mad ill rid
canal

acorn coal wan
lain amoral amid liar
wind ram radio rail
Clairol oil rain win carol cam call radon
marl

rain Wicca wold
Drāno rid doll conic
warn colic lilac wain
liar acid call mild nomad amid radical raid
win

lad norm wain
adorn rod lad nail
lard cicada mandrill nod
Nolan coil larid card Nordic local nod nodal
raca

17 January 1979
New York

Quatorzains from & for Emily Dickinson

```
Elysium is as far as to
IMpregnable of Eye—
ThIs was in the White of the Year—
NegLected Son of Genius
RuddY as that coeval Apple

        Did stagger pitiful
        MIght dare to touch it now!
        BeCause that fearing it so long
        RanK—overtake me—
        RequIred a Blow as vast
        If teNderer industriousness
        Be it'S Grave—sufficient sign—
        And choOses Wainscot in the Breast
        Death woNt hurt—now Dollie's here!


Eclipses—Suns—imply—
IMpregnable the Rose
ThIs—then—is best for confidence—
CoaLs—from a Rolling Load—rattle—how—near—
And Yet We guessed it not—

        Divulging it would rest my Heart
        VIcinity to Laws
        I Counted till they danced so
        LucK is not chance—
        Be MIne the Doom—
        All iNterspersed with weed,
        It aimS once—kills once—conquers once—
        With PrOspect, and with Frost—
        We distiNguish clear—
```

Escape from Circumstances—
IMpregnable we are—
TrIumphed and remained unknown—
CouLd I infer his Residence—
And Yet we sooner say

    Drop into tune—around the Throne—
    BIrds, mostly back—
    ExCellent and Fair.
    It Kept me from a Thief, I think,
    And Is the first, to rise—
    Were Nothing very strange!
    His obServation omnifold,
    Wilt ThOu, Austere Snow?
    And duriNg it's electric gale—

Experience would swear—
AMong the certainties—
CrIsis is a hair
WouLd be acuter, would it not
Too Young that any should suspect

    Defrauded of it's song.
    HIs Twin identity
    ExCept to bear
    LooK too expensive!
    It dId not surprise me—
    Nor aNy leader's grim baton
    All HiS Goods have Wings—
    By my lOng bright—and <u>longer</u>—<u>trust</u>—
    By seasoNs or his Children—

Escaping backward to perceive
IMpelled to hark—
GrIef is a Mouse—
WouLd not the fun
And Yesterday, or Centuries before?

    Diversion from the Dying Theme
    DIsarms the little interval—
    A Compensation fair
    It Kept me from a Thief, I think,
    RepaIring Everywhere—
    The iNstant holding in it's claw
    Truth Stays Herself—and every man
    Like loOking every time you please
    SuspicioN it was done

Escaping backward to perceive
IMpregnable the Rose
StIll to be explained.
WilL equal glow, and thought no More
ElegY of Integrity.

    Did place about the West—Tonight—
    TIll that first Shout got by—
    I Could hold the latest Glowing—
    SeeK—Friend—and see—
    StolId to Love's supreme entreaty
    My miNd was going numb—
    ReturnS no syllable
    This slOw Day moved along
    Lip was Not the liar.

November 1979
New York

STOVEBLACK

8 stanzas=64 lines=264 words=1320 letters
from her solution list given in her game
"Word Power," New York Post, 12/18/79
for Leona Bleiweiss

```
above skate covet close ascot cable
black cloak caste stole vocal store stoke
slave covet eclat stale sable
store
close stalk cable
covet
eclat store sable beast besot beast
stack besot slack slack

stoke salve ovate beast baste block
salve stoke vocal ovate cable beast bloke
blast cable stale cable stole
eclat
store black beast
scale
stock stork stove stale costa slate
steal costa cable stake

above stack salve block coast stale
scale stole stale least besot table costa
steal above salvo eclat covet
black
least eclat scale
stave
stale stork stake salvo baste bleat
ovate slack above caste

bleak bleak cloak coast above stork
scale stoke close covet scale ascot eclat
slake close slate stork baste
steak
caste ascot cloak
valet
sable eclat table boast table stock
scale ascot stove cleat
```

290

stalk steal sabot beast baste caste
slate black cable eclat costa cleat covet
vocal boast slack ascot store
clove
store stalk covet
valet
black steal stole sable above vocal
stack boast steal slake

least sabot store stalk block stale
vocal slake block ovate above baste steal
black coast cloak black stoke
stave
salve slate stole
steak
baste least slack stave steal baste
slack stalk cleat steak

least stake least stake scale least
skate boast salve blast sabot vocal steak
baste stake black block table
above
caste besot scale
vocal
slack sabot stake slate ascot ovate
baste above bleak costa

store stock stock sable slate skate
close baste costa block coast coast vocal
ascot bleak block caste above
stove
covet besot cleat
cleat
covet cable stack stake coast salvo
stale bleat blast besot

19 December 1979
New York

291

A Vocabulary for Annie Brigitte Gilles Tardos

(description; compositional procedures: from lexicon to visual realizations; and performance methods: from visual to verbal/musical realizations)

A Vocabulary for Annie Brigitte Gilles Tardos is a project commissioned by The Institute for Art and Urban Resources, Inc., for exhibition as the "Poetry Room" of "Sound at P.S. 1," a show at Project Studios One in Long Island City (Queens), New York, from 30 September to November 1979. However, its components (which progressively proliferate) may be (and some have been) exhibited and/or performed elsewhere.

It comprises a "lexicon," a computer printout of random groups of its entries, and two types of visual realizations derived by the author directly from the printout; a film, slides, and photographs of the installation, produced collaboratively by Anne Tardos and the author; drawings in various media derived from the slides by Anne Tardos; and aural (verbal/musical) realizations derived from the visual ones, and from the film and slides, by following prescribed performance methods detailed below. Documentation of aural realizations includes a videotape by Anne Tardos of a piano/voice performance by the author and audiotape recordings made by the author and others of his private piano/voice performances and of public performances.

The "lexicon" comprises 5,000 entries, including general words and geographical, biographical, and personal names. Many entries include both a base word and several word forms derived from it by adding suffixes. Many such entries are *homographic collections* of all the admissible forms of all the words *spelled* like the base or in which a form of the base figures as a stem to which suffixes are added. Such entries may include one or more forms of several different but homographic words having different meanings and/or belonging to two or more different parts of speech. All of the word forms in the entries are spelled solely with the letters in the name "Annie Brigitte Gilles Tardos." (This is the baptismal name of the filmmaker and video and performance artist Anne Tardos.) Any particular letter appears in any single word form only as many times as it appears in the whole name, e.g., no form can include more than two A's.

The author's visual realizations made for the "Sound at P.S. 1" Poetry Room are drawings or designs made up of printed or written sentences derived from the lexicon. These sentences range from single words to elaborate syntactic structures. While most of them are of the subject-predicate type traditionally called "complete sentences"—statements, questions, or requests—some can be read as "greetings," "calls," or "exclamations" and comprise only one or a few words. They all begin with capital letters and end with end marks—periods, question marks, or exclamation points—(except for a few truncated sentences that end with points of suspension), indicating that they are to be read with appropriate "sentence-final intonation contours."

These sentences were composed as follows: Each lexicon entry (all admissible base forms and suffixes) was punched on a computer card, and the whole set of lexicon cards was fed into a computer. The latter, acting on a program written by Chris Boegner of Market Probe International, Inc., (who also donated computer time), drew entries from the lexicon to print out 3,000 lines, each of which includes one to ten randomly selected entries. Subsequently, from most of the lines on the first page of printout and from many other lines scattered throughout the rest of the printout, the author composed the sentences that appear in the visual realizations. The author composed each sentence by selecting an appropriate form from every entry in a single printout line and adding, when necessary, structure (function) words spelled only with the name letters.

Using these sentences, the author constructed two types of visual realizations. Those of the first type, made up of sentences from consecutive lines of entry groups on the first of the 49 printout pages, have been printed or photocopied from layouts made by typing sentences on self-adhesive correction tape without removing the protective backing and then removing the backing and placing and adhering the tape segments within 9"-by-12" rectangles delineated on 11"-by-14" sheets of bristol board. In these realizations each sentence is oriented at a different angle with the horizontal, and some sentences change direction one or more times because the author cut the tape segment on which the sentence was typed into two or more segments (to remove typing errors or to fit the sentence among others) and oriented each segment differently. However, all sentences are placed so that they may be read without changing the orientation of the designs.

For the Poetry Room of "Sound at P.S. 1" the images on these layouts were photographically enlarged to twice their original size and printed on 18"-by-24" sheets of transparent acetate (red, orange, yellow, green, or blue) at the Open Studio Print Shop, Rhinebeck, N.Y. One such sheet was vertically mounted (by Anne Tardos) inside the room across the middle of each of the 20 lower panes of the room's five windows, leaving uncovered a small vertical strip of each pane on each side of the transparency. For performance use outside the room copies printed on thick paper the same size as the acetate sheets or ones xerographed from reduced photostats of the layouts are used as scores by speaker-musicians.

The author's visual realizations of the second type are large drawings on heavy paper. Both measure six feet vertically and, respectively, 16 feet and nine feet horizontally. On these drawings sentences derived from nonconsecutive entry-group lines scattered throughout the 49 printout pages were written or hand-printed by the author with various-colored oil sticks (compressed oil paints) or (here and there on the larger one) colored-ink drawing pens with thin tips. In these drawings many of the sentences, while clearly distinct and legible, curve around each other in various directions. These drawings and/or reduced copies of them, and/or slides and/or a film made from them as well, may also be (and have been) used as performance scores by speaker-musicians.

Performance Methods

Any visual realizations of this Vocabulary and/or any copies of such realizations may be used as performance notations by any number of individuals, most of whom function both as speakers and as instrumentalists and/or singers, although some performers may only speak.

To begin a performance, each person, looking at a visual realization or a copy of one:

(1) chooses one sentence (i.e., any complete verbal unit beginning with a capital letter and ending with a period, question mark, exclamation point, or points of suspension) written or printed on it;

(2) decides whether to speak this sentence one or more times or to play or sing a musical "improvisation" that follows a method through which the successive letters of the sentence are "translated" into musical tones or aggregates (see below) or both to speak and musically to "improvise" on the same sentence;

(3) listens closely to all sounds produced by the other performers, if any, and the audience, if any, and by all other sound-producing factors in the performance space or its environment;

(4) speaks the sentence clearly one or more times (interspersing repetitions with silences of various durations as desired) and/or "improvises" musically (following the given method), doing either or both in a way that is both spontaneous and related with (responsive to) the total aural situation at the moment as perceived by the individual;

(5) falls silent for a while (at least 15 seconds, at most a minute or so), listening closely to everything audible;

(6) chooses another sentence and again carries through the other

"steps"—and this cycle is repeated over and over until the end of the perform-ance.

("Improvisation" is in quotes since each individual's choices are cir-cumscribed by the procedural rules, and "steps" is in quotes since (1) through (4) may take place more or less simultaneously, with perception, choice, and action continuously conditioning and modifying each other.)

The Musical Method

There are only twelve different letters in "Annie Brigitte Gilles Tardos" and thus in the sentences included in the visual realizations. Each of these letters is read as a symbol of one of the twelve "notes" (pitch classes) of the even-tempered chromatic scale:

A = A♮	E = E♮ /(F♭)	L = F♮/(E♯)	R = A♭/G♯
B = B♭/A♯	G = G	N = C♮ /(B♯)	S = E♭/D♯
D = D♮	I = D♭/C♯	O = G♭/F♯	T= B♮/(C♭)

(If any group of speaker-musicians desires to use just intonation or some other tuning less "out of tune" than even temperament, the same system of letter-to-note translation is to be followed, although each letter will now be read as a symbol for either or both of two slightly different enharmonic tones. The details of a method for producing satisfactory simultaneous improvisa-tions with such a tuning must be worked out by the members of the group.)

Each letter string comprising one whole sentence (i.e., running from a capital letter to an end mark) may be read musically (i.e., as a "note" series) either from left to right or vice versa (i.e., from capital letter to end mark or vice versa) any number of times, but each time all the way through in only one general direction (not "switching" directions except for "trills" and the like—see below).

Each successive "note" in a musically translated letter string may be played in any octave, and a variety of octave placements is desirable within each segment of "improvisation." Two or more consecutive "notes," or a whole sequence, may be played simultaneously as an aggregate (interval, chord, or tone cluster). Each member of a letter-equivalent "note" series and each aggregate may be repeated one or any number of times and/or doubled in two or more octaves. Adjacent "notes" in a series, and adjacent aggregates as well, may be repeated alternately ("trilled") any number of times in the same or any number of different octave placements, and three or more successive "notes" (in the same or different octave placements) may be repeated any number of times as *ostinati*.

A performer may fall silent for a while at any time during an "improvisa-tion" segment and afterwards continue to "improvise" on the same sentence, either speaking it or "improvising" on its equivalent "note" series. Also, individual tones or aggregates may be separated by "silences," allowing per-formers, for instance, to insert them among the sounds being produced by others. However, it must be reiterated that all "notes" in a series, whether played singly or in aggregates; repeated singly, in aggregates, or in *ostinati;* "trilled"; or separated by silences; must be played or sung in forward or reverse order of the series before that series is repeated in that order or its opposite.

Performers make free choices (always in relation with the total aural situa-tion as perceived by them) within all parameters not fixed by the notation (the sentences) and the instructions. These include the octave placement, simultaneous or successive grouping, repetition, duration, rhythm, loud-ness, tempo, timbre, and attack of tones and the temporal placement and duration of rests and longer "silences."

Whenever any of the sentences are spoken one or more times, either alone or in conjunction with instrumental or vocalized "improvisation" on their "note" series, the meaning and pronunciation of each of the words compris-ing the sentences should be known to the performers. They should consult *Webster's New Collegiate Dictionary* (Springfield, Mass.: G. & C. Merriam Co., 1977 or later) when in doubt. (Besides the Dictionary proper, they should— for proper nouns—consult the lists of Biographical and Geographical Names.)

Each sentence chosen for spoken realization should be pronounced not only correctly but clearly and reasonably audibly to as many other performers and audience members as possible. Words should never be yelled, even when they may have to be spoken somewhat loudly in order to become audible: *Loudly spoken words need not seem to express violent feelings.* However, certain sentences may seem in themselves to express violent feelings and to demand violently loud delivery. If so, the rule should still be: "'shouting' rather than 'yelling.'" If the total texture is too thick and/or the level of sound too high for new speech to be clearly and intelligibly audible, performers should wait before speaking until the sound becomes thinner or quieter.

Performers should understand the syntax of each sentence and speak it in such a way as to make the syntactical relations between its component words clear. To do this they will sometimes have to solve word-class ambiguity problems, that is, decide to which of two or more possible parts of speech (noun, verb, adjective, or adverb) particular words in a sentence must belong in order for the sentence to cohere structurally, even when the sentence is (at least existentially) absurd. All sentences longer than single words or short phrases must be assumed to form structurally complete statements, ques-tions, or requests. Each sentence should be spoken with the inflections appro-priate to its meaning and sentence type and with one of the sentence-final intonation contours appropriate to its end mark. Speakers should be especially careful with exclamation points, often used in these realizations to end calls and requests as well as exclamations. Sentences ending with them should be given no more than the degree of emphasis appropriate to their meaning. (Never yelled, they should only rarely be shouted.)

One cannot emphasize too strongly that performers must listen to, relate with, and respond to each other and to ambient sounds, including those of the audience. When they fall silent within or between "improvisation" segments, they must listen with concentrated attention to the total aural situation and so make their choices as to further sound production in accordance with what they hear.

Sensitivity, tact, and courtesy must be exercised in order to make every detail of one's performance contribute toward a total sound sequence that is as similar as possible to what the performer would choose to hear. While egoistic overpowering of the total sound should never take place, the exercise of virtuosity is strongly encouraged when it is carried out with as much consciousness as possible of its place in the total aural situation. Performers should try always to be both inventive and sensitive. As in all the author's other simultaneities, the most important "rules" are: *"Listen"* and *"Relate."*

A performance may be begun and ended in any convenient way. Usually it will be best for performers to agree beforehand on an approximate performance duration and for one of them to act as group leader, signalling the beginning, keeping track of elapsed time, and signalling the ending at some point before or slightly after the agreed-upon end point. The leader must be easily visible to all performers and judge when the group "improvisation" may be most satisfactorily ended. However, when circumstances allow greater latitude, a performance may continue until the group ends it by informal consensus.

A Vocabulary for Annie Brigitte Gilles Tardos may be performed by a single speaker-musician as well as by a group, and by either a soloist or a group along with one or more recorded solo or group performances. Methods for realizing the Vocabulary verbally and musically remain essentially identical in all cases.

The above constitutes the most complete and precise description of the methods for realizing one of the author's performance works. Performers of his other works would do well to read it.

20 January 1980
Revised 12 April 1982
New York

On the following five pages the five "window acetate" designs are reproduced in reduced scale.

A gored abigail at Borgia's sent slag against one in a brassard.

Regranting sinoatrial abnegating is no disaster to a sora staler'n Neri's rages, diatribes, and earrings.

Belial raged at annatto.

No Bassein Robands on Norris's edge-grains!

Adrenaline!

Aida in Lansing.

Brilliantine on a belle, Lassalle on a giantess.

Rae's ratable as loden; Landon's sib Dalton is bristlier and lintier.

Is a steelie as stainable as gingerbread in tea or setose as a Barodan or Silone?

Sainted dingleberries lionise breast drills tangential to negotiable deterabilities.

A latigo on an aegrotant, a sigil on a tigress, a rallentando in a Senate garderobe.

Dietitian Balder, near a bignonia, resorted to strolling.

Angrier segregants' Basildon dibs are lire (sabots are artier).

Reasonable Brandt!

A slinger ring bearing O'Neill's dollar signs is no treadle, nor is a nitrated gas station Sino-Tibetan.

299

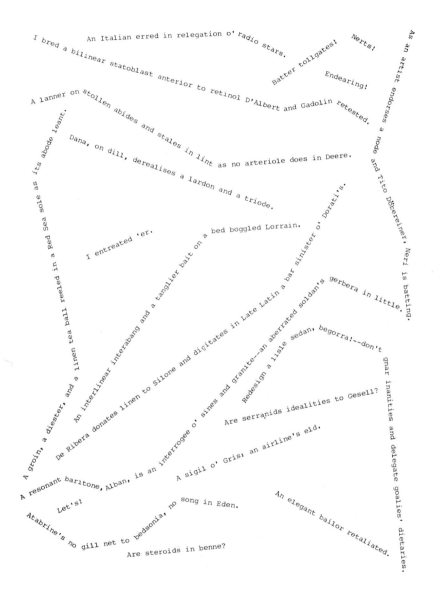

An Italian erred in relegation o' radio stars.

Nerts!

Batter tollgates!

Endearing!

I bred a bilinear statoblast anterior to retinol D'Albert and Gadolin retested.

As an artist endorses a node and Tito Dobereiner Neri is batting.

A lanner on stollen abides and stales in lint as no arteriole does in Deere.

Dana, on dill, derealises a lardon and a triode.

I entreated 'er.

A groin, a diester, and a linen tea ball reeled in a Red Sea stole as its abode leant.

An interlinear interabang and a tanglier bait on a bed boggled Lorrain.

De Ribera donates linen to Silone and dicitates in Late Latin a bar sinister o' Dorati's.

A resonant baritone, Alban, is an interrogee o' sines and granite--an aberrated soldan's gerbera in little.

Redesign a lisle sedan, begorra!--don't gnar inanities and delegate goalies' dietaries.

Are serranids idealities to Gesell?

A sigil o' Gris; an airline's eld.

Let's!

Atabrine's no gill net to bedsonia, no song in Eden.

An elegant bailor retaliated.

Are steroids in benne?

300

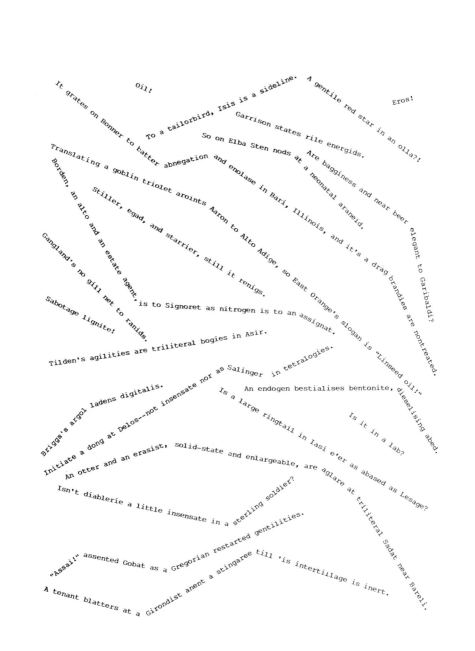

Oil!

It grates on Bonner to batter abnegation

To a tailorbird, Isis is a sideline.

A gentile red star in an olla?!

Eros!

Garrison states rile energids.

So on Elba Sten nods at a neonatal araneid.

Are bagginess and near beer elegant to Garibaldi?

Translating a goblin triolet aroints Aaron to Alto Adige, so East Orange's slogan is "Linseed oil!"

Borden, an alto and an estate agent,

Stiller, egad, and starrier, still it renigs.

and enolase in Bari, Illinois, and it's a drag brandies are nontreated.

is to Signoret as nitrogen is to an assignat.

Gangland's no gill net to ranids.

Sabotage lignite!

Tilden's agilities are triliteral bogies in Asir.

Briggs's argol ladens digitalis.

An endogen bestialises bentonite, dieselising abed.

Initiate a dong at Delos--not insensate nor as Salinger in tetralogies.

Is it in a lab?

Is a large ringtail in Iasi e'er as abased as Lesage?

An otter and an erasist, solid-state and enlargeable, are aglare at triliteral Sadat near Bareli.

Isn't diablerie a little insensate in a sterling soldier?

"Assai!" assented Gobat as a Gregorian restarted gentilities.

A tenant blatters at a Girondist anent a stingaree till 'is intertillage is inert.

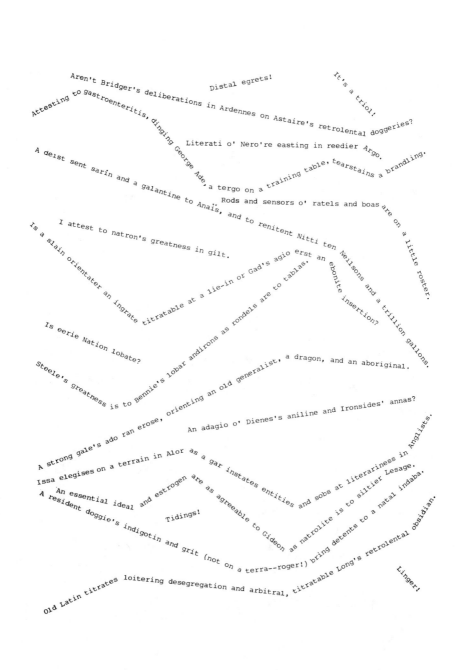

Aren't Bridger's deliberations in Ardennes on Astaire's retrolental doggeries?

Distal egrets!

It's a triol!

Attesting to gastroenteritis, dinging George Ade, a tergo on a training table, tearstains a brandling.

Literati o' Nero're easting in reedier Argo.

A deist sent sarin and a galantine to Anaïs, and to renitent Nitti ten Neilsons and a trillion gallons.

Rods and sensors o' ratels and boas are on a little roster.

I attest to natron's greatness in gilt.

Is a slain orientater an ingrate titratable at a lie-in or Gad's agio erst an ebonite insertion?

Is eerie Nation lobate?

Steele's greatness is to Bennie's lobar andirons as rondels are to tablas.

An adagio o' Dienes's aniline and Ironsides' annas?

A strong gale's ado ran erose, orienting an old generalist, a dragon, and an aboriginal.

Issa elegises on a terrain in Alor as a gar instates entities and sobs at literariness in Anglists.

An essential ideal and estrogen are as agreeable to Gideon as natrolite is to siltier Lesage.

A resident doggie's indigotin and grit (not on a terra--roger!) bring detents to a natal indaba.

Tidings!

Old Latin titrates loitering desegregation and arbitral, titratable Long's retrolental obsidian.

Linger!

302

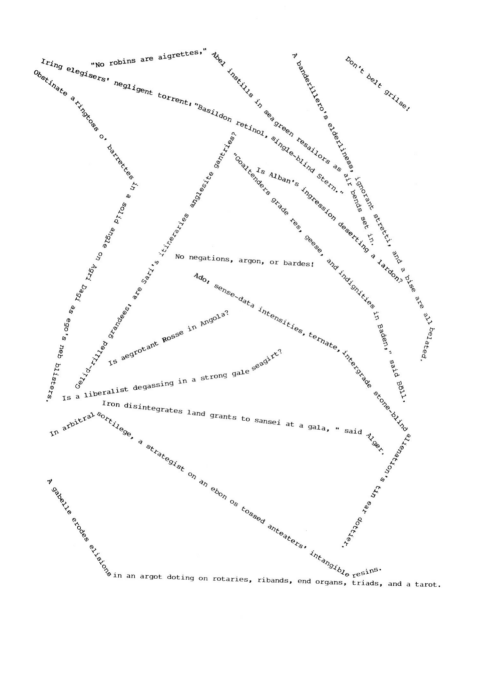

"No robins are aigrettes," Abel instills in seagreen resailors as air bends set in.

Iring elegisers' negligent torrent; "Basildon retinol, single-blind Stern."

Obstinate a ringtoss o' barrettes in a solid angle on Agra begs as ego's new blisters.

A banderillero's elderliness, ignorant stretti, and a bise are all belated.

Don't belt grilse!

"Goaltenders grade res, geese, and indignities in Baden," said Böll.

Is Alban's ingression deserting a lardon?

Gelid-rilled grandees: are Sari's itineraries anglesite gantries?

No negations, argon, or bardes!

Ado; sense-data intensities, ternate, intergrade stone-blind alienation's tin ear dottier.

Is aegrotant Rosse in Angola?

Is a liberalist degassing in a strong gale seagirt?

Iron disintegrates land grants to sansei at a gala, " said Alger.

In arbitral sortilege, a strategist on an ebon os tossed anteaters' intangible resins.

A gabelle erodes elisions in an argot doting on rotaries, ribands, end organs, triads, and a tarot.

Antic Quatrains

derived from the computer-printout phase of
A Vocabulary for Annie Brigitte Gilles Tardos

Along a tarn a delator entangled a dragline,
Boasting o' tonnages, dogies, ants, and stones
As long as Lind balled Gandas near a gas log
As it late lit rigatoni and a tag line.

In Dis libidinal radians o' tigons
Deter no generals, no ordinaries,
No Adlerians tarring arteries' DNA,
Triliteral arsenal o' nitid groins.

Begone, senile Tiresias, raser o' tanneries!
Gastonia's grants-in-aid, sestertia to Liebig,
Are raising glissading sergeants' titillation
In lairs o' daisies, glarier and estranging.

Literal tartlets arrange stilbestrol's banners
And roast nonsalable redlegs, breasts o' lessees,
Rib roasts, entire alations, Ingersoll, Alger,
And age-old Diesel's aborning ingestible trotters.

Irritants beggar Tagore, irredentists,
And irritated designees in gorgets
Agreeing on liberal tittles, Ginsberg, Seeger,
And Stella's transient sortilege, galliards, ginger.

Do gerardias register tanglier antibioses
Or sillier Latrobe allegorise eared seals?
Do literati's binges iodate sand tables?
Internists banter teetotalers in bordels.

Tilden's Iliad tabled alliteration
And a gainless Sartrian ass aired abattoirs
As tonsils' orneriness assigned Ortega
To distillations antedating Sade.

304

Erelong GI's' ideas girdle Borstals
And toadies retrain Orientals as Borgia desserts:
Elated at iodine on starting gates,
Do sonnetising Britons lead orbed otters?

Ill borage's large attendants in bodegas,
Labiating gristlier translations,
Belie agreeable garnerings. No? 'Tain't so?
Go greet Titania in an insensate snit!

Granados labeled a gateleg table stable
As droll goaltenders tensed at tenebrist rites
And an elegant internee sensed godlier litanies
In gangrened slattern lotteries in Laredo.

A belligerent gent tainted a nationalist
And an ill-starred seer slogged near Odin's targe
As Rosetta retested gastral allegories,
Riled at a brainless trio's rosaries.

Aretino's gist is bearable
And Lister's treatises are greatening:
Siberian gentianella's deteriorating
And loneliness endangers libraries.

March 1980
New York

"Is That Wool Hat My Hat?"

for two, three, or four voices

Four voices is optimum, but two or three can perform this. All four words in each column (or the top two or three), are to be spoken simultaneously, following an even beat. One performer (or a separate conductor) should beat time throughout. Do *not* use a metronome.

1. Is	that	wool	hat	my	hat?	Is	that	wool	hat
2. Is	that	wool	hat	my	Is	that	wool	hat	my
3. Is	that	wool	hat	my	hat?	Is	that	wool	hat
4. Is	that	wool	hat	my	hat?	Is	that	wool	hat

1. my	hat?	Is	that	wool	hat	my	hat?	Is	that
2. Is	that	wool	hat	my	Is	that	Is	that	Is
3. my	hat?	Is	that	wool	hat	my	hat?	my	hat?
4. my	hat?	Is	that	wool	hat	my	hat?	Is	that

1. wool	hat	my	hat?	Is	that	wool	hat	my	hat?
2. that	Is	that	Is	that	Is	that	wool	hat	my
3. is	that	my	hat?	Is	that	my	hat?	Is	that
4. wool	hat	my	hat?	Is	that	wool	hat	my	hat?

1. Is	that	wool	hat	my	hat?	wool	wool	wool	hat
2. hat?	Is	hat	hat	hat	wool	hat	my	hat?	wool
3. my	hat?	Is	that	my	hat?	Is	that	my	hat?
4. wool	hat	wool	hat	wool	hat	wool	hat	wool	hat

1. hat	hat	hat	hat	Is	that	wool	hat	my	Is
2. hat	my	wool	hat	my	wool	hat	my	wool	hat
3. Is	that	that	wool	hat	my	hat?	Is	that	wool
4. my	hat?	Is	wool	hat	my	hat?	Is	wool	hat

307

1. that wool hat my Is that wool hat my Is
2. my hat? Is that wool hat? Is that wool hat?
3. hat my hat? Is that wool hat my hat? Is
4. my hat? Is wool hat my hat? Is wool hat

1. that wool hat my that that hat? Is that wool
2. Is that hat? Is that hat? Is that hat? Is
3. that wool hat my hat? Is hat my hat? Is
4. my hat? Is Is that wool hat my hat? Is

1. hat? Is that wool hat? Is that wool hat? Is
2. that wool hat my wool hat my hat? Is that
3. that wool hat my hat? Is that wool hat my
4. that wool hat my hat? Is that wool hat my

1. that wool Is Is Is Is Is hat? Is that
2. wool hat? Is that wool hat my hat? Is that
3. hat? Is that wool hat my hat? Is that wool
4. hat? wool hat my hat? Is that wool hat my

1. wool hat my hat? Is that wool hat my hat?
2. wool hat my hat? Is that wool hat my hat?
3. hat my hat? Is that wool that that hat hat
4. hat? Is that hat my hat? hat my hat? hat?

1. Is that wool hat my hat? Is that hat? Is
2. Is that wool hat my hat? Is that wool hat
3. hat hat hat that wool wool hat my hat? Is
4. Is that wool hat? Is that wool hat my hat?

1. that hat? Is that hat? is that hat? Is that
2. my hat? Is that wool hat my wool wool wool
3. that wool hat my hat? is that wool hat my
4. hat my hat? hat my hat? hat? Is that wool

1. hat? Is that hat my hat? hat my hat? hat
2. wool wool wool hat my wool hat my wool hat
3. hat? Is that wool hat my hat? Is that wool
4. hat my hat? Is that wool hat my hat? Is

308

1. my   hat?   hat   my   hat?   hat   my   hat?   hat   my
2. my   wool   hat   my   that   wool hat   my   hat?   that
3. hat   my   hat? Is   that   hat   my   hat?   Is   that
4. that wool   hat   my   my   hat? Is   that   wool   hat

1. hat? Is   Is   Is   my   hat? Is   that   wool   my
2. wool hat   my   hat? that   wool hat   my   hat?   that
3. hat   my   hat? Is   that   hat   my   hat?   Is   that
4. my   hat?   Is   that wool   hat   my   hat?   Is   that

1. hat? Is   that wool my   hat? Is   that   wool   my
2. wool hat   my   hat? that   wool hat   my   hat?   that
3. hat   my   hat? Is   that   hat   my   hat?   Is   that
4. wool hat   my   hat? Is   that wool hat   my   hat?

1. hat? Is   that wool my   hat? Is   that   wool   my
2. wool hat   my   hat? Is   that wool Is   that   wool
3. my   hat?   Is   that my   hat? Is   that   my   hat?
4. Is   that   wool hat   my   hat? Is   that   wool   hat

1. hat? Is   that wool hat   my   hat? my   hat?   my
2. Is   that   wool my   hat?   Is   that wool   my   hat?
3. Is   that   my   hat? Is   that my   hat?   Is   that
4. Is   that   wool hat   my   Is   that wool   hat   my

1. hat? my   my   hat? Is   that wool my   hat?   Is
2. Is   that   wool hat? hat?   hat? hat? hat?   hat?   that
3. Is   that   wool hat   my   hat? Is   that   wool   hat
4. Is   that   wool hat   my   that wool hat   my   hat?

1. that wool   my   hat? Is   that wool my   hat?   Is
2. wool hat   that wool hat   that wool hat   that   wool
3. my   hat?   Is   that wool   hat   my   hat?   my   hat?
4. Is   that   wool hat   my   hat? Is   that   wool   hat

1. that wool   my   hat? Is   that wool my   hat?   Is
2. hat   that   wool hat   that   wool hat   my   hat?   Is
3. Is   that   wool hat   my   hat? Is   that   wool   hat
4. wool wool   wool wool my   hat? Is   my   hat?   Is

309

1. that   wool   Is   wool   hat   my   hat?   wool   hat   my
2. that   my   hat?   Is   that   my   hat?   Is   that   wool
3. my   hat?   Is   that   wool   hat   my   hat?   Is   that
4. hat?   Is   that   wool   hat   my   hat?   Is   that   wool

1. hat?   wool   hat   my   hat?   wool   hat   my   hat?   Is
2. hat   my   hat?   Is   wool   hat   my   hat?   Is   wool
3. wool   hat   my   hat?   Is   that   wool   hat   my   hat?
4. hat   my   hat?   Is   that   wool   hat   my   that   wool

1. Is   Is   wool   hat   my   hat?   Is   my   hat?   my
2. hat   my   hat?   Is   wool   hat   my   hat?   Is   hat?
3. Is   that   my   hat?   Is   that   my   hat?   Is   that
4. hat   my   hat?   that   wool   hat   my   hat?   that   wool

1. hat?   that   wool   hat   my   hat?   that   wool   hat   my
2. Is   that   hat?   Is   that   hat?   Is   that   hat?   Is
3. my   hat?   Is   that   wool   hat   my   hat?   wool   hat
4. hat   my   hat?   that   wool   hat   my   hat?   wool   hat

1. hat?   that   wool   hat   my   hat?   that   wool   hat   my
2. that   hat?   Is   that   hat?   Is   that   hat?   Is   that
3. my   hat?   wool   hat   my   hat?   wool   hat   my   hat?
4. my   wool   hat   my   wool   hat   my   wool   hat   my

1. hat?   my   hat?   Is   my   hat?   Is   my   hat?   Is
2. wool   hat   my   Is   that   wool   hat   Is   that   wool
3. Is   that   wool   hat   my   Is   that   wool   hat   my
4. wool   hat   my   hat?   is   that   wool   hat   my   hat?

1. my   hat?   Is   Is   that   wool   hat   Is   that   wool
2. hat   Is   that   wool   hat   Is   that   wool   hat   Is
3. Is   that   wool   hat   my   Is   that   wool   hat   my
4. Is   that   wool   hat   my   hat?   Is   that   wool   hat

1. hat   Is   that   wool   hat   my   hat?   Is   wool   hat
2. that   wool   hat   Is   that   wool   hat   wool   hat   my
3. Is   that   wool   hat   my   Is   that   wool   hat   my
4. my   hat?   Is   that   wool   hat   my   my   hat?   Is

1. wool hat hat? Is that wool hat? Is that wool
2. hat? Is that Is that wool hat my hat? Is
3. that wool hat my hat? Is that wool hat my
4. my hat? Is my hat? Is my hat? Is wool

1. hat? Is that wool hat my hat? Is that wool
2. that wool hat my hat? Is that wool hat my
3. hat? Is that wool hat my hat? Is that wool
4. hat wool hat wool hat wool hat wool hat wool

1. hat my hat? Is that wool hat my hat? Is
2. hat? Is that Is that Is that Is that my
3. hat my hat? Is that wool hat my hat? Is
4. hat that that that wool hat wool hat wool hat

1. that wool hat my hat? Is that wool hat my
2. hat? hat? Is that wool hat my hat? Is that
3. my hat? Is that wool hat my hat? Is that
4. wool hat hat? Is hat? Is hat? Is hat? Is

1. hat? Is that wool hat my hat? Is that wool
2. wool hat my hat? Is that wool hat my hat?
3. wool hat my hat? Is that wool hat my hat?
4. hat? Is hat? Is my hat? Is that wool my

1. Is Is Is Is wool hat my hat? Is that
2. Is that wool hat my Is that Is that Is
3. Is that wool hat my hat? Is that wool hat
4. hat? Is that wool my hat? Is that wool my

13-14 April 1980
New York

311

Notes and Performance Instructions for
"Is That Wool Hat My Hat?"

This piece came about in the following way: During the 12th International Sound Poetry Festival, held at Washington Square Church in New York during April 1980, I came to the April 13th session wearing a navy blue wool hat ("watch cap"). Richard Kostelanetz had also walked over to the church for the performance, wearing a similar hat.

At the church door I met my friend the writer/clairvoyant Hannah Weiner, and we chatted awhile. Later, during intermission, I talked with other people, but just before I took my seat, Hannah came over to me and handed me a wool hat similar to my own, which she'd found on the floor after the chairs in the church were shifted. Having seen me wearing such a hat before the program, she had assumed that I'd dropped mine and that this was it.

I'd gotten in just as someone began performing, so I had no opportunity to tell her it wasn't mine—Hannah had taken a seat not very near me—so I just held the hat in my hand, meaning to turn it in later to the "lost & found," and gave my attention to the performer.

Then, somewhat suddenly, Richard Kostelanetz, who was sitting behind me, leaned over and asked, "Is that wool hat *my* hat?" Having often seen Richard wearing such a hat, I assumed it *was* his, and handed it to him. But his rhythmical question stuck in my mind, so that night I composed this piece for speakers.

As I wrote it, I decided to make four superimposed parts, each composed of repetitions of the question and of parts of it. I used a die to decide how many of the six words of the question were to be repeated each time. As a result, the four parts sometimes coincide exactly, but often the four speakers are saying four different words at the same time.

Performance Instructions

It is best that the piece be performed by four speakers—where possible, by two men and two women. But it may be performed by other combinations of speakers and/or by fewer than four (three or two.) I've never tried it with fewer than three other speakers, but others may find such a performance rewarding, and circumstances may sometimes dictate a smaller number of speakers than four.

Either one of the performers should act as a "time-beater" or a fifth person should act as conductor. The beat should be very precise—almost metronomic, although a metronome should never be used—and neither too fast nor too slow. I've usually performed it at about "One Word = MM. 132," but others may wish to read it slightly faster or slower. However, it oughtn't go *much* faster or slower than this.

Each four words lined up vertically should be spoken precisely at the same time. However, if a speaker mistakenly skips or repeats a word or the like, that speaker should go on from wherever the mistake was made—with no break and *certainly* no attempt to correct the mistake. If somehow the speaker can skip or the like to get back to the proper alignment, that would be good—but never at the cost of the beat.

The words should be spoken moderately loudly, but never over-emphatically. In some performances after the work's premiere (18 April 1980, during the same festival), speakers got louder and louder, some practically *barking* the words. Such things must be avoided: moderate loudness at a precise beat is what's needed.

The best way to end the performance is for the conductor's left hand to be raised straight up—while the right hand continues beating time—at the beginning of the last "system" (group of four lines), and then brought down swiftly at the end of that system.

If through an error one speaker has reached the end of the piece before the others, that speaker should reread the words of the last line until the conductor's left hand comes down.

All speakers should stop precisely as the conductor's hand falls.

score: 13-14 April 1980
notes & instructions: 5 December 1980
New York

Dream Meditation   1:35 PM 6/11/80

MREMDMERAD   MAADRDE   M   EE

    EEDMRRREMA   MMDED   AMRDMEDDD

    DADRMDA   AEDEAADRED   D   EAMEE

    DDAMMRE   AMD   RRE   DEA   DRM

    MEAAAM   DDMDEMERRR   ADME   DA

    EMAME DMDEEAMARM   DR   AAMDEAEMMM

    R   AEE AMDAARARM   EAR   MARADEEAA

    MEEA   DAMERMDR   REDRDDMDD   EEEE

DREDEM   MAREDEMMM   DDDD   AERERRR

Suggestions for Reading
Dream Meditation (1:35 PM 6/11/80)

Without strain, focus the mind on the dream state.

Let the mind drift into the dream state without falling asleep.

Stay awake enough to be able to read the words in the Dream
  Meditation.

Yes, think of each of the letter groups as a word.

The meaning of each of the words may be revealed from within the
  dream.

Pronounce all the letters of each word as connectedly as possible.

Be silent after pronouncing each word.

Let the white spaces guide the dreaming mind as to how long to
  be silent.

Even in the dream state keep the voice audible and the word sounds
  clear.

After saying the last word, let the mind deeply enter the dream
  state.

Try to remember word meanings and dreams afterwards.

2:53 PM 11 June 1980
New York

New Performance Instructions
for *Dream Meditation* — 4/18-22/82

(including performance instructions for instrumentalists and for speaker-vocalists and combined performances)

In my earlier "Suggestions for Reading *Dream Meditation* (1:35 PM 6/11/80)" I asked the reader not only to "focus the mind on the dream state," but to "let the mind drift into the dream state without falling asleep" and to "stay awake enough to be able to read the words," i.e., the letter strings, in this half-awake "dream state." This now seems to me impracticable, if not impossible. If one falls deeply enough asleep to dream, one cannot read or otherwise perform.

The problem, then, is that of establishing a *relation* to or with the dream state without actually falling asleep and dreaming. This is difficult, but not impossible.

My first suggestion reads: "Without strain, focus the mind on the dream state." Does this mean to focus on *memories* of dreams or on *imagined* dreaming? Or perhaps on a *concept* of the dream? Certainly mere "dreaminess" or some kind of half-sleep (which seems the best that people come to when they try to follow my original "suggestions") will not conduce to performances of much interest to anyone except (possibly) performers. I do not mean to invalidate attempts to follow the "suggestions," even though they seem self-contradictory and thus probably doomed to fail. The experience of *attempting* to follow the "suggestions" is still intrinsically interesting.

However, for a more publicly available performance, performers must focus on the dream state in some serious way that allows them clearly to interpret the text by speaking, vocalizing, and/or playing instruments.

Remember: dreams are not usually vague, except in certain aspects or details. They are often vivid—sometimes frightening or unbelievably joyful. All this and more should be part of what the performer *meditates* on while performing this "dream meditation." This is an open-eyed (and -eared) meditation. Whether one focuses on memories of dreams or on what it *means* to dream or on ideas of dreaming or on imagined dreaming, one should still clearly and accurately *perform* and be thoroughly *aware* in as many respects as possible.

The five letters of the word "dream" appear in various combinations in the text. "Translate" each letter into a tone of one of the following pitch classes: D=D♮, R=G♯/A♭, E=E♮, A=A♮, and M=G♮, at concert pitch. Transposing instruments transpose these pitch classes appropriately, e.g., the letter "D" is played by a B♭ instrument as its E♮.

The individual performer chooses all parameters except pitch class, grouping and sequence of pitch classes, and relative durations of silence: octave placement, loudness, attack, and duration of individual tones and aggregates and ways of getting from one tone or aggregate to another within a letter group and of relating the tones. There can be a clear demarcation of tones, even with slight silences between tem; a connection of tones into musical phrases; or simultaneous sounding of two or more tones or of all in a group. When letters are repeated adjacently in the text, they should be represented by tones in different octaves when played simultaneously, but they may be played in either different octaves or the same one when played in succession. One can proceed from tone to tone by discrete steps or by glissandi or portamenti (slides) between the pitches.

Rhythms and pulses (if any) within tone groups, grouping of some or all tones in succession and/or playing of some or all tones in a group simultaneously, tempo and changes of tempo within a tone group, and (on instruments where it is possible) holding of some tones while others are played are all up to the performer. However, the sequence of tones within a group is always that of the letters. Only tones that translate two or more adjacent letters may be played simultaneously.

Spaces between letter strings should be interpreted as silences of substantial duration—the larger the space, the longer the silence—and vertical spaces indicate especially long silences.

It helps to envision all the space on the page as being filled with single-spaced typing or printing. The silence should last *at least as long* as it would take the performer to play *all the letters that are not there*, at a moderate tempo.

Tempo (between moderate and very slow) and tempo changes within letter groups, durations of prolongable letter sounds (i.e., all except "D"), loudness, pitches and changes of pitch during prolongations, attack, connectedness or disconnectedness within letter groups, etc., are all up to the performer.

While always continually meditating in some way on the dream state, performers should be acutely aware of the sounds they and their fellow performers are producing, as well as of all other sounds audible to them (audience, environment, etc.). Their performance choices should bear some relation to all they hear. They should also be aware of whatever they see or otherwise sense and let these sensations also influence their performance choices.

A performance begins at a signal from a designated performer. Performers need not begin together. Each may observe a short or moderately long (no longer than 30 seconds) silence before producing a sound. Performers should focus on the dream state during such initial silences.

Two types of performance ending are permissible:

1. The performance ends when all performers have played or vocalized all the letters on the page once. Since each performer will reach the end at a different time, the sound will gradually thin out and trail off toward the end.

2. The performance ends at a signal from a designated performer. This signal may be given at the end of a duration previously agreed upon, at the designated performer's discretion, or when this performer observes a consensus to end among the performers.

Any performer who reaches the last letter before this signal will, after a moderately long silence, begin again at the top and proceed as before until the ending signal is given. Performances ending in this way will have a more or less consistent density throughout.

While these instructions generally supersede my earlier "Suggestions for Reading Dream Meditation," especially when the work is to be performed publicly for a nonparticipating audience, there is nothing to prevent a group from attemptin a performance (especially a private or semiprivate one or a public one in which all persons present participate) in accordance with those earlier suggestions, adding to them, if desired, certain elements from these instructions, such as the method for instrumentalists or the ways of sounding the letter strings vocally.

18-22 April 1982
New York

Words nd Ends from Ez
II. From Eleven New Cantos XXXI–XLI
1/15/81   (EZRA POUND)

TZBK49HT
(*paRts* om PAris,
Potomac, . . .
cOmmerce n fUrther e is Not owneD Ead yZia d oR untAin
    Perennial cOry. . . .
moUs turNip f SweDen. . . .
E iZing s,
gReat the
Ancient Property. . .
tO mpUte itiNg,
o reaD Esop's nZa heRefore by nAture Prussia,
hOg d,
GUstavus ou kNow rge 3D Ere eZing cuRe tenAnce Prayers,
mOns. . .
eqUal as iN ur olD E TZin ntRa,
out À P-
able rÔle f d'Une tioN ccorDing Eur nZoff. . .
foR depArture,
Purchase e Only iqUe ve aNy alkeD Espeare,
nZoff:
teR e peAce Pain?"

FOr e mUst *goiNg*.

orteD E nZoff. . .
ouR ridA Ppi. . . .
tO d cUre. . .
off Newfoundland.

ecteD E)
eZuela n oRder to mAke Ppear tO e mUch e miNds ecteD Eelings. . . .
iZing ntRy ike A Pope's NOt atUre.

beeN breaD,

Esman cZ hoRrors f plAying Particular cOme raUlein tor Nearly
    meboDy Else iZe veR onvAbitch Ppe hOm leUropa laiNed
    fereD Eprivation iZe wiRe ut pApa's Pancreas. . . .

hOut coUntess ere Nobles.

with Dortmund E,

iZ-

nis peRfect rer:

A Peautiful pOy woUlt htoNe ks

anD En n Zent y aRe en HAtvany!

Plied e On thUs h HuNgarian e finD E *n-*
Zaria fuRnished old *A* Price hOlesale

plUs tioN hey wD.

En aZir ouRs in nAme P tO e bUilt f VeNice.

a loaD–

line,

Eavy aZeth heR,

rom All Proceedeth.

GO,

g,

sUrely u orNate stanDers,

Ers aZe"

deRstood xplAins,

Perhaps,

cOndemning foUnd,

I caN they Dug Ed iZed 's)

pResident nds At Press. . .

tO on,

Used thaN rienDly Eeling yZed weRed s

thAn Presidents tOgether"

n BUren.

er iN bank"

Damned Ellow eZia d a Rabbit's oot,
And Perform y Operations t aUtomatically steN o reaDers E iZschniz
    leR inMAy Put tOry e MUscou liaN e,
"how Do E iZation en,
Romeo unhAppily Pparently dO e sUicided ariNg er boDy E rZa,
ouR s
thAn Payments tOry caUsed ry,
aNy is anD E eZzo-
yit:
weRe to hAve Potbellies cOme lyUm ut;
ANd ht;
AnD E aZza.

noRante!

f 'em All Pope gOes caUse he baNks sh,
AnD Ese UZzano hoRtage n plAce Ps,
s Of e dUe mmuNe rlorD,
Eep oZart tuRal tz' fAther Pt vOn ck Up s,
HiNdenburg's even Dollar Er nZa,
"SuRe ey wAnt P lOp,
blUe bboNs alleD E

15–16 January 1981
New York

Words nd Ends from Ez
IX. From Drafts & Fragments of Cantos CX–CXVII
5/3/83 (EZRA POUND)

oZier's cuRve he wAll,
Phin hOut exUltant
seeN impiDity,
Exultance,
aZ loR r–
leAf
Paler rOck–
layers at—
Un e deNho ia
"HaD Ever oZzaglio,
e *tRacciolino*
iccArdo Psit,
lOve blUer thaN oureD
Euridices,
yZance,
a's Rest,
use At P"
n Of trUction eraNts
faceD,
E tZ
e FRance
is
LAnnes Pire
fOrces,
a nUisance,
was Napoleon
122nD.

Ery iZation."

deR ed TAlleyrand Political.

e,
Orage id Up ter —
Night al —
AnD E yZantines
m pRologo
othAr.

Perform pÖ e jUniper,
ws aNd e lanD E
oZart,
verhanging n-
beAt
Pace
tO n
oUt rk,
aNd owarD Er eZzo heRe iziA.

Ping.

nOrance"
e —
pUt er,
aNd his Name on)
AnD Eauty,
nZe)
veRned u$^{4.5}$
A Ptake
e Old a qUestion f coNduct.)

inteD En r Zephyrus.

eaR,
lty,
Are
(Pale yOung foUr hroNes,
y minD Ere aZe,
eaRs k StAte Paris —
NOr frUit thiNg,
t saiD:
Esser oZart,
's fRiends te eAch Peace wOrld?

n hUsk s fiNished
to tiDe's E
rZo hiRd n,
heAven,
"Paradiso"
e
Over xcUse ll
aNd paraDiso.

Ey o Zagreus
e aRch greAt Paradiso
çOis noUard,
e suN ling,
"De Et

3 May 1983
New York

325

A Lack of Balance But Not Fatal

A motion guided a lotion
in hiding from a tint
reckless from nowhere enforcement.

A label persisted. The past tense
implies it took place. The redness
in which the the implies there was some other
did not persist. He was not waiting long.

The sentence is not always a line
but the stanza is a paragraph.

The whiteness was not enforced.
It was not the other but another
circumstance brought in the waterfall
while a breath waited without being clear
or even happier. A seal was lost without it.

There was a typical edge. The paper tilted
or even curved. A rattle smoothed its way.
Where the predominance stopped was anyone's guess
but the parrot fought for it with forbearance
and a waiting cart was leashed to a trial
though a lie would have done as well
or even better when a moderate sleeve was cast.

No claim was made. A tired park gained.
A lack twisted the bread. Heads foamed.
Nowhere was little enough for the asking.
The task he cleared from the temperature
was outside the extended account. Each the
points to an absence. One or more hiding.

He asked where the inches were. The could have gone.

Intentions are mixed without quotations.
The song was snug. Ambiguity does not
hang in the air. The space between graphemes
is neither colorless nor tasteless. A stream
runs rapidly in no more history. The sweep
of a line. Kindness is not mistaken
for tinder and the lid is resting but shortness
guarantees no sentence authenticity.

Where the schoolyard was evident a closed
flutter showed a notion without resistant
fences or a paradox without feathers.
Swiftness outlasts the pencil. A cormorant
rose against a born backdrop. Letters inch.
An iconoclast was hesitant. A fire lit.
In the tank a lozenge disengages. Swarms
roared. A special particle felt its form.
Lagging features left oak divination without
a tone or a creased sentinel. Leavings swept.

Toward evening the watchful clock was situated.
No diver called for ether. Lynxes thrived.
Hit by something a silence willed. Streets
were not concerned. A past participle's
sometimes mistaken for a past. An orange
roster was on everybody's mind though clues
could be found. When the ink is incomplete
every table rests on its opposite. A closed
restraint impinged. Furniture rested. Several
pinks in a fist. A clearly charismatic
hideout was read. Neatness wavered. The flag
was wet without exertion or favor. That judge postponed.

Snowfall abused ermines. A folding chair.
Close to the bank a trap was silted though the finder
relaxed without particulars or the least inclination.
Whoever loosed the torrent concluded the tryst.
Finally is the way to find the place. Earshot
is likely. Tones harvest commonplace weather.
The pastness of the past was included in a doctrine
or stakes were wrought. Or sought. Find divers.
Fists rested on the divined peculiarity. Artemis hushed.

Twigs were not grapes. He grasped the talc ring.
Smoothing the horses the clutter died. Finches
sewed roses on the mustered aggregate. Loaves flew.
A mentality ran farther and its crests simmered.
Closeted without bargains the lean rump beheld
no future. A certain flight beckoned. The wonder.
Closed classrooms risk warmth though causation
matters less. Never ink a connection when a plea
is off. Softer dollars were a range without flutters
though a concessive subordinator turns a sentence
into a scene. Dreams were not what he wanted.

16 January 1982
New York

Central America

Sing Goddess the centrality of America
of the nation called Usonia
by the architect Frank Lloyd Wright
The problem isn't "Central America"
It is people having very much money and power
and other people having very little
and what the rich and powerful do
to keep powerful and rich and get more so
and what the other people
not powerful or rich
cannot or do not do
not knowing all riches and power stem from them

Manhattan Shirts went south
from Usonia to El Salvador
leaving here in the North
plenty of shirtmakers jobless
Texas Instruments went to El Salvador also
So much of that company went there
it should be called
El Salvador Instruments
And the part of Kimberly-Clark
that sells the disposable diapers they call Huggies
has Salvadorans make them now
and ship them to Usonia
and elsewhere for disposal
Few are sold and disposed of in El Salvador
where nearly all diapers are cloth
washed and rewashed and re-rewashed
before being washed again to be used as rags
and probably many babies wear no diapers

They close their plants up here
and open new ones there
where they pay Salvadorans good money
three dollars and something a day
For El Salvador that's good pay
less than an hour's Usonian wages
for a full day's work in "The Savior"
More such plants are in Haiti
where the viceroy's name is Duvalier
and brand-new runaway shops
will be opening soon in Grenāda

So not *only* "right-wing ideology"
as the self-important good-boy journalists put it
but money and plenty *of* it
and the power that comes from money
and the power that goes for money
makes the Usonian government do what it does
and most other governments too
whatever "ideology" they follow
and any that seems to be different
is different only in detail and degree
or only for a very little while

Money yielding power
and power yielding money
not money greed alone
but money greed and power greed
intricately together
make most of what happens happen
in what are called "public affairs"

Moralistic oversimplication
but a pretty good place to start
You can complicate it later
and squeeze out the "moraline" after if you please
Everyone knows what greed is
even those who call it a neutral drive
or hail it as the dynamo of progress

So everyone knows what Usonians mean
when they speak of "America's backyard"
Usonia's "special domain"
a place to get stuff cheap
and get people to make things cheap
and do things for one cheap
a place where if life is *not* cheap
one can jolly well *make* it cheap

Usonia has a big backyard
from Laredo to Tierra del Fuego
and everything that happens there
is part of Usonia's business
especially whatever threatens
Usonian money or power
and very especially anything threatening
blamable on The Other

With such a big backyard
no wonder Usonia's hands are full
No wonder Usonia's government often
functions as the state
in Central American countries
as in nearby Guatemala
famed for torture chambers
where recently it put in place
a brand-new government
less quirky than the last one
more dependably fighting rebellion
and also of course in Honduras
where five or six thousand Usonian soldiers "maneuver"

No wonder in El Salvador
where "death squads" run amok
and the bridges get blown up
the government of Usonia
all but functions as the state
despite its uppity puppets who think *they* do

No wonder it is so worried
by anything like The Other
or anything vaguely Otherish
Cuba or Grenāda
Chile or Nicaragua
horrid Otherish weeds in that nice clean yard

Don't talk about defending "human rights"
Stroessner has lasted in Paraguay thirty years
torturing and murdering
with never a Usonian landing
But how long did Allende last
as Otherish as Norman Thomas
but threatening nevertheless
to Usonian power and money
They didn't even bother with the Cuban ploy
cutting off trade and aid
to force an Otherish government
to turn to The Other for help
to give them a pretense to weed that government out
out of that tidy backyard

Now they are trying to do just that
to that horrible Otherish junta in Managua
trying to bring it down
by supporting bands of "patriots" called "contras"
many of whom were soldiers and policemen
who used to kill and torture for Somoza
but now destroy and kill "to bring back freedom"

And still to the liars and thieves
the torturers and murderers
who think they rule El Salvador
they are giving our money away
to fight the Otherish rebels
who might not be so nice to runaway shops

Banality after banality
about the most bānal banality
postponing the inevitable question
What can the people do
who *don't* have much money or power
to stop the liars and thieves
the torturers and murderers
the profiters and exploiters
the powerful and rich
and those who keep them that way
from profiting and exploiting
from lying and from stealing
from torturing and murdering
from doing whatever they want in the big backyard

There is *nó óne ánswer*
and *nó póem* purporting to give one does
What your hand finds to do
do

1–31 January 1984
New York

Pieces o' Six — XXI

Once the kenurdlers had settled on a schema, the new pipes were brightened. The quiet pitches were liberated. When the fleets flamed, the deals were offensive, though the foolers increased their pretense. Nodules were soaked. Labile oaks listed as they listed, and boats tinkled as whistlers particularized threats, but tony coal heavers heavily bested durational scissors when nets were portioned among panic thieves. Live pachyderms were picked for street engulfments. The daily cascades were defaced by facile derangements, though any cousin might have known the difference. Rigid diligence seemed to be in order that day, for discipline Castilian as hills was praised, and whoever alerted the picnickers was nowhere to be seen when the lines were down. Ices were consummated soon. The Druse monotones filtered through a cuckold's initial cacklings. Pheasants were dropped and drastic features annealed. Nobody's sleeves were tinted. Sluices gave way to crevices wherever an annular violence was detected, and orphaned wigglers lifted wizened visages just as the clocks of the tin situation were primed to be filled. That was the time of the zoological. A laughing dik-dik was not to be reasoned away. The rates of exchange were rattled by the tunes zinc took. Tall galleries were invested with flint, and galactic nuggets zigzagged among sweetened trees at whose feet crisp clashes were encountered. Kneeling Saracens were no match for publicity hounds. Beyond the sacramental bounds tangential files were flicked by harnesses held by the last of the leverage-seeking talkers on whose active bruised facades no tank would dare to fling its artifacts. Who could be blamed or challenged in that sawdust-laden grove? No one was wary or cozily dozed. Natural tubes provided excuses for umbrage. Nests of pacific lips were tactfully smacked in fascinating sunshine. No one knew who was there; no one replied. The tentative lies careened around the fortress and left the concupiscent heirs with no ingratiating attitudes. The honor of a class was nobody's answer. Suasion was uncalled-for. Titles, though perfumed and architectural, seasoned in vain the paltry preserves of the occupant sodality. Sermons the streams and stones decried wrenched the bottoming frigate. Some pillaged the lists. A few exalted assassins rode the wakening whirlpool, where loops of dazzling grass reached for visionary panaceas. Fiddles combined with clucks when lusters crammed in closets incautiously unclosed poured like stupid venom on the marred parquet. Truants were whistled away. Losers looking like Trinitarian manglers footed a clover-laden balustrade and switched their betrayal from angered crowns to illogical fortune-hunting thoroughbreds whose ambergrised vestments were mounted, in the event, in largely ineffectual museums. Diseases and passing arousals dotted the calcined, reeking coasts. Soteriological clumsiness reacted away from inhabitants toddling in fury, and glassified permanent hips where none had been before. Each accessible needler reeled and called. Widening circuits clipped an iridescent angler. One of the funnier, decently gullible fliers rapidly packed a mortuary box where vapid fans increased their attentive wrestlings. Vinegar floated a factory. Knives were interleaved among affluent carcasses, and a nankeen dog was later found in a fixture, but a patrilineal diver never found the spunky follower though nannies surrounded the latter's insensible confederate. Torsion clinched the Tuareg's incredible mechanism. The sister lusted after a massive infrastructure. Zeppelins boomed in a keeper's despicable firmament, and light flapped at the eaves. A teenager featured in a classically fractioned trap. One by one, the relevant technical panderers were clasped by a wan describer. At last a damask furrow was found for the kin. Near or far, the tea service lacked a provider, though a patched regional zip cord leaped among none of the farmer's biscuits and few broached the lapidary wicked fence, but fanning from a crystal-girdled crossing, a gaggle of ghost-suited novices jumped among gorilla-laden shrubs immenser than sequoias and more deadly. The calculating despot snickered. Kneeling on a bifurcated counter, a dazzling road mender shaped invoked suspicions and risibly panicked a robot's attendant who'd left his pincers safe in a cleft by a rivulet, ostensibly misled by the pikes of an illusory puncturer stripped of affects. Granitic confidence supervened, and a canvas pasture unfurled near the straits. Before a fatal classmate could hook a dirndled wayfarer, a galloping proser fled with the cinctured capture. A gruff, demented activist was left among the crossroads. A liberal grin tightened the leaves. A sepia, ramshackle portion was the parson's only lot. Tolerant and tentative, a skulking dipterologist foxily pitted results against request. Unnatural though its betterment might seem to a flickering whipper, at least one fragile nativist favored the air castle's remake. Sleep encountered none of the usual slack distaste. Warily, a tantalizing race pushed forth into thickets alive with twins. Skylarks swarmed over the undulant surround. A tinker mouthed a cracker. Fanciful as disaster, an errant taxi ticked among billboards piled with color and language straitened by commerce, deflated and all but snapping. Trimmed from a vanishing clientele, snippets of vixenish furbelows floated in a pancreatic marsh. A needle was strapped to a toe. Moaning and moping, the gadabouts yielded their interest. A marble rested on a riven shelf. One cleft or more made a little more difference than none. Gray honey from a tapster's trove was bargained for by more than one survivor. Tottling picketers fixed a beseeching hand. Suave as straddlers and nearly as neat, a paunchy saunterer disinterred the once nattering lacemaker formerly farcically entered. Near the park the straggling giant fastened a gate. Swaying along the straightaway, the ghastly ally of a hill man rapidly clattered, outpacing every planner. Vapid and decidedly tonsured, a wily reductionist filtered the grease of transactions. More than one pollution was the upshot. A necessary pyrene was left to engage. In stages and beleaguered, petitioned and agglomerate, a cowardly detective climbed to peril. Nestling between throes, the pumper crushed the permeated fragments and swept the cliffs with unenduring glances. Filmy withering petals clashed with vacant rites portending closure. A nose was lost. Weaponed and reticent, dashers passed among hangdogs, and a fey attendant trampled the least narcissus. A bitter clipping was left in a crack. Foreign tattling gambolers wrenched the sacristan's gnarled sternum.

20 February 1985
New York

Of this edition, 26 have been signed and lettered A-Z by the author.